30/10/07

10.8.1

CHARISMATIC CHRISTIANITY

Charismatic Christianity

Sociological Perspectives

Edited by

Stephen Hunt
Lecturer in Sociology
University of Reading

Malcolm Hamilton
Head of Department
Department of Sociology
University of Reading

and

Tony Walter
Reader in Sociology
University of Reading

First published by
MACMILLAN PRESS LTD
Houndmills, Basingstoke, Hampshire RG21 6XS
and London
Companies and representatives
throughout the world

ISBN 0–333–66598-8

A catalogue record for this book is available
from the British Library.

This book is printed on paper suitable for recycling and
made from fully managed and sustained forest sources.

Transferred to digital printing 1999

Contents

Notes on the Contributors

Paul Chambers is a tutor and Ph.D. student in the Department of Sociology and Anthropology, University of Wales, Swansea. He is currently completing a three-year research project examining church growth and decline in south Wales.

Paul Freston wrote a doctoral thesis at the University of Campinas on evangelicals and politics in Brazil. He has published extensively on the sociology of Protestantism and taught sociology at the Federal University of São Carlos.

Malcolm Hamilton is a senior lecturer in the Department of Sociology at the University of Reading. In the field of the sociology of religion his publications include *The Sociology of Religion: Theoretical and Comparative Perspectives* (Routledge, 1995) and *Sociology and the World's Religions* (Macmillan, 1997, forthcoming).

Stephen Hunt is a lecturer in sociology at the University of Reading. He has written extensively on various aspects of the Charismatic movement, as well as publishing widely on political movements and political extremism.

Douglas McBain has long been involved in Baptist Renewal. He is now the president of the Baptist Union. His books include *Discerning the Spirits* (Marshall Pickering, 1986) and *Fire over the Waters* (Darton, Longman & Todd).

Keith Newell is a graduate in sociology from the University of Durham. From 1972–4 he belonged to a Christian community at Potters Green, Coventry, and since then has been associated with a number of Charismatic communities.

Martyn Percy is chaplain and director of theology at Christ's College, Cambridge. He has published widely in the field of sociology and theology with *Words, Wonders and Power: Understanding Contemporary Christian Fundamentalism and Revivalism* (SPCK, 1996) numbered among his books.

Philip Richter is a Methodist minister and sociologist, currently director of the Church Leaving Research Project, Roehampton Institute, London. He is co-editor of *The Toronto Blessing – Or Is It?* (Darton, Longman & Todd, 1995).

William Thompson is a lecturer in sociology at the University of Reading. He researches into moral panics, and has published several books and articles on contemporary Christian activism including the British satanic abuse allegations.

Tony Walter lectures in sociology at the University of Reading. His books include *The Eclipse of Eternity: a Sociology of the Afterlife*, *Pilgrimage in Popular Culture* (both Macmillan) and *A Long Way from Home* (Paternoster).

Andrew Walker is senior lecturer in theology at King's College, London. He is also director of the Centre for Gospel and Culture. He has written extensively on Pentecostalism and contemporary Christianity and his publications include the bestselling *Restoring the Kingdom: the Radical Christianity of the House Church Movement* (Hodder & Stoughton, 1987) and *Harmful Religion* (SPCK, 1997).

Nigel Wright is the senior pastor of Altrincham Baptist Church and previously senior lecturer in Christian theology at Spurgeon's College. He is author of ten books and co-author of the bestselling *Charismatic Renewal: the Search for a Theology* (SPCK, 1995).

Introduction
Tongues, Toronto and the Millennium
Stephen Hunt, Malcolm Hamilton and Tony Walter

In 1967 a popular New Zealand Christian magazine published a letter written by a concerned church minister, a certain Revd Boniface (Boniface, 1967). His complaint was that the emerging force of neo-Pentecostalism was divisive since it created major divisions within Baptist and Brethren churches, and disrupted the Anglican way of life. He also raised a profoundly pertinent question. Was this new movement 'the most important development in Christianity in 1600 years or a tremendously dangerous psychological delusion'?

History may prove it to be neither. Ultimately, neo-Pentecostalism could turn out to be a very small paragraph in the story of Christianity. Nonetheless, it has not prevented those sympathetic to the movement using various criteria to boost the claim that it marks a significant 'move of God'. One of its leading apologists Peter Wagner (Wagner, 1992) argued that, on a global scale, it is the most significant non-political and non-military social movement in the latter half of the twentieth century. Even allowing for exaggeration the scale of the movement cannot be ignored.

This book does not seek to consider the psychological well-being of those involved, but it does attempt to answer some other questions. What is the nature of the beast? What is the significance of this growing religious phenomenon? How has it evolved in the last 30 years? To what extent is it a manifestation of the modern, or even post-modern, world? The chapters of this book explore different perspectives. Most of the chapters are concerned with the British experience. Indeed, there is good evidence that the contemporary British scene is a very good indicator of recent trends, although we leave scope in Chapter 9 for Paul Freston to range wider in looking at developments in Latin America.

Some chapters are written by sociologists, some by theologians. Some by those who have a foot in both camps. We have also included

1

contributors who are 'insiders' to counter the tendency of the outside observers to be less than charitable in their analysis. Hence, there are included those who have lived within the neo-Pentecostal world, and even one who has left it behind.

At this juncture we merely attempt to flag up a few precursory observations. The first is that there is a problem of definition. This accounts for the discrepancies in the figures presented as to the scale and influence of the new movement.[1] The earlier Pentecostal movement, with its alleged beginnings at the Azusa Street mission in California in 1906, is now typically referred to as classical Pentecostalism. On a global basis it has produced its own denominations which have come to take their rightful place alongside the other mainstream historical churches. Neo-Pentecostalism, otherwise known as the Charismatic movement, is the contemporary counterpart. It includes those churches within the established denominations that have been open to Pentecostal influence through the dynamics of Charismatic Renewal, along with itinerant ministries and para-church organizations outside of these structures.

The superficiality of these classifications is apparent in that they describe the same thing, namely an emphasis upon the charismata: glossolalia, prophecy, healings, words of knowledge and other so-called supernatural gifts of the Spirit. These gifts are often identified as distinguishing characteristics not only because the older Pentecostals and Charismatics regard them as crucial, but also because they have rarely been manifested in the history of the Christian Church (Carrol, 1966). The other identifiable feature is the doctrine of 'the Baptism in the Spirit', deemed an essential part of the born-again Christian experience. Both the charismata and the 'second baptism' had been used by Pentecostals from the beginning of the twentieth century as a self-affirming emblem of sanctity and separation. However, the entire Pentecostal movement is evolving so rapidly that it is not entirely clear whether these distinctive hallmarks still hold.

For adherents, there may be a psychological need to establish a beginning. Charismatic folklore locates the start of the renewal movement within Episcopalian circles in Van Nuys, California in 1960 (Bennett, 1970) and the Church of the Redeemer in Houston, Texas, with outbreaks of tongue-speaking.[2] Some 30 years on it is apparent that the entire neo-Pentecostal movement has gone through, and continues to go through, a process of metamorphosis. Indeed, the wind of change that the wider Pentecostal movement has brought to Christianity from the beginning of the twentieth century has never stopped blowing.

However, this wind is prone to rapid changes of direction, depending on local climatic conditions. For those involved, the Spirit may appear to move where it wishes, but the movement that claims to represent its will is buffeted by social and cultural gales. It also appears to be subject to sociological laws. The early Renewal movement had begun as an endeavour to bring new life to the churches at a time of numerical decline. Simultaneously, it also attempted to counter the growing routinization and bureaucratization of church life. But the roots of neo-Pentecostalism lay not only in the state of the mainline churches, but in a response to wider society.

Precisely how neo-Pentecostalism relates to contemporary society is perhaps the key question. Arriving at a categorical answer is not easy since the movement is one of contradiction, paradox and internal dilemmas. The main contradiction is that it appears to resist secularizing forces while simultaneously endorsing some aspects of present day culture.

A ready-made framework is that of secularization. Theories of secularization focus upon a number of themes, although here we can only detail them superficially. Most converge upon the dynamics of 'modernization' – another difficult concept to come to terms with. Usually modernization denotes the interrelated processes of industrialization, rationalism, the break up of community, and pluralism. In one way or another all these trends appear to engender disbelief, or at least the decline, and perhaps the inevitable disappearance, of religious faith.

These common themes still persist in the work of numerous sociological writers. The central notions of the perceived demise in the impact of religious doctrines, loss of social prestige, and the demise of civic religious institutions, are supplemented by the greater conformity of religion to 'this world'. There are the accompanying dynamics of rationalization and disenchantment, and the withdrawal of religion into the private sphere. Simultaneously, the contemporary world appears to encourage religions to display various expressions of anti-modernism. The need for religious meaning still persists, new religious movements, some appearing archaic in form, fill the breach. At the same time traditional faiths under threat of decline or extinction may spawn new forms of fundamentalism and a sectarian backlash.

. There appears sufficient here at least to account for the early stages of the Charismatic movement, as well as its persistently contradictory nature. Nevertheless, today there are ample developments in the religious sphere to suggest an exploration of post-modernist themes. At least some sections of the movement are becoming increasing experiential, typified by the so-called Toronto Blessing which took both long-time Charismatics and observers by surprise. Characterized by some extraordinary physical phenomena and esoteric experiences, it swept through Charismatic networks at a remarkable pace. The charismata were being driven to their logical, or perhaps illogical conclusion.

Post-modernism, suggesting that key aspects of the *modern* world have disappeared or dissolved, presents us with another concept which is extraordinarily difficult to grapple with. The contemporary epoch is post-industrial and consumer-led. Rationalism is questioned. Grand narratives, including the taken-for-granted foundations of modernism, not least of all notions of 'progress', are eaten away by subjectivism. In this post-modern world the monolithic culture disintegrates, a process intensified by the dynamics of globalization.

Putting all this together there is much to vindicate the view of Lyotard (1984) who insists that the cultural shifts of the contemporary world have been so enormous over the last two decades that there are no available paradigms for understanding it. All previous sociological constructs and interpretations, including those of religion, struggle to keep pace. The secularization thesis looks less secure. But we are not there yet; the post-modern world is perhaps heralded prematurely. This does not help our enquiry as to where neo-Pentecostalism fits in. The problem is that it displays attributes which are, sometimes simultaneously, anti-modern, modern, and post-modern.

ANTI-MODERN?

Does neo-Pentecostalism exhibit the backward-looking fundamentalism and reactionism often attributed to its predecessor? Does it take an uncompromising or even hostile stance towards the outside world? The early Charismatics in Britain have followed the evangelical tradition of repudiating the term 'fundamentalism'. Indeed, the term 'renewal' was preferred both to signify the return of the charismata to the contemporary church and to differentiate it from the revivalism and anti-intellectualism associated with American fundamentalism.

Beyond that, there was no clear agreement, at least by Charismatics in the established churches, as to what their movement signified. Some believed that God was preparing to bring spiritual life back into denominations marked by stagnation and worldliness. Others put the emphasis upon the universal Church rediscovering Christian unity and consequently gaining the strength to reassert itself in an ever increasingly secular world (Harper, 1965). This was sometimes accompanied by a sense of exclusiveness, even elitism. The first Pentecostals saw their movement as the 'Latter Rain' of God pouring out His Spirit in the Last Days. The Charismatics used similar terms such as 'revival', 'awakening', 'outpouring' and many believed that renewal signified a return to the early church experience. At times the hopes of renewal and revival were linked to millenarianism. A return to unity, true spiritual experience and the gifts of the Spirit all seemed to point towards the restoration of God's true church.

Others, like Hollenwerger (1966), have argued that the Charismatic movement is fundamentalist. It largely adheres to the inerrancy of the Bible, opposes theological liberalism, and embraces 'a complex, systematic worldview in its own right'. However, fundamentalism suggests more than a Biblical literalism and an uncompromising turn of mind. It concerns attitudes towards secularity. In particular, some commentators have identified a certain tension with the world characteristic of sectorianism.[3] Neo-Pentecostalism appears to be in some respects, a 'deviant' religious minority with a distinct worldview (McGuire, 1982, pp.218–20). This hostility has sometimes had profound repercussions, as examined in Chapter 8 by Bill Thompson who points out that Charismatics have often been at the forefront of moral campaigns in Britain. Driven on by an uncompromising worldview they have social agendas, not always easy to discern and often pursued in an aggressive and controversial way.

There is another sense in which the Charismatics could be seen as backward-looking. In the *Heretical Imperative* Peter Berger (1979) compares the strategies open to a religious tradition undermined by modern rational scepticism. Conservatives confront the world unashamedly with the uncompromising Word of God, while liberals compromise the faith in order to be relevant to modern man. A third alternative is what Berger terms the Inductive Possibility; the attempt to rediscover the human experience of the divine as the starting point for religious reflection. Although Berger himself does not explicitly do so, it is more than tempting to put Pentecostalism within this framework.

Harvey Cox comes close to this (Cox, 1995, pp.81–3) when he suggests that Pentecostalism seeks a 'primal spirituality', in its attempted restoration of the spiritual experience which began the faith. To be more specific, this includes firstly, 'primal speech' – the ecstatic utterance of glossolalia. In an age of ultra-specialized terminology and contrived rhetoric, speaking in tongues is 'a language of the heart'. This is accompanied secondly, by 'primal piety', the resurgence of archetypal religious experiences of trance, vision, healing and dreams. Here is a primal mode of praise and supplication of what Durkheim called 'the elementary forms of religious life' (Durkheim, 1961). Finally, there is the 'primal hope' that looks forward to the dawn of a new age, a millennial heaven on earth.

Gaede (1981, pp.181–8), in modifying Berger's typology, firmly places Pentecostalism within a fourth category, inductive orthodoxy, which emphasizes the psychological need to 'live out the Word' through an experience-led fundamentalism. Likewise, Chalfont et al.'s work on classical Pentecostalism (Chalfont et al., 1987) demonstrates the appeal of a close relationship between evangelism, a literal interpretation of the Bible and religious experience including glossolalia, prophecy, healing, deliverance, miracles, and other paranormal experiences. Such experiences, interpreted through Biblical literalism, not only carry profound religious significance and meaning, but simultaneously demonstrate the 'power of God'. This is the basic recipe for Pentecostal growth.

Many of these apparently backward-looking tendencies were to be seen in a larger measure in Britain's Restorationist churches. The term 'restorationist' denoted a distinctive theology and reflected a profound disenchantment with the established denominations as individuals sought to recreate the 'true Church'. Walker identified the Restorationist churches, in their early stages at least, as decidedly more sect-like and they constituted 'the most significant religious formation to emerge in Great Britain for over half a century' (Walker, 1985, p.28). Restorationism seemed more active in demonstrating the power of God, restoring a 'lost' Church and rebuilding the Kingdom of God. It represented, in the words of Grace Davie, 'a desire for something special or distinctive about religious activity' (Davie, 1994, p.34).

The Renewal movement sought only to revive the mainline churches within their traditional structures. The early Restorationist leaders believed this imposed severe limitations and that God wanted an all-encompassing transnational Church, not 'the abomination of demonstrations'. The shortcomings of Renewal were said to be its lack of discipline and authority, unbiblical teachings such as infant baptism, and curiosities such as vicars with their shirts on the wrong way round. The post-millenarianism which Restorationism encompassed showed a tendency towards universalism, exclusivism and spiritual elitism. Much of this was reflected in church life systematically structured around what was understood to be the New Testament pattern. But the Kingdom did not come. In the 1990s the movement fractured. There was good evidence to suggest Restorationism was capitulating to the very secularization to which it was opposed. Ideology, attitudes towards ecumenism, contrasting dispositions towards the world, and much more divided the movement. This is discussed in some detail by Nigel Wright in Chapter 3.

There was another side to the equation. Neo-Pentecostalism has attracted a fairly distinctive middle class clientele. Why this has been the case is complex and various explanations have been offered. Wallis, in his survey of new religions (Wallis, 1984), suggested that movements such as neo-Pentecostalism help their followers cope with their life experiences and compensate for the difficulties thrown up by the modern world, notably rationalization and the bureaucratization of life. David Martin (1978, pp.41–3) has argued that neo-Pentecostalism represents a grass-roots initiative providing spiritual certainty, esoteric symbols, and a prophetic criticism of society through eschatological and mystical yearnings. In the increasingly bureaucratic nature of the workplace it was the middle classes who were perhaps most vulnerable. The Charismatic movement offered to them an enticing way to overcome feelings of social isolation and alienation.

Like other new religious movements neo-Pentecostalism could be interpreted as providing a subculture into which people could occasionally or permanently retreat from the impersonal modern world (Wilson, 1982). It means a departure into a world where males are allowed to cry in public meetings, where glossolalia is understood to have therapeutic qualities, where the laying-on of hands becomes a means of transmitting spiritual experience, while embracing friends and strangers alike becomes a means of sharing it. Thus this stress upon the charismata marked a rejection of what the modern world was all about and at its inception dovetailed well with the 1960s counter-culture's devotion to spontaneity, that is, to yield to impulse by disregarding intellectual and rational control (Balswick, 1982).

One possibility was opting out altogether into a communal life. In the 1970s sociologists suggested that modern religion was reflecting 'the search for community'. One of the significant aspects of the Renewal movement was its ability to spawn 'intentional communities' (Elbert, 1988), this being particularly strong within Roman Catholic renewal. This appeared to indicate that the Charismatic movement has satisfied yearning for community and a re-establishment of social bonds at a time when impersonal bureaucratic structures have come to dominate society, traditional communities have broken up, and social and geographical mobility have weakened wider social relationships and networks.

The secular equivalents to intentional communities have been notoriously short-lived and some Charismatic ones have also struggled to survive. Others like the Jesus Fellowship, have flourished, but not without difficulties. Keith Newell in Chapter 6 discusses the problems of surviving on an island in a sea of secularity and the inherent contradiction of sustaining an existence dedicated to 'coming out of the world' and the need to evangelize and expand.

MODERN?

In contrast to evidence of anti-modernism, neo-Pentecostalism, in no uncertain terms, also reflects the modern world. Andrew Walker in Chapter 1 has few doubts that the entire Pentecostal movement has been thoroughly modern. There is good evidence that the Charismatic Renewal movement, which sought to revive the established churches, was conceding much to the modern world. A sign of this, as pointed out by Douglas McBain in Chapter 2, is that the Renewal movement has always tended to meet opposition from conservative forces within the Church which means that its growth has never been a straightforward one.

Among the classical accounts of secularization is that of Bryan Wilson which includes the suggestion that ecumenical initiatives are themselves an indication of the weakness of religion (Wilson, 1966). Rival denominations can afford to bicker over theological differences if they feel sufficiently strong, but when they lose numbers and/or confidence then joining with others becomes a more attractive proposition.

The grass-roots Charismatic approaches across the Protestant–Roman Catholic divide in the 1960s cannot be underestimated. In fact, they may be the most enduring aspect of Renewal. From the very beginning Christians began to discover that they were brothers and sisters under the skin; all one in the Spirit. There were many roads to reconciliation. Perhaps it was a sign of the times that in the 1960s the classical Pentecostal churches, which had hitherto distanced themselves from the established churches which they deemed hopelessly lost, reached out to the rest of Christendom through the initiatives of key individuals.

Ecumenism also incorporates aspects of liberalism, although we must be careful how the term is used here. At the very least it suggests the recognition and legitimacy of pluralism and an acknowledgement that other faiths may have something going for them after all. Developments within the Roman church were particularly significant. The emergence of the Charismatic wing of Roman Catholicism virtually coincided with the Second Vatican Council (1962–5) which encouraged experiments both with liturgy and theology. While some of the more modern-orientated positions were condemned, neo-Pentecostalism itself was deemed worthy of endorsement.

We can look at modernist tendencies from another direction. The link between classical and neo-Pentecostalism should not be overstated; important theological and ecclesiastic difficulties remain. Charismatic worldly accommodation has long been contested by the older Pentecostals with the jibe that there was a tendency for the Charismatics to be too worldly and lacking in puritan attitudes.

This accusation has not been without some substance. There has always been a tendency for neo-Pentecostalism to endorse certain modern trends. In this they are not alone. Bebbington (1989, pp.272–3) has argued that in Britain various strands of evangelicalism have successfully adapted to cultural changes without, for the most part, losing their integrity. In many cases, however, modern Charismatics were going further. In some strands of the movement there was a more overt dedication to improving this-wordly conditions, not retreating from them. Visions of human potential, of health and wealth, are perhaps most clearly seen in the American Faith ministries that appear to marry a motivation derived from instrumental rationalism, albeit within a worldview embedded in rather primitive notions of metaphysical causation.

Among the Charismatics there has also been something much more basic to be observed. At one level a peculiarity of modern culture which is particularly conducive to the growth of new religions is the expression of *individual* experience. The Charismatics' emphasis on experience is in danger of accommodating itself to the very forces of secularization to which it is opposed. Nuanced slightly differently, one could say that the charismata enabled Christians to be spontaneous and individualistic while remaining thoroughly spiritual. The age-old question of the relationship between faith and culture remains: has the Charismatic movement sold out to the secular cult of impetuosity, or has it radically Christianized it? One can say, at least, that by opting for the modern pursuit of experience, neo-Pentecostalism mediates between the legalism of fundamentalism and the relativism of liberal theology.

If this premiss is correct it should not surprise us that Wallis firmly put the neo-Pentecostals in the world-accommodating camp (Wallis, 1884). Sociologists have long argued that religious groups must either choose between their fundamentalist beliefs or compromise them by accepting modernizing trends. Wallis suggests that both responses can be made at one and the same time by some religious groups, that is, religious movements may react against society while simultaneously celebrating a number of its major features. Steve Hunt, in Chapter 4, maintains that the Charismatics have become very proficient in holding this tension. This is exemplified by the spectacular growth and theological construct of John Wimber's Vineyard ministry which has shown that this strategy is effective in the highly diverse contemporary spiritual marketplace.

Choosing a religion in this marketplace of faiths also hints at a certain rational instrumentalism which is a theme recently developed by some American writers (Iannaccone, 1990; Stark and Bainbridge, 1985). In essence, that religion can be marketed and likewise consumed. There is, however, a danger of stressing too many economic metaphors. Religious belief by its very nature does not easily lend itself to notions of rational choice. Nonetheless, such theories may be more convincing when they argue that the decline of civic religion does provide a kind of level playing field for religious groups to compete on.

British Charismatic congregations tend to demonstrate the kind of belonging that American writers such as Wuthnow (1993) call a 'new voluntarism'. This form of association, also found in secular groups, encourages people to pick and choose until they find the religious identity best suited to their tastes, and is evidence of the growing emphasis on achieved over ascribed religious identities. Religious collectives have become one place where people derive and create their own self identities (Wuthnow, 1993, p.189). This 'new voluntarism' in religious belonging, however, may be fundamentally unstable since it is not essentially rooted in any sense of community. This may be one of the reasons why Charismatic churches are notoriously short-lived and prone to internal conflicts. The tendency is examined in Paul Chambers' discussion of divisions within a Charismatic church in Chapter 7.

POST-MODERN?

Around Pentecost Sunday in 1994 outbursts of uncontrolled, if not hysterical, laughter occurred during services in British Charismatic churches. While some members of congregations floated to the floor 'slain in the Spirit' allegedly under the power of God, others staggered around in what has been designated as a 'spiritual drunkeness' –

laughing or displaying slurred speech, spasms of the limbs and, later, a variety of animal noises including those imitating dogs, cattle and chickens. There was the 'Toronto twitch', pogoing, frantically running around the church, playing at being motor cars, and women symbolically birthing the Kingdom. This was the much reported and much discussed Charismatic phenomenon that has come to be known as the 'Toronto Blessing'. The Revd Boniface would have been most perplexed.

Besides these physical manifestations there were more esoteric experiences. There were prophecies, 'pictures', visions of angels. At one Baptist church members were asked to come to the front of the congregation and share their experiences of God's blessing, Toronto-style. A young woman excitedly told how she had seen the Lord during a mid-week prayer group. Evidently, Jesus had playfully thrown rainbows at her and bid her to do the same to those praying around her.

There was the enduring theme of revival. According to the senior pastor of the Toronto Vineyard church, *the* Church was being prepared for

> ... probably the greatest harvest in the world ... we could be moving towards the last move of God ... the real power is coming. God is saying just get used to it.

> (John Arnott, 1994)

Philip Richter, in Chapter 5, argues impressively that the Toronto Blessing was an attempt to prevent the Charismatic movement ossifying, stagnating and becoming like a formal church organization dominated by a rational bureaucratic structure. In one respect there was nothing new here. Indeed, the wheel had turned full circle. Routinization had come to haunt the movement after a mere decade. When it began to consolidate its position in the churches in the late 1970s its increasing respectability and official recognition defused its potency, allowing the pendulum of power to swing back to the mainline denominations (Reed, 1991). This was especially so among Roman Catholics where the Charismatics became merely another conservative faction under the authority of the church's hierarchy.[4]

So long as Charismatics did not themselves form their own denominations, they could rely on the administrative structure of the denominations of which they were part and did not need to encumber themselves with bureaucratic structures. They could thus represent the 'anti-structure' that Victor Turner (1974) has suggested is the sociological basis of spirituality. However, as Charismatic groups grew beyond the size where everyone knew everyone else and as more complex hierarchies of leadership were required, how could effective organization be achieved without eroding the very spontaneity and ecstasy on which the movement was founded?

The mass meetings which had Charismatics gathered together from across the denominations fell into decline by the late 1970s. The vigour of the movement had begun to falter. At one level Renewal had left an indelible imprint upon the established churches. Charismatic worship, symbols and culture (although not necessarily Charismatic theology) had penetrated nearly every corner of Christendom. At the same time speaking in tongues and the 'second experience' of Baptism in the Spirit were not always insisted upon as signs of belonging to the born-again community.

Here was one of the central contradictions. Renewal was, as much as anything, about church growth, yet converts could not be pressurized into displaying Charismatic credentials. Charismatics were thus compromising their distinctive dogma and losing their exclusivity. The religious market metaphor reasserts itself. However, the Charismatics have never quite fitted the rational-choice/lifestyle scenario. In seeking religions reflecting personal taste born-again Christians are as likely to be seeking highly charged emotional experiences as much as anything else. This was what many of the new independent Charismatic ministries were offering to what Walker (1983) called 'spiritual nomads'.

One appraisal of contemporary Christianity views it as becoming part of the entertainment industry of western culture (Noll, 1994), offering much to the consumer side of post-modernist society. Post-modern society produces a culture of the consumer, a culture in which what matters is not what is true or what is meaningful, but *pzazz*, what catches the eye, for only that which catches the eye will sell (Davie, 1994, ch. 10). If religion is to compete in a post-modern world it too must offer eye-catching wares, which is precisely what neo-Pentecostalism does. God has to top last year's eye-catching interventions in this world with something even more eye-catching this year.

The movement has increasingly appealed to members of a society who have grown up with the three-minute culture of the television and have come to expect instant satisfaction. It offers spiritual excitement through what Wilson (1982) calls 'proximate salvation'. It satisfies an impatient demand to consume experience 'now', tending towards what might be termed an over-realized eschatology where the expected Kingdom to come is manifest today. But the 'now' and the 'new' have no sense of continuity nor church history, no patience with dogma nor ecclesiastical authority.

The problem with such an analysis, however, is that the post-modern looks rather like the anti-modern; ecstatic religious experience looks both ways. McDonnell maintained that with neo-Pentecostalism the tendency towards raw experience belongs to a post-literary culture. The whole movement is experience-orientated, unstructured, spontaneous, inward-looking, almost atomistic in its concern for the 'now' 'at a level which, like tongues, is unutterable' (McDonnell, 1972, p.5).

The Toronto Blessing appeared to indicate in one sense that the movement was turning back on itself. A statement produced by a conference of seasoned Charismatics, sceptical of recent developments, reveals that they relate spiritual innovation to the social conditions of the contemporary world, however that world is defined, to an extent that is alien to at least some in the movement. The statement also provides a wry sociological insight and indicates the extent of the neo-Pentecostal journeying when it states:

> that the prophecies concerning a great outpouring of power in the last days upon an elite company of believers is a dangerous eschatological teaching that has no foundation in scripture. It is, nevertheless, a teaching that has great appeal in an age characterized by a sense of powerlessness. In times of economic hardship, unemployment, breakdown of social order there is a general and widespread feeling in society of being driven by forces beyond human control.
>
> (A Report of a Leadership Consultation on the Current Situation in the Charismatic Churches, 1995, p.12)

The Toronto Blessing is clearly an extremely complex phenomenon. Like neo-Pentecostalism itself, it may be many things. Such esoteric movements may mark an attempt to revive an increasingly beleaguered worldview in a world where there are few certainties. It might be seen as a kind of 'ghost dance' within Christianity. In other words, a nihilistic millenarian movement that is going nowhere in particular. It might also represent a coming together of the Charismatic tribes. In Durkheim's terms it may have been a great gathering of effervescent enthusiasm, a refreshing experience of what neo-Pentecostalism is all about. If so it might once again herald the ecumenical, signifying the weakness of the movement rather than its strength.

At this stage we are clearly asking fresh questions. Do these developments augur well for the future of the movement? Are the foundations sufficiently secure to give it a lasting endurance? Perhaps that depends on your perspective. In the final chapter Martyn Percy steers clear of the clutter of subjectivism when he considers the future prospects.

The preceding chapters also provide some of the answers. They indicate that much has happened in the last 30 years. At the end of his gospel, St John says there were so many things that Jesus had done that all the books in the world could not relate them. There are many things that neo-Pentecostalism has done in His name. The contributions which follow document a few of them.

NOTES

1. One estimate from a source sympathetic to the movement puts the total number of Pentecostals and Charismatics at 4.3 billion; D. J. Hasselgrave, *Today's Choice for Tomorrow's Mission* (Grand Rapids, MI: Zondervan Publishing House, 1992).
2. In the case of Roman Catholic Charismatics, the universities of Duquesne in Pittsburgh, Notre Dame and Michigan State were the cradles of the charismatic experience before it spread widely through the Catholic world; E. D. O'Connor, 'A Catholic Pentecostal Movement', *Ave Maria*, vol.105, no.22, June 1975, pp.3–10.
3. Notably, C. Y. Glock and R. Stark's classic work *Religion and Society in Tension* (New York: Rand McNally, 1966).
4. In some respects the writing was always on the wall for the Roman Catholic Charismatics. Movements feeding into Catholic renewal, such as the Catechumenate and eucharistic celebrations not only concerned themselves with rediscovering the Spirit but also advocated the recovery of long-neglected aspects of specifically Roman Catholic church life; K. McDonnell, 'Catholic Pentecostals. Problems in Evaluation', *Dialogue*, Winter, 1970; E. O'Connor, *The Pentecostal Movement in the Catholic Church* (Notre Dame: Ave Maria Press, 1971).

BIBLIOGRAPHY

John Arnott, *Receiving the Spirit's Power*, audio tape, Toronto Vineyard Church, 1994.

J. D. Balswick, 'The Jesus Movement: A Sociological Analysis', in E. Barker (ed.), *New Religious Movements: Studies in Religion and Society, 3* (New York: Edwin Meller Press, 1982), pp.259–66.

D. W. Bebbington, *Evangelism in Modern Britain: A History from the 1730s to the 1980s* (London: Unwin Hyman, 1989).

D. Bennett, *Nine O'Clock in the Morning* (Plainfield, NJ: Logos International, 1970).

P. Berger, *The Heretical Imperative* (Penguin: London, 1979).

Revd H. G. Boniface, *Church and People*, 11 August 1967.

R. L. Carrol, 'Glossolalia: Apostles to the Reformation', in W. H. Horton (ed.), *The Glossolalia Phenomenon* (Cleveland: Pathway Press, 1966) pp.67–94.

H. P. Chalfont, R. E. Beckley and C. E. Palmer, *Religion in Contemporary Society* (Palo Alto, CA: Marxfield Publishing, 1987).

'Charismatic Crossroads', *A Report of a Leadership Consultation on the Current Situation in the Charismatic Churches*, 1995.

H. Cox, *Fire From Heaven: The Rise of Pentecostal Spirituality and the Reshaping of Religion in the Twenty-First Century* (Reading, MA: Addison-Wesley, 1995).

G. Davie, *Religion in Britain since 1945: Believing Without Belonging* (Oxford: Blackwell, 1994).

E. Durkheim, *The Elementary Forms of Religious Life* (New York: Collier Books, 1961).

P. Elbert, 'Renewal Movement "losing the war"', *Eternity*, no.33, Nov. 1988.

S. Gaede, 'Review Symposium', *Journal of the Scientific Study of Religion*, no.20, 1981, pp.181–8.

M. Harper, *As at the Beginning* (Plainfield, NJ: Logos International, 1965).

P. Hocken, *Streams of Renewal: Origins and Early Developments of the Charismatic Movement in Britain* (Exeter: Paternoster Press, 1986).

W. Hollenwerger, *The Pentecostals: The Charismatic Movement in the Churches* (London: SCM, 1966).

L. R. Iannaccone, 'Religious Practice: A Human Capital Approach', *Journal of the Scientific Study of Religion*, no.29, 1990, pp.297–314.

J. F. Lyotard, *The Post Modern Condition* (Manchester: Manchester University Press, 1984).

D. Martin, *The Dilemma of Contemporary Religion* (Oxford: Basil Blackwell, 1978).

K. McDonnell, *Pentecostals in the Modern World* (Notre Dame: Ave Maria Press, 1972).

M. McGuire, *Pentecostal Catholics: Power Charisma and Order in a Religious Movement* (Philadelphia: Temple University Press, 1982).

M. A. Noll (ed.), *The Scandal of the Evangelical Mind* (Leicester: Intervarsity Press, 1994).

R. Reed, *From Movement to Institution: A Case Study of Charismatic Renewal in the Anglican Church in Canada*, Paper Presented at the 21st Annual Conference of the Society for Pentecostal Studies, Florida, 1991.

R. Stark and W. Bainbridge, *The Future of Religion* (Berkeley, CA: University of California Press, 1985).

V. Turner, *The Ritual Process* (Harmondsworth: Penguin, 1974).

P. Wagner, *Warfare Prayer* (Venturer, CA: Regal Books, 1992).

A. Walker, 'Pentecostal Power. The "Charismatic Renewal Movement" and the Politics of Pentecostal Experience', in E. Barker (ed.) *Of Gods and Men: New Religious Movements in the West* (Macon: Mercer University Press, 1983) pp.89–105.

A. Walker, *Restoring the Kingdom: The Radical Christianity of The House Church Movement* (London: Hodder & Stoughton, 1985).

R. Wallis, *Elementary Forms of New Religious Life* (London: Routledge, 1984).

B. Wilson, *Religion in a Secular Society* (London: C. A. Watts, 1966).

B. Wilson, 'The New Religions: Preliminary Considerations', in E. Barker (ed.), *New Religious Movements: A Perspective for Understanding Society* (New York: Edwin Mellor Press, 1982), pp.16–31.

R. Wuthnow, *Christianity in the Twenty-First Century: Reflections on the Challenge Ahead* (Oxford: Oxford University Press, 1993).

1 Thoroughly Modern: Sociological Reflections on the Charismatic Movement from the End of the Twentieth Century

Andrew Walker

INTRODUCTION

When the 'Marches For Jesus' began in our cities in 1989 it was said by some of the organizers that marching on the streets was a way of 'shifting the demonic atmosphere': they believed that cities and regions of the world could be controlled by 'territorial spirits'. Indeed, these days, demonic infestations, which are legion, seem to be bound up with well known and much sought after exorcists: Bill Subritzky from New Zealand, Derek Prince from the United States, Peter Horrobin from Lancashire, and the Revd Arbuthnot from the London Healing Mission, are just some of the people who have a 'special ministry' in the realm of unclean spirits.[1] Such beliefs and practices might seem evidence enough that the Charismatic movement is pre-modern, a throwback to a primitive or animistic religion – to an era, as Rudolf Bultmann would have put it, when it was only possible to believe in such things before the advent of wireless and electric light.[2]

And it is not just a question of demons: oil miraculously appearing on hands at Kensington City Temple, London, it has been rumoured (a feature of the American healing movement of the 1940s), roaring and laughing at the height of the 'Toronto Blessing' of the 1990s, and that mainstay of classical Pentecostalism, *glossolalia* – all these phenomena seem to inhabit a cultural universe beyond the ken of modernity. So one might be tempted to think that such religious supernaturalism in the modern world is culturally misplaced. To read the religious supernaturalism as primitive, however, is not only usually reductionist in intent but it is also empirically indiscriminate: if Charismatic religion

17

is a throwback then what are we to make of *The X Files*, alternative medicine, crystals and star gazing, the late modern fascination with the weird and the unexplained, the replacement, we might say, of 'mere Christianity' with the merely strange? We might want to offer the rationalistic or aesthetic judgement that these things are bizarre or bewildering – even a form of pre-millennial tension or post-modern fragmentation – but hardly, I would have thought, be satisfied with the epithet 'pre-modern'.

Perhaps we would be on surer sociological ground if we were to reserve judgement on the pre-modern or primitive status of Charismatic phenomena and note that they appear to be firmly fixed to those religious movements that can be seen to be not so much pre-modern as anti-modern. Following Troeltsch and Weber's classic division into church and sect there have been few sociologists[3] who have not viewed Pentecostalism and its many Charismatic mutations as 'culturally denying' in some sense and thus resistant to modernity. In Niebuhr's seminal *Christ and Culture*, for example, it is quite clear that all things Pentecostal would fit his rubric of 'Christ Against Culture'.[4] Admittedly, theologian John Howard Yoder and sociologist Bryan Wilson would prefer the notion of 'conversionist' to describe the sectarian nature of Charismatic groups, but like Neibuhr and Troeltsch before them they too accept that such sects are still essentially resistant movements to the modern world; certainly not institutional and symbolic carriers of modernity.[5]

A proper case could be made that some expressions of Charismatic religiosity cannot be classified by sectarian notions of conversionism,[6] but in this chapter I prefer not to become embroiled in typological issues but rather to argue that Charismatic Christianity is neither essentially pre-modern nor anti-modern. On the contrary, I shall argue, it has embraced modernity either begrudgingly (making Pentecostalism reluctantly modern) or with enthusiasm (with the result that Pentecostal religion can be called thoroughly modern). Such a revisionist historiography seems apposite as we near the end of the century for we can now look back on 100 years of Pentecostal and neo-Pentecostal religion. I do not wish to assert that there are no world-denying elements in Charismatic Christianity, nor no anti-modern aspects to such movements – especially when second adventist hopes are high – but more plausibly to argue that Charismatic Christianity is more modern than not.

REVIVALISM IS ITSELF A MODERN PHENOMENON

Pentecostalism, and its Charismatic outcrops, is the twentieth century's most successful embodiment of revivalism. Revivalism itself came into being at the dawn of the Enlightenment and thus can be properly classified as a modern phenomenon. I have argued elsewhere that the literary culture that developed with the invention of printing in the late fifteenth century facilitated not only critical rationality but also individualism and pietism.[7] The Age of Reason was also the age of revivals. Both John Wesley and Jonathan Edwards, born in 1703, were admirers of science. Edwards may have been a high Puritan but he was considerably influenced by John Locke and Isaac Newton.

The Methodist revival in Europe and the First Great Awakening in New England have to be seen, in my opinion, as part of the cultural shift from feudalism to capitalism. In the United States in particular the revivals ensured the successful transmission of Protestant religion from feudalism into the modern era but they also sounded the death knell for the already crumbling Puritan covenant of 1620. To see the eighteenth century revivals as the cultural carriers of modernity may seem a strange idea because we tend to think of them in opposition to the Enlightenment preoccupation with rationality, deism and unitarianism. Or again we may be reminded that Gotthold Lessing characterized the Enlightenment as a 'big ugly ditch' that halted historic Christianity in its path.

But the early revivals were not opposed to critical rationality, individualism and progressivism in themselves. Jonathan Edwards, for example, may be remembered for his frightening sermons on God's wrath and eternal perdition but he also provided a thoroughly modern psychological account of the revivals and his own wife's religious experiences.[8] Perhaps the most convincing evidence of the modernizing tendencies of early revivalism comes from Jon Butler's revisionist accounts of the American Awakenings (especially the Second Awakening at the advent of the nineteenth century) where he demonstrates that the passion and piety of the revivals also fuelled the progressivist vision of the American dream. The Puritan vision of the 'city set upon the hill' settled down to a dream of a decent and respectable life in the new Republic. When revivalistic fervour cooled it left a strong residue of ascetic Protestantism, with its commitment to literacy and hard work, and in time provided a ladder of social mobility.[9]

The early revivals had unintended consequences not least because their emphasis on experience and the self was not only thoroughly modern in itself but was also conducive both to the religious freedom of the Republic and to the pietistic but theologically non-specific 'civil religion' of middle America.[10] More obviously revivals were themselves aided both by the technology and the principles of modernity. Not only is this the case with the appropriation of firstly the telegraph and later the phonograph for the more routinized revivals and urban missions of the nineteenth century, but it is also the case that revivalists came to see their campaigns in terms of pragmatic techniques. This assertion does not hold for The First Awakening or the 1801 Cane Ridge revival in Kentucky: the first revivals were too new, spontaneous and unexpected to be honed into a technique. But the assertion does hold for Finney's great revivals of the early years of the nineteenth century. As he says in his *Lectures On Revival*: 'A revival is not a miracle, or dependent on a miracle, in any sense. It is purely philosophical results of the right use of constituted means as much as any other effect produced by the application of means.'[11]

Henceforth American Camp Meetings, holiness gatherings, revivalistic campaigns became formatted and routinized: nightly meetings, demotic preaching and singing, altar calls, 'anxious benches'. To this was later added mass publicity, showmanship and most important of all business acumen. George Thomas goes so far as to say that nineteenth century revivalism was isomorphic with the rise of early forms of modernity.[12]

The early revivals, then, contributed to the advancement of modernity because they provided a value matrix conducive to the ascetic Protestantism of early capitalism. The enthusiasm, freedom, individualism and moral values of the revivals entered the mainstream of American society: revivals helped reinforce the work ethic and the expressivism so dear to the heart of nineteenth century America. They also provided a legitimate context for public emotion which in time became transferred to the secular contexts of baseball, football and politics. Vestiges of early revivalism remain in American religious life today through the legacy of sacred songs, vernacular preaching, special conventions and visiting speakers. The long term and lasting effects of the revivals, however, have not been the continuation of an evangelical Camp Meeting tradition but the establishment of numerous denominations and established sects, the contribution to civic life through the building of hospitals and universities, and the provision through education and self-help of a ladder of social mobility from the working class to the middle class.

The thesis that classic revivalism was both a contributor to the modernizing process and in turn adapted to the modernizing process seems less contentious if we contrast these revivals with the millennialism of early Charismatic religion. Pentecostals were convinced that the end of the world was imminent, whereas a proper modern confidence characterized the great revivals – of Wesley, Whitfield, Edwards and Finney. Certainly these founding modern evangelists could see Lessing's ditch as an obstacle in their path but they were convinced that they could jump across it and ride on into a hopeful future. For them there was hope in the future, for there was to be a future. In short, modernity was a challenge but it was not a catastrophe which heralded the end of time as it did for Pentecostals.

It is interesting to compare the optimism of the late eighteenth century/early nineteenth century American revivals with the outbreak of Irvingism in London in the 1820s. Irving can properly be seen as the 'morning star' of Pentecostalism[13] and is certainly the most interesting precursor of twentieth century charismatic Christianity. For our purposes in this chapter what is interesting about Irving is not the outbreak of tongues in Regent Square in October 1830, nor even the establishment of 12 apostles in the wake of his ministry. For us what is striking is that Irving, the Albury circle of which he was a part, and their prophetic journal, *The Morning Watch*, were all convinced that the French Revolution signalled not only the end of an age but the end of time. Irving believed that modernity was essentially evil and was to be resisted: the role of the saints was to endure the coming crisis until the eagerly awaited, and soon to be expected, Rapture.

Irving, unlike Edwards and Wesley, was deeply romantic. Attached to Coleridge and an upholder of feudal traditions, Irving had no place in his worldview for the future. The only future for modern culture was its eventual destruction. The immediate future of the Church was to be snatched from the world like a brand from the burning coals.[14]

The American counterpart to this eschatology of disaster began in New York State in the 1820s with the Church of the Latter Day Saints (they too were tongue-speakers in the early days) and it continued with William Miller in the 1830s. Despite the failure of Miller's predictions, modern day millenialism entered the American bloodstream like a foreign body opposed to the health and progress of the cultural organism. We not only think of the Christadelphians, Seventh Day Adventists, and Jehovah's Witnesses, but also of an abiding fascination with the final things by the ever-growing evangelical movements from the 1860s onwards. Consequently the optimism of the First and Second Great Awakenings, of early American revivalism, was dampened by pessimistic rumblings fuelled by the many holiness movements that emerged from the Camp Meetings and disaffected Methodism. In time America was to become the homeland of modern millenialism under the enormous influence of Schofield's theories of Dispensations outlined in the Bible that bears his name and which was first published in 1909.[15]

PENTECOSTALISM AS TWENTIETH CENTURY REVIVALISM

There are a number of reasons why Pentecostalism can be seen as anti-modern in contradistinction to the modernizing tendencies of the early revivals. First, from the early days of Charles Parham at Kansas in the 1890s and Pastor Seymour in Azusa Street in Los Angeles from the first decade of the twentieth century, the manifestations of tongues, prophecy, exorcisms and so on, led to almost universal condemnation by what Irving used to mockingly call 'the religious world'. The jerks and barks of Cane Ridge were outlandish enough for many mainline Christians, but claims that the charismata of the New Testament had been restored to the modern world of science and steam trains seemed preposterous.

Second, the fact that such 'signs and wonders' were appearing among black and white uneducated people was considered to be evidence of their lack of plausibility. The fact that early Pentecostalism was a religion of the dispossessed has been exaggerated[16] but it is true that the majority of the early Pentecostals were working class. For Marxists, as for Anderson years later, Pentecostal experience was an example of 'false consciousness':[17] economically deprived working men and women were turning their backs on the promise of progress through revolutionary struggle and were being hoodwinked by immediate emotional satisfaction on the one hand ('the Baptism of the Spirit') and a false earthly utopia on the other hand (the literal thousand year reign of Christ and the saints).

And this leads us to the third, and in the light of our earlier section on revivals, the most important reason why Pentecostalism has been understood to be against modernity. The new revivalism was 'birthed', to use Charismatic nomenclature, in adventist hope. Pentecostal revival was itself seen by its members as a sign of the end-time. Following Parham, many of them also initially believed that the tongues were the evangelistic means whereby the whole world could receive the good news of the gospel.[18] So early Pentecostalism adopted a conversionist modus operandi because it thought that the time was short, the fields already 'white unto harvest', and that revival – spearheaded by the miracle of tongues – would sweep millions into the kingdom of God as the precursor to the end of the world.

The revivalistic fervour predicated upon Charismatic experience and millennial excitation led either to a hostile stance to the world or an indifferent attitude to civic responsibility and the lure of modern progress. Pentecostals were certainly not right-wing in their early days but rather apolitical and culturally denying.

The antagonistic attitude of the other churches to Pentecostals also facilitated the Pentecostal rejection of both the established churches and the secular world. In this respect at least, when coupled with adventist fervour, classical Pentecostalism was, unlike the earlier revivals, initially anti-modern. However, like those revivals, Pentecostalism, over time, became at the very least an unwitting symbolic carrier of modernity as well as falling prey to the secularizing tendencies of the modern world. Its modernizing tendencies, however, vary between classical and neo-Pentecostalism on the one hand and between the First and Third Worlds on the other hand. Before we proceed to demonstrate this there is one obvious, and much cited, objection to the claim that Charismatic religion is thoroughly modern. This objection is to insist that Pentecostalism is, on the contrary, thoroughly fundamentalist and thus anti-modernist. I believe, at best, that this argument is a red herring, but because of its plausible appeal and widespread acceptance I will deal with it now in the form of an excursus.

PENTECOSTALISM AS FUNDAMENTALISM

Many of the early Pentecostals were pleased to boast of their fundamentalist allegiance. Official support was widespread for the *Fundamentals* published between 1912 and 1916 by leading conservatives from the Princeton School of Theology and their allies. Words like 'inerrant' and 'fundamentalist' appeared in many a Pentecostal confession of faith. In Great Britain only a few years ago the magazine of the Elim Church bore the legend on its front page that it was 'Pentecostal, Evangelical, Fundamental'.

There are, however, a number of problems in identifying Pentecostals with fundamentalists. The most obvious one is to show that the second generation of Pentecostals, both renewalist and independents, are not wedded to a fundamentalist epistemology. This is clearly so for

many Anglican and Catholic renewalists but it can also be said to be
the case for 'new church' leaders like Roger Forster of Ichthus and
Gerald Coates of Pioneer.[19] Furthermore it could not unreasonably be
said that the recent and brief history of the Toronto Blessing demonstrates that Biblical fidelity is not paramount for the new generation of
Charismatics; it is difficult to see how, for example, one could ground
the Toronto Blessing in Biblical narrative or scriptural proof texts.[20]

It might seem that this argument is sleight of hand as neo-Pentecostals
are only distant cousins to their classic brethren. This objection is
epistemologically quite strong – neo-Pentecostals are not typically
wedded to holiness traditions as classical Pentecostals are – but it is
phenomenologically weak: modern Charismatics and Pentecostals are
much the same. Admittedly, renewalists are gentrified Pentecostalists
but they are not a different genus, and the sociological distinctions we
might have made, even ten years ago, between classical and neo-
Pentecostal are now difficult to sustain in the light of new Charismatic
alignments and the syncretistic tendencies of late Pentecostalism.[21] These
days classical Pentecostals feed off the independent or so-called 'new
churches' who feed off renewalists who in turn feed off classical
Pentecostals. If you visit Kensington Temple in London, for example,
it may formally be Elim Pentecostal but it is awash with the methodologies of John Wimber and Rodney Howard Browne, Morris Cerullo,
and the indomitable style of its own Colin Dye. Despite its virtually
white leadership Kensington Temple also reflects the earlier Camp
Meeting style of its large Afro-Caribbean membership.

Alternatively you can visit St Andrew's, Chorleywood, and be introduced to Anglican renewals, with its Wimber clinics, Toronto swoon-
ing, and whiffs of Pentecostal holiness prophecy via visits from some
of the Kansas City Prophets (who themselves hark back to the healing
revivals of North America in the 1940s under the controversial William
Branham).

But if we were to accept the sleight of hand argument we would
still have to contend with Don Dayton's revisionist history of American classical Pentecostalism in which he contends that Pentecostalism
is certainly pietist and rooted in holiness traditions but it is only incidentally fundamentalist.[22] Fundamentalism was in the air before Pentecostalism came into being. To assert your evangelical legitimacy in
the early part of the twentieth century you had to sport your fundamentalist credentials. And Pentecostals craved legitimacy among their
evangelical peers even if they were indifferent to everyone else. Fundamentalism, in other words, acted as a useful legitimation for a move-

ment that wanted to demonstrate that it was faithful to New Testament Christianity.

Dayton's revisionism is particularly compelling if we look at the more extreme developments of Pentecostalism, for Charismatic Christianity has not always been tied to orthodox belief despite the fundamentalist label. Oneness Pentecostalism, for example, which developed soon after the revivals of Azusa Street in Los Angeles, was heretical in its understanding of God and refused to use the Trinitarian formula for baptism.[23] Again if we turn to the Christology of William Branham in the 1940s we find something more akin to Arianism than the orthodoxy of the Nicene Constantinopolitan creed.[24] And it is clear that if Charles Hodge of Princeton, or B. B. Warfield, the intellectual architects of fundamentalism, were to investigate the hermeneutics of say Kenneth Hagin and Kenneth Copeland of the Faith Movement they would turn in their graves.[25] Indeed in many ways the Pentecostal revivals by their very volatile nature have been a challenge to the scholastic rationalism of the fundamentalist movement. Pentecostals have certainly been Bible lovers but they have also been moved by the Spirit, spoken prophetic words and received new revelations.[26]

Ironically if we were to take issue with Dayton and see (to use a pre-modern analogy) Pentecostalism as essentially rather than accidentally fundamentalist then this would actually strengthen our argument that Pentecostalism is modern. This is so because fundamentalism, despite its resistance to modern thought, is itself, modernist. The Princeton theologians in the last quarter of the nineteenth century were convinced that the new higher criticism that was emerging from the German Liberal School of Theology, of Ritschl, Harnack *et al.*, when coupled with the evolutionary theories of Charles Darwin, posed serious threats to the truth claims of historic Christianity. In particular it was felt that redactive criticism and the like called into question the reliability of the Biblical record.

In this respect fundamentalism was part of the religious resistance movement to modernism at the end of the nineteenth century. Rome resisted through Vatican I and the papal dogmas, Protestantism through fundamentalism. Fundamentalism, however, unlike Vatican I was thoroughly modern in method and intent. Nineteenth century philosophers and scientists were looking for rational foundations of reality, so some conservative theologians felt it wise to do the same as part of an apologetically aimed strategy against modernism. The Princeton school alighted on a foundation which they believed would rationally shore-up the truth claims of Christianity.[27] To paraphrase a well known fundamentalist book: Christianity is true because the Bible tells us so. And the Bible can be trusted, so the argument went, because God Who is Truth has revealed Himself as truth in the sacred text. The Bible by virtue of this fact is *ipso facto* both the vehicle and the locus of truth.

The sting in the tail for what was an essentially rational epistemology raised to the status of religious dogma is, that as the Bible, as God's book, is true, it can never contradict itself: the Bible is no longer merely 'infallible' to use a well seasoned Reformation word, it is also 'inerrant'. In practice, however, the notion of inerrancy is problematic because this new foundation of truth (unknown in dogmatic form by the Fathers or the Reformers) had to deal with the tricky problem of textual contradictions which appear to be legion. Furthermore many, but not all, of the early fundamentalists recast the first two chapters of the book of Genesis as scientific accounts of the creation of the world so that the Bible was now set up in opposition to biological science as well as German theology.

The high tide of fundamentalist scholarship passed with the First World War where in many evangelical and Pentecostal circles it became ensnared with dispensationalist theories of prophecy. It also became increasingly sectarian and in time even anti-intellectual. After the debacle of the Scopes monkey trial in America in 1925 fundamentalism became an object of ridicule in most theological circles and despite its resurgence in the 1980s through tele-evangelism it is now in retreat in many American evangelical seminaries.[28]

This does not alter the fact that early fundamentalism was a rational, not to say modern(ist), attempt to underpin the truth of the Bible by a tendentious theory of the inspiration of scripture. Nevertheless fundamentalism, by virtue of its Biblicism, succeeded in constraining and controlling Pentecostal theology and practice: it kept the new enthusiasm within the evangelical fold and curbed its volatile excesses by an insistence on Biblical fidelity.

THE MODERN TENDENCIES OF NORMATIVE CLASSICAL PENTECOSTALISM

If we grant that classical Pentecostalism was anti-modern in its revivalistic days we do so simply because it was adventist and quite literally 'other worldly'. Over time, however, as the routinization of charisma set in Pentecostalism trod the well worn path of American nineteenth century urban missions with all their pragmatic tendencies and replete with the latest modern technologies. On the one hand Pentecostals, unlike Methodists and Anglicans, have not adopted a modern scriptural hermeneutic nor acceded to Enlightenment doctrines of progress and critical rationality. On the other hand, Pentecostals have been open to modern technologies, advertising and management techniques. Their commitment to demotic hymnody – no doubt in order to subvert popular culture – has meant in effect that they have been far more at home with mass media and consumer culture than many of their mainline counterparts.

Furthermore, the fact that the Pentecostals of the twentieth century have not been perceived to have joined the societal mainstream as obviously as Methodists did in the nineteenth century is partially a question of their anti-worldly ideology but also partly a question of a slower assimilation of modern values. Pentecostals, in the First World at least, have been reluctant modernizers and have become thoroughly modern by a slow process of cultural osmosis rather than through ideological acceptance of the modern world. In Great Britain, for example, before the First World War, Bible Colleges were originally eschewed as unnecessary for spirit-filled Christians. By the 1920s, however, the Elim Pentecostal Church had established a Bible College therefore ensuring the professionalization of its pastors and hence contributing to the gradual modernization of the church. This process has taken some 40 years to come to fruition. Today, the Elim Bible College has become Regent's Theological College complete with a director for studies with an earned Ph.D., an undergraduate BA and a new MA course. The Assemblies of God College at Mattersey Hall in the North East of England has a similar story to tell.

It is David Martin's recent studies, however, that provide the most convincing evidence of the modernizing tendencies of Pentecostalism.[29] For if Pentecostals have been a little slow off the mark in diving into the modern stream in Europe and North America, the opposite can be said of South America. Pentecostalism is the fastest growing Christian religion in the Third World and in some Central and South American countries Pentecostals already number some 40 million which is approximately one in ten of the population.

To be a Pentecostal in South America is to be a modern in capitalist guise. Pentecostal leaders are not only Spirit-led but also entrepreneurs and small businessmen. 'The Evangelical poor,' on the other hand, says Martin, 'have adopted a discipline of life: no drink or drugs, no fiesta, but hard work, careful budgeting, honesty, family integrity, and discipline in the home. According to social workers their children may

well perform above average at school.'[30] Despite the neo-Marxist rhetoric
of Catholic liberation theology, Catholicism has not been a successful
agency of modernity in South America, but Pentecostalism would appear
to be so. This is not just because Marxism is losing out all over the
world to free enterprise, but because in South America Marxist Catholics
are clearly outnumbered by the many traditional Catholics who support
the feudal structures of the traditional landowners. Pentecostals, by
contrast, are for free expression, free enterprise, democracy, hard work,
individualism and the Holy Ghost. They are thoroughly modern but
with 'signs following'.

At the very least upholders of the view that Pentecostalism is anti-
modern will have to, in the light of the empirical evidence, revise
their thesis to say that Pentecostalism might be said to be reluctantly
modern in the First World of advanced industrial societies, but in the
Third World Pentecostalism would appear to be at least as significant
a modernizing agency as Methodism was in Britain and North America
in the eighteenth and nineteenth centuries.

Classical Pentecostalism since Azusa Street has always been an
amalgam of ancient and modern – 'a traditional service in the modern
manner' as the advertising slogan goes. A feature of my own studies
among the so-called house churches or new churches, who are hybrids
of classical and neo-Pentecostalism, is that rational and economic goals
are often set and adhered to in a sensible manner but these would
often be buttressed by Charismatic reinforcements. Bryn Jones of Covenant ministries, for example, offered a perfectly rational argument to
me as to why he had pioneered new churches along the west coast of
Scotland, England and Wales, but also offered the insight that 'we had
a prophecy about that'.[31] Gerald Coates of Pioneer is a very successful
Christian leader in Britain, well organized, hi-tech, pragmatic and modern,
but he also takes notice of dreams, prophecies, promptings.[32]

(How many secular business agencies, we wonder, take advantage
of New Age methodologies to improve their performance indicators?[33]
Such activities are surely typical of late or post-modernity rather than
indices of anti-modern sentiment.)

To suggest that classical Pentecostalism is at the least reluctantly
modern and at the most thoroughly modern is not so much to point to
its use of modern tunes, new technologies and secular business techniques – though these are not without significance – but to register the
fact that Pentecostalism has ministered to the poor and the disinherited
in a culturally appropriate manner and in so doing has initiated them
into the working processes and value systems of modernity. In short,

Pentecostalism for the working classes has been a continuation of the ascetic Protestantism of Puritanism and the revivals of the Great Awakenings. It has provided modest but real social mobility for working class families in Europe and North America and a fast-track modernizing programme for many in the Third World. Even if we want to apply a Marxist perspective to the phenomenon of Pentecostalism (which we mentioned earlier) and criticize it in terms of religious opium and 'false consciousness' this is not to deny its modernizing tendencies but rather to discredit its revolutionary potential.

FROM CLASSICAL PENTECOSTALISM TO CHARISMATIC CHRISTIANITY

It is surely no coincidence that when Pentecostalism was transformed from its working class style to its middle class one we had moved from early to late modernity: an era that with the advent of consumerism in the 1950s saw the demise of ascetic individualism and the rise of hedonistic individualism.[34] When in the 1960s middle class members of mainline churches claimed the 'Baptism in the Spirit' as their own, classical Pentecostalism found itself with what was initially perceived to be a rival in the revivalist stakes.[35] This new, or neo-Pentecostalism, was not only different in terms of social status and organization but also in tone.

We noticed it first in the name used to tag the new enthusiasm. The specialist and non-threatening adjective 'Charismatic' replaced the proper noun Pentecostal. This was affixed to the altogether more restrained and non-evangelistic badge of belonging known as 'Renewal'. To be in the Charismatic Renewal was to be still a committed Anglican or Catholic, Baptist or Presbyterian. A renewalist was for praise and sanctity, a devotee of religious experience, but he or she was not a revivalist. Those in the Renewal found themselves in ever larger circles, and in increasingly successful ventures, but they moved together, with each other: they did not evangelize the unchurched in any systematic way as the Pentecostalists had done in the flush of the revivals.

Gradually as the Renewal grew tendentious Pentecostal doctrines were dropped, such as the two-stage experience of conversion and Spirit baptism (which was inherited in part from the holiness days of belief in the 'second blessing' of sanctification). Charismatics during the late 1960s underwent what I earlier called a process of gentrification: they sported bishops and canons from the Church of England among their number, nuns and priests from Rome, and even a cardinal from Belgium. Theological literature of a scholarly fashion flowed from the pens of Charismatic apologists.[36] They also attracted pop stars in their orbit such as Sir Cliff Richard, and even for a time captured Bob Dylan who gravitated for a season to a Vineyard church in California.

To be a Charismatic, then, was phenomenologically identical to being a Pentecostal but culturally redefined by class, taste and the late modern preoccupation with therapy and self-fulfilment. Chorus singing, clapping and dancing were incorporated into the new enthusiasm but Charismatics preferred their own tunes and songs – more middle of the road rock and modern anthem than Redemption Hymnal and Moody and Sankey.[37] They maintained interest in physical healings but moved deeper into a realm of inner healings. People in the Renewal were in touch with themselves as well as with God. As the Hobbesian and hedonistic individual replaced ascetic individualism in the larger culture so the Renewal reflected these changes in its style of worship and experientially driven theology. If Pentecostals in the First World were reluctantly modern in their early days, renewalists were thoroughly modern from the start.

The 1960s was a revolution of experience – sexual and chemical – and in some quarters this revolution was seen as counter-cultural. The Charismatic movement in the churches reflected the idealism, the heightened experience, and the hedonism of this counter-culture even though ideologically they were opposed to each other. Within a few years the Renewal also folded back into classical Pentecostalism. Songs, ministries and styles began to cross over the classical/neo-Pentecostal divide. Oral Roberts, for example, during his successful reign as a tele-evangelist from the late 1970s to the mid 1980s became a Methodist. Like those other Pentecostalists, Jimmy and Tammy Bakker (unlike Jimmy Swaggert), he dropped the strident fundamentalism and evangelistic fervour of his earlier days in favour of a folksy, cosy approach.

Tele-evangelism itself reflected the narcissistic streak of American hedonism. Christianity was repackaged so that increasingly there was little emphasis on asceticism – what you could do for God – towards self-gratification – what God could do for you. Steve Bruce superbly captures this mood change.

> The broad road is the pursuit of self-fulfilment, self-satisfaction, and self-esteem. The 'power of positive thinking', roundly criticised by conservative Protestants for its 'this worldly' orientation when it was

presented by Norman Vincent Peale in the 1950s, now informs most religious television. This is less of a change for Robert Schuller (like Peale a Reformed Church minister and a man who has never claimed to be a fundamentalist) than it is for Oral Roberts, Jim Bakker, or Kenneth Copeland, but the ghastly punning title of Schuller's *The Be Happy Attitudes* will stand as a sign of the orientation of most televangelism.[38]

Not only tele-evangelists got in this groove. Writing in the 1980s James Davison Hunter demonstrated that evangelicals generally, and Charismatics in particular, were borrowing heavily from secular therapeutic models and looking for life-enhancing satisfaction. Here are some of the typical titles Hunter selected from the Christian bookshelves:

- *Transformed Temperaments*
- *Defeating Despair and Depression*
- *God's Key to Health and Happiness*
- *Feeling Good about Feeling Bad*
- *How to Become a Happy Christian*
- *How to Become Your Own Best Self*[39]

NEO-PENTECOSTALS, INDEPENDENTS AND CHARISMATIC REALIGNMENTS IN LATE MODERNITY[40]

If by neo-Pentecostalism we mean specifically the Charismatic Renewal Movement in the mainline denominations then I think we have to say that it existed in a pure form for only a very few years – say from 1965 to 1980. The 1970s was the decade of its greatest influence when barely a major denomination had not been flooded with the new songs, the excitement and the renewal of religious commitment. Looking back it was the Kansas City Conference of 1977 that stands out as the Woodstock of Charismatic ecumenical experience. At Kansas the Renewal seemed at its most joyous and least strident. Final and formal worldwide recognition for the Renewal came in 1980 at Bossey in Switzerland when the World Council of Churches held its one and only consultation on the movement.[41] By the time I wrote 'A new light for the churches' for the Agenda page of *The Guardian* newspaper on 24 November 1980 the Renewal was already waning.

Writing now over 15 years later I think that although the Renewal was analytically distinct from classical Pentecostalism – not least because it was middle class and non-denominational – I now think that it was never a totally distinct phenomenon; it was never exclusively middle class or totally free from sectarianism.[42] Neither did it totally free itself from Pentecostal theology and practices. Fr Peter Hocken has demonstrated that a number of independent movements, classical streams and new renewal groups not only overlapped but intertwined in Great Britain from at least the 1960s.[43] Men from classical Pentecostal backgrounds, such as David du Plessis from the Assemblies of God and Cecil Cousens from the Apostolic Church, had considerable influence on the theology and belief systems of the burgeoning Renewal. Maverick groups, such as the North American healing movement of the 1940s and the 'Latter Rain' movement of Canada in the 1950s provided numerous personnel who found their way into the Renewal in one way or another.

From the late 1970s until the present time what we have seen since the heyday of the Renewal is the emergence of numerous independent ministries, maverick organizations, new networks of churches, parachurch groups. These new movements did not destroy the Renewal movement but they did rival it, then penetrate it, and eventually alter its nature. In the 1980s, for example, by far the most significant Charismatic growth in Great Britain came from the so-called Restorationist house churches. These were certainly not renewalist for they taught a radical separationist doctrine and condemned the historical churches as moribund. With their commitment to apostolic and prophetic leadership, and their 'shepherding' or discipleship doctrines, these independent churches were in effect a threat both to the Renewal and to classical Pentecostalism. Restorationism was not a new version of classical Pentecostalism as I mistakenly thought in 1985: it was a syncretistic amalgam of classical, renewalist and independent streams.[44]

Restorationists were like renewalists in terms of their middle class affiliation and their emphasis on experience and new songs. They were also similar to classical Pentecostalists in two respects: they were more enthusiastic about evangelism that the renewalists, and they regrouped themselves into enclaves that were sociologically sectarian in character. It could also be said of Restorationists that they were a throwback to Irving and the Catholic Apostolic Church (CAC) of the 1830s.[45] Like the CAC, Restorationists initially thought that their movement in itself heralded the end of time. In this sense they were millennial and one might have expected them to be anti-modern. However, unlike both Irving and early Pentecostalism, Restorationists were optimistic about the future and were committed to the establishment of a powerful Church before the thousand year reign of Christ.[46] This 'eschatology of victory' led them to be optimistic about the future, and by the early 1980s their business acumen and organizational flair lent them a thoroughly modern air.

By the mid 1980s, however, strange things began to happen. As Bryan Wilson put it to me at All Souls, Oxford, religious changes were taking place at a bewildering pace in the late twentieth century.[47] This speeding-up process meant that Christian religious formations were coming and going, starting and stopping, with the speed we associate with New Religious Movements. Restorationism in a ten-year period, for example, underwent the kind of growth, changes, splits, and realignments, that took Elim and the Assemblies of God 60 years to undergo.

With the advent of niche marketing, video and audio tape sales, rapid movement from country to country, and the beginning of information technology, Charismatic Christianity went into overdrive in the late 1980s. The Evangelical Alliance persuaded most of the house churches, now being called 'new churches', to join them. The family oriented Spring Harvest celebrations became a catch-all Charismatic supermarket where classical Pentecostals, renewalists, independents and non-Charismatic evangelicals came together. In 1993 some 80,000 people attended Spring Harvest.

Meanwhile a Californian Charismatic, John Wimber, made considerable impact in Britain from 1984 onwards. Initially popular with Anglican renewalists through his connection with the late Canon David Watson, Wimber soon appealed to the new churches too. Terry Virgo, Restorationist apostle of New Frontiers in Hove, became a close friend. Wimber majored on spectacular 'slaying in the Spirit', and wherever he went there was, as Nigel Wright put it, the smell of cordite.[48] Wimber was controlling but Californian in style not strident in the Bible-Belt tradition.[49] Wimber prefigured what was to come in the 1990s in the form of Benny Hinn's spectacular ministry and the mayhem of the Toronto Blessing.[50]

Following Wimber's success many of the Restorationists 'loosened up' and began to work with people that they had earlier eschewed. Gerald Coates, for example, apostolic leader of Pioneer in Cobham, Surrey, went on to become a national church leader working with the ecumenical Youth With A Mission (YWAM) and Roger Forster of Ichthus in South London to establish the Marches For Jesus as a worldwide phenomenon by 1994.

If this were not enough the classical Pentecostals began to make a comeback. Elim and Assemblies of God recovered from the raiding parties made on their fellowships by Restorationists. Kensington City Temple in London (Elim) probably has the largest church membership in Great Britain. Their leading pastor, Colin Dye, now has one of the highest profiles of any Charismatic leader in England.

In the 1990s, however, British Pentecostals appear virtually indistinguishable from renewalists and independent Charismatics in terms of hymnody and practices. All these groups, regardless of social class or denominational affiliation, cross over in terms of their songs, video ministries, paperback tales of the miraculous, favourite gurus and so on. They are all open to penetration from overseas ministries: Kenneth Copeland, John Wimber, Morris Cerullo, Derek Prince from America; Rodney Howard Browne and Reinhart Bonnke from South Africa; and Bill Subritzky and John Smith from New Zealand. All have been blown over by the Toronto Blessing.[51]

The last two decades have seen Charismatics riding a roller coaster of excitement that to the sober outsider seems almost, at times, like a frenzy. There seem to have been more demons, more outlandish experiences, a greater thirst for new things, than ever classical Pentecostalism knew. We can not put this down to millenialism even though a literal millennium approaches and may yet make its impact in terms of adventist excitation. Neither can we talk of revivalism being the cause of such excitement in the sense of church growth resulting from evangelization. Charismatic growth has resulted primarily through recycling Christians from one denomination to another, or renewing pockets of established denominations and sects.

Perhaps we cannot altogether account for these directional changes (given their multi-causal nature), but we can usefully attempt to characterize them. The argument of this chapter has been that the Charismatic movement has followed the same contours of secular modernity from its early to its late phase: it has in fact been for the spirit of the age rather than against it. It has perhaps, in David Harvey's understanding of late capitalism, capitulated to the consumer and experiential hedonism of late modernity and become commodified and corrupted.[52] It has arrived, at the dawn of the new millennium, as no longer reluctantly or thoroughly modern but ultra- or hyper-modern.

The hyper-modern status of the Charismatic movement is highlighted by the so-called 'Toronto Blessing' from 1994 to the present time. Whether the laughing experience has come in Toronto fashion, complete with growls and jerks, or in the Rodney Howard Browne guise – no animal noises but gales of uncontrollable laughter – Toronto has become a watershed in Charismatic experience. Toronto has not yet been shown to be the prelude to a nineteenth century style religious awakening like Finney in America or a twentieth century style revival like Roberts in Wales. So what has it been? Sociologically, at least, it seems clear, that it has been a craze.[53]

Toronto is phenomenologically similar to some of the lesser known aspects of Wesley's and Edwards' revivals and some of the excesses more usually associated with the New Age human potential movement. On the other hand it has not been typical of classical Pentecostalism: falling like ninepins, guffawing and gasping, uncontrollable crying and laughing, are not unknown in the older revivals but they were untypical or epiphenomenal. Powerful preaching, the gifts of the Spirit of 1 Cor. 12, chorus singing and conversion were their hallmarks. Classical Pentecostalism could certainly be said to have been thaumaturgical but Toronto has developed a style, inherited from Wimber, that we might call theanthropic therapy. This is reflected in the emphasis by Toronto enthusiasts on God visiting his people, blessing them, playing with them, releasing them and refreshing them.

Indeed for many touched by Toronto it has been impossible to interpret it with the theological tools to hand. In a way Toronto has been an abyss of primordial experience – a disintegration of liturgical and Biblical norms. Many who looked into the abyss have abandoned Charismatic affiliations altogether. Peter Fenwick, for example, respected elder statesman from the Sheffield House Church, sees Toronto as Pentecostalism gone mad. Others, such as Clifford Hill, sociologist and prophet, see the whole thing as an omen of disaster. Former enthusiasts for Toronto, such as Holy Trinity Brompton, are now concentrating on *Alpha* courses as God's direction for the future.[54] John Wimber has disowned Toronto and excommunicated John Arnott, pastor of the Toronto Vineyard Church. Some people, somewhere, are still falling over, giggling, and feeling blessed, but the momentum of the movement is passing. The craze, like modernity, seems to be fading with a final gasp.[55]

But in many ways Toronto can be seen as the logical outcome of recent Charismatic developments. Over the last ten years Charismatic Christianity has drunk deeply at the well of modern cultural forms: the 'clinics' of John Wimber; the concern with inner healing; the endless in-house entertainment of conference, convention and celebration – for all the world like a spiritual equivalent of the rave culture. No longer restrained by fundamentalist edicts, or the mainline theology of writers like Anglican Tom Smail and Catholic Steve Clark,[56] Charismatic Christianity increasingly appears fey and orphic.[57]

When all is said and done as we near the end of the twentieth century the defining theologian of the Charismatic movement will turn out not to be a Jonathan Edwards, a Charles Hodge, or even a Charles Parham: they were all too constrained within the bounds of historic orthodoxy. The theological father of the movement will turn out to be none other than the father of modern liberal theology, Friedrich Schleiermacher, who in rebelling against German rationalism and classical theology arrived at a religion of feeling and God consciousness which he managed to meld with the pietism of his Moravian background. Charismatic Christians have not formally followed Schleiermacher for he is associated with liberalism but they have unwittingly followed his direction because of their growing tendency to allow experience to become the touchstone of orthodoxy.[58] This touchstone is not a return to New Testament Christianity, as is believed, but a thoroughly late-modern concern with the self and its satisfaction.

Pentecostalism rushed into the twentieth century like a hurricane at Azusa Street, Los Angeles, in 1906. Perhaps it finally blew itself out at Toronto Airport in 1994. Azusa Street acted as a beacon to enthusiasts from many countries: pastors and church leaders came to see the revival for themselves and through them the Pentecostal blessing was diffused and distributed throughout the world. Toronto has repeated history in this respect but because of air travel and the Internet the diffusion has been far quicker – perhaps too quick to have a lasting effect. Churches take time to build up and establish themselves, but Toronto may have been merely a new experience in a dying modern world that treasures novelty for its own sake and craves signs and wonders as its daily fare.[59]

CONCLUSION

Neo-Pentecostalism has been more thoroughly modern than its classical counterpart but also more open to the cultural obsessions of late-modernity. I believe that classical Pentecostalism has on the whole been modern in a positive sense though more obviously so in South America and South Korea than in Europe and North America. At the very least Pentecostalism throughout the world has not only provided meaning and succour to its adherents but it has also equipped many of them with the values of ascetic Protestantism so useful to the modern enterprise, and so essential for social mobility in a capitalist economy.

Conversely, with the possible exception of the early Renewal movement, neo-Pentecostalism has overstressed self-experience and what Jung
Ha Kim has called 'supply side spirituality'.[60] As modernity has waned
this concern with the self and commodity religion has run the risk of
becoming an indulgence if not a sinking into decadence. Arguably this
decadence has infiltrated classical Pentecostalism, unleashing the narcissistic and irrational forces that were latently there but mostly kept
under control.[61] But because of the pluralistic nature of late-modernity
the inevitable syncretistic strands of a religion of experience have become increasingly volatile. Far from seeing Pentecostalism rushing into
the new century with the force of the old I believe that it will be
buffeted by theological confusion and social fragmentation.

If we follow Zygmunt Bauman[62] instead of Harvey and see the modern
world not as decaying but as fading – in transition to a post-modernity
– we must ask whether Charismatic Christianity is well equipped to
survive in the future. Post-modernism not only eschews the metanarrative
of rational discourse but it also distrusts the lordship of the self and
inner experience. If the world emerges like Foucault's landscape, where
reality is seen as a discursive achievement and the certainty of universal truths are denied, what will Charismatic utterances mean? It mat-
tered not in modernity if tongues were interpreted as babblings because
they were seen to release or realize the self. But with the self on hold
what will glossolalia come to signify? On the day of Pentecost xenoglossy
was seen as a reversal of Babel – a time when charismata as gifts
from God indicated His presence. Real presence – any wager on tran-
scendence – as George Steiner has shown[63] is a problem in post-modern
understanding. Given such a linguistic turn will xenoglossy and
glossolalia[64] be a return to a new Babel where tongues will be seen as
meaningless noise – a sign of absence – of the *deus absconditus*?

We should, however, be careful not to confuse post-modernism as
intellectual fashion with a genuine cultural shift to a post-modernity.
'Perhaps' I wrote recently, '. . . postmodernism is not the ideology of
the future, of the Internet, mass culture and cultural pluralism. Instead
it is the language of limbo; the go-between gossip of transition; the
discourse of leave-taking, travelling from modernity to the not yet.'[65]
If post-modernity turns out to be a new cultural era we can expect that
it will share as many continuities with the past as discontinuities so
there is no doubt that Pentecostalism will survive in the future. In the
Third World, for some time to come, it will no doubt continue to be
thoroughly modern. But in the post-industrial societies a different religiosity is likely to abound. It will be one that will not repudiate the

past. Nor will future religion always be wanting God to be doing a 'new thing' which late-modern Charismatics have craved. A post-modern religion will certainly look for a 'form of life' and a narrative of belonging but it will not trust experience to be at the heart of things. It will be one that will open up to other living traditions. It will be one that will value story over feeling, narrative over experience, icon over text, prophecy over tongues.

In fact such a religion is happening right now under the nose of the Charismatic movement. Like a phoenix from the ashes the alternative liturgical movement is emerging from 'happy clappy Bappy' land, as the Revd Nick Mercer calls it,[66] and is merging with Celtic spirituality, Taize chants, Eastern Orthodoxy, Reformed Theology, Charismatic happenings. Such a syncretistic mix may or may not end up Christian, as the Nine O' Clock Service[67] forewarns, but then neither will it any more be modern.

NOTES

1. See S. Hunt, 'Giving the Devil More than His Due: Some Problems with the Deliverance Ministry' in A. Walker and L. Osborn (eds) *Harmful Religion: studies in religious abuse* (SPCK forthcoming).
2. R. Bultmann, 'New Testament and Mythology' in H. W. Bartsch (ed.), *Kerygma and Myth* (London: SPCK, 1955), p.5.
3. A. Walker 'Fundamentalism and Modernity: the Restoration Movement in Britain', *Studies in Religious Fundamentalism*, ed. L Caplan (London: Macmillan, 1988).
4. R. H. Neibuhr, *Christ and Culture* (London: Faber & Faber, 1952).
5. See J. H. Yoder, 'A People in the World: Theological Interpretation,' in *The Concept of the Believer's Church*, ed. H. L. Garrett, Jr. (Scottdale, PA: Herald Press, 1969), pp. 252–83 and B. Wilson, *Sects And Society* (Greenwood: Press, 1978).
6. The Renewal movement, for example, resides in the historic churches and can hardly be said to have majored on revival.
7. A. Walker, *Telling The Story: gospel mission and culture* (London: SPCK, 1996), pp.61–74.
8. J. Edwards, *Religious Affections*, ed: J. Smith (New Haven: Yale University Press, 1979, 2 vols).
9. J. Butler, *Awash in a Sea of Faith: Christianizing the American People*. Studies In Cultural History (Cambridge, MA: Harvard, 1990). See also N. Hatch, *The Democratization of American Christianity* (New Haven, CT: Yale University Press, 1989).
10. See R. N. Bellah, 'Civil Religion in America,' *Beyond Belief: Essays on*

Religion in a Post-Traditional World (New York: Harper & Row, 1970), pp.168–89.

11. Quoted in J. Seel's 'Modernity and Evangelicals: American Evangelicalism as a Global Case Study' in P. Sampson, V. Samuel and C. Sugden (eds), *Faith And Modernity* (Oxford: Regnum Books, 1994), p.293.

12. ibid. p.293.

13. See D. Allen, *The Unfailing Stream: A Charismatic Church History in Outline* (Tonbridge: Sovereign Word, 1994), chap. 6.

14. See A. Walker, *Restoring The Kingdom: the radical Christianity of the house church movement* (London: Hodder & Stoughton, 1985), chap. 11.

15. It is not without irony that Schofield learned his millennial theories from the writings of John Nelson Darby one of the founders of the Brethren movement which through its own prophetic conferences at Powerscourt in Ireland were feeding off the same adventist theories as Irving and the Morning Watch. Mark Patterson, a doctoral student at King's College, London, thinks that it might be established that Darby's dispensationalism actually led back to the Albury group and possibly Irving himself.

16. In Britain, for example, leadership initially came from the upper class Revd Boddy in Sunderland. The so-called 'Cambridge Seven' which included Cecil Polhill were from aristocratic backgrounds. Polhill, it could be argued, helped bankroll the Pentecostal movement and certainly kept Boddy's influential journal, *Confidence*, alive.

17. R. M. Anderson, *Vision of the Disinherited: The Making Of American Pentecostalism* (Oxford: OUP, 1980).

18. There was a confusion among Pentecostals between the glossolalia of St Paul in his letter to the Corinthians (I Cor. 12, 13, 14) – the normative experience of Pentecostal tongues – with the xenoglossy of Acts 2 when according to St Luke's account people in Jerusalem could hear the disciples speak in their own natural languages.

19. See G. Coates, *Divided We Stand* (Eastbourne: Kingsway, 1986).

20. In one of the most innovative and intelligent defences of the Toronto experience, Patrick Dixon prefers science and history, rather than Biblical exposition, to make his case. See his *Signs of Revival* (Eastbourne: Kingsway, 1994).

21. Class distinctions still count. Renewalists are still primarily middle class; whereas Pentecostals are still primarily working class and lower middle class.

22. D. Dayton, *Theological Roots of Pentecostalism* (Grand Rapids, MI: Zondervan, 1987).

23. This was not, as is often thought, because they were anti-Trinitarian but because they were Sabellian and hence denied the unique and distinct persons of the Godhead in favour of a threefold modalistic presentation of a monistic God.

24. Branham not only had trouble with defining Jesus as truly God but he also was tainted, in the eyes of many Pentecostals, because of his association with Oneness theology.

25. See T. Smail, A. Walker and N. Wright, 'Revelation Knowledge and Knowledge Of Revelation: The Faith Movement and the Question of Heresy, *Journal of Pentecostal Theology*, vol.5, 1994, pp.57–77.

26. Curiously modernist Harvey Cox has come to see Pentecostalism in a more positive light precisely because of its experiential nature. See his *Fire From Heaven: Pentecostalism, Spirituality, and the Reshaping of Religion in the Twenty-first Century* (New York: Addison-Wesley, 1994). I think Cox is projecting twentieth century self-expressionism into, what I think will be, an altogether different future. See my conclusion in this chapter.
27. A. Noll, comp. & ed., *The Princeton Theology 1812–1921: Scripture, Science, and the Theological Method from Archibald Alexander to Benjamin Beckeridge Warfield* (Grand Rapids, MI: Baker Book House, 1983).
28. Notably Fuller seminary in California.
29. D. Martin, *Tongues of Fire: The Explosion of Protestantism in Latin America* (Oxford: Basil Blackwell, 1990).
30. D. Martin, 'Latin America Pentecost' *Leading Light*, vol.3/1, Summer 1996, p.13.
31. Interview at Church House, Bradford with Bryn Jones on 28 June 1989.
32. In interview with Gerald Coates, op. cit., he told me of a woman's dream about a new direction in his life where he began to dress differently and change his hair style. While dashing off to the airport to meet an important contact he suddenly realized his blazer and new haircut were just as in her dream.
33. *The Sunday Times* reported on 22 September 1996 in its financial section that the European Bank had programmed astrological configurations as part of its financial forecasting.
34. See D. Bell, *The Cultural Contradiction of Capitalism* (London: Heinemann, 1976).
35. See W. T. H. Richards, *Pentecost is Dynamite* (Lakeland: Cox & Wyman, 1972).
36. Most notably from Roman Catholics. For example, D. L. Gelpi, SJ, *Pentecostalism: a Theological Viewpoint* (USA: Paulist Press, 1971).
37. In Martyn Percy's unpublished paper, 'Sweet Rapture: Subliminal Eroticism In Contemporary Charismatic Worship' he demonstrates that by the time of Wimber (1980s) the jolly refrains of classical Pentecostalism, such as 'In my heart there rings a melody', or 'Since Jesus came into my heart' had been replaced by romantic and intimate songs. This theme continues to the present time. For example:

> I will be yours, you will be mine
> Together in eternity
> Our hearts of love will be entwined
> Together in eternity, forever in eternity.

(Brian Doerkse, 1994, in song book, *Isn't He/Eternity: Intimate Songs of Praise and Worship*, Anaheim: VMI Publishing, 1995).
38. S. Bruce, *Pray TV: Televangelism in America* (London: Routledge, 1990), p.237.
39. J. Davison Hunter, *American Evangelicalism: Conservative Religion and the Quandary of Modernity* (New Brunswick, NJ: Rutgers University Press, 1983).
40. By late modernity I am signalling consumer capitalism rather than affirming a Marxist theory of capitalist development.

41. I was at the consultation representing the British Council of Churches with Professor James Dunn and the Revd Michael Harper.
42. See my concept of the 'sectarian implant' in 'Harmful Religion', *Leading Light: Christian Faith And Contemporary Culture*. vol.2/2, Autumn 1995, pp.5–7.
43. P. Hocken, *Streams of Renewal: Origins and Early Development of the Charismatic Movement in Great Britain* (Exeter: Paternoster Press, 1986).
44. See my *Restoring The Kingdom*, op. cit.
45. Not least in their espousal of apostles and prophets.
46. It was envisaged that powerful Christian communities and businesses would flourish.
47. A. Walker, *Restoring The Kingdom*, op. cit. (1988 edn) p.333.
48. A phrase he frequently used in a lecture series on the Charismatic movement organized by the C. S. Lewis Centre in the early 1990s entitled 'The love of power and the power of love'.
49. See M. Percy's *Words, Wonders and Power* (London: SPCK, 1996).
50. For a less than enthusiastic view see C. F. Porter and P. Richter, *The Toronto Blessing – Or is It?* (London: DLT, 1995). cf. D. Roberts, *The Toronto Blessing* (Eastbourne: Kingsway, 1994).
51. This probably does not hold for the remnant of British Catholic renewalists. The rise of the Evangelical Alliance and the numerous independent Protestant groups has not been conducive to Catholic sentiments.
52. D. Harvey, *The Condition of Postmodernity: An Enquiry Into the Origins of Cultural Change* (Oxford: Basil Blackwell, 1989).
53. John Moore adopted this category from Smelser's typology of changing collective behaviour to investigate Catholic renewal in the 1960s. See his 'The Catholic Pentecostal Movement' in M. Hill (ed.) *Sociological Yearbook of Religion, 6*, (London: SCM, 1963).
54. *Alpha* is a course of Christian initiation, not dissimilar to the early Church catechumenate but with the expectation that it will lead on to personal conversion and perhaps the Baptism in the Spirit.
55. This seems to have led to two reactions; either waiting for the next big wave of revival, or realizing that Toronto is a bridge too far and retreating into a more 'business as usual' (normative) Pentecostalism.
56. See T. Smail, *The Giving Gift* (London: DLT, 1995) and S.B. Clark, *Redeemer* (Ann Arbor, MI: Servant Press, 1992).
57. One of the themes of Harold Bloom in his *The American Religion: The Emergence of the Post Christian Nation* (New York: Simon & Schuster, 1992).
58. Such a generalization probably does not hold across the board. I doubt if this is a fair assessment of Anglican Renewal Ministries, for example, nor the ecumenical movement associated with Fr Michael Harper and the Sword And The Spirit communities. And although this trend can be seen in many new churches it would be a distortion to say it is an accurate characterization of Ichthus communities and all those within the Pioneer network of churches.
59. Although Professor William Abraham of Southern Methodist University and Dr Graham MacFarlane of London Bible College (both excellent scholars and men whose judgement I value) feel that Toronto, although a mixed blessing, has more to recommend it than I can see for the moment.

60. Supply side spirituality like supply side economics is a feature of an abundant or affluent ideology. A demand-side spirituality would be more concerned with the fight for justice and deliverance associated with the poor. See J. H. Kim, 'Sources Outside of Europe' in P. Van Ness (ed.) *Spirituality And The Secular Quest*, World Spirituality Series (London: SCM Press, 1996), p.63.
61. Nowhere is this more obvious, in my opinion, than in the recent fascination with demons. See my chapter 'The Devil you Think You Know' in T. Smail, A. Walker and N. Wright, *Charismatic Renewal: The Search for a Theology* (SPCK new edn 1995, pp.86–105).
62. See, for example, his *Intimations of Postmodernity* (London: Routledge, 1992).
63. G. Steiner, *Real Presences: Is There Anything In What We Say?* (London: Faber & Faber, 1989).
64. Notwithstanding my earlier distinction between tongues as natural languages and ecstatic utterances, they are both treated in the New Testament as post-Pentecostal experiences.
65. A. Walker, *Telling the Story*, op. cit. p.180.
66. Former vice-principal of London Bible College and now an Anglican priest in the liberal Catholic tradition.
67. Under the leadership of the Revd Chris Brain, the Nine O'Clock Service moved from Wimber neo-Pentecostalism to Matthew Fox neo-Paganism. See R. Howard, *The Rise And Fall of the Nine O'Clock Service* (London: Mowbrays, 1996).

2 Mainstream Charismatics: Some Observations of Baptist Renewal

Douglas McBain (with additional material provided by Stephen Hunt)

It is common in justifying an analysis of the Pentecostal scene to quote impressive statistics. The figures look even more spectacular when those of the classical Pentecostals are amalgamated with their contemporary Charismatic variant, and independent ministries with the renewed wing of the established mainline churches. From one perspective it is not unreasonable to merge them together since there is a considerable overlap of both theology and ethos. In combining all the streams of Pentecostalism David Barrett estimates that in 1970 there were some 68,000,000 people involved in the wider movement worldwide. By 1990 the figure had grown to approximately 405,000,000. The prediction is that by the year 2000 the total number will be in the region of 619,000,000. This number represents no less than 29 per cent of the entire Christian population of the world (Barrett, 1988).

To be sure, the spread of Pentecostalism has been extraordinary by any standards. However, the statistics do not tell us much about the complexities of the numerous strands of the movement. Moreover, they say little about the ebbs and flows, the rapid changes which have taken place, and the important variables which allow differential growth in a variety of cultural contexts. In this chapter we attempt to do justice to some of these key aspects by examining the Charismatic Renewal movement in the historical churches in Britain.

We might well consider the important aspects of renewal through the prism of experience of the Baptists over the last 30 years. There have been many developments which the Baptists have shared with other denominations, but there are many others which are unique to themselves. These experiences say a great deal about the contemporary church. Simultaneously, they provide indicators as to the vigour and the future prospects of the wider renewal movement, as well as its long term health.

REVERSING DECLINE

Renewal movements in the established churches, as Pousson (1994) points out, are far from new. By the end of the eighteenth century, for example, practically all Christian denominations throughout the western world, including Orthodox, Catholic and Protestant churches, had been 'renewed' in one way or another. Those representing Protestantism during this period included Pietism, Puritantism, Moravianism, the Evangelical Revival in England and the related Wesleyan revival, and the Great Awakenings in the American colonies.

The context of renewal in the mid-twentieth century Church was that of a very different cultural milieu. Secularization confronted the Church, not so much with the blinding science which challenged it in the eighteenth century, but with disbelief and a parallel decline in church attendance. The common experience of the established denominations, to which their annual statistical returns continue to bear dismal testimony, is of a steady numerical decline. Although the various types of churchmanship have affected the extent of the demise, with those of a conservative evangelical theology having fared relatively better than liberal or middle-of-the-road churches, the overall trends have been similar.

In contrast, 41 per cent of the highest proportion of growing churches, in terms of congregations in Britain, has occurred among the Charismatic evangelicals (Brierly, 1993, p.153). A movement which was unknown in 1960 has proliferated in such a way that it is now clear that a high proportion of the most numerically robust churches are moving in that direction. Peter Brierley, concluding from his 1989 church census, points out that

> The Pentecostals, Baptists and Independents have the most growing churches with Methodists and other Free churches least... By far the highest percentage of growing churches were charismatic evangelical ones which had more than two in every five of them actually growing.
>
> (Brierly, 1993, p.131)

There is good reason for singling out the Baptists to appreciate developments, and explore the issues. With reference to renewal, Bebbington maintains that it was the Baptist Charismatic congregations which were growing most markedly. This appeared to put the Baptists in a notable position since Bebbington also ventured that 'the Charismatic movement was poised to become the prevailing form of Protestantism in 21st century modern Britain' (Bebbington, 1983, p.247).

Thirty years earlier it was a very different story. In 1969 a commission had been established by the Baptist Union in Britain to examine prospects for the denomination in the coming years. In 1971 the commission issued a report entitled *Ministry Tomorrow* which provided many positive comments, but also dropped a bombshell in that it stated that in the future the Baptists would only be able to pay between 300 to 400 regular ministers. This drastic reduction was attributed to financial shortcomings resulting largely from declining congregations. There were no initial suggestions of how that decline might be halted (*Baptist Times*, Dec. 1971).

By the mid-1960s however, the characteristic experiences associated with renewal were already observable in some Baptist churches. From these early years renewal meant an intensely personal spiritual encounter for ministers and lay people alike. While the spread of renewal might partly be attributed to the encouragement of a number of widely dispersed church leaders, the movement, in many respects, was initiated at the grass roots with the impetus coming from ordinary people responding to their own experiences. There was, by way of illustration, the remarkable conversion of a Jamaican woman who had a vision of Christ in her kitchen. Before the vision she was never in church, but immediately afterwards presented herself at the manse door of a surprised Baptist minister, asking for baptism. The prayer meetings she attended were novel and disconcerting. She had her own prayer language. Though she had no previous links with any Pentecostal group, what she was doing was what was later understood to be speaking in tongues.

Such accounts stimulated curiosity, but also highlighted the sense of spiritual inadequacies in the mainstream churches. They also coincided with episodic experiences of spiritual baptism by some of those in prominent positions within the denomination. A number of leading Baptist ministers had already become aware of a common Charismatic adventure as early as the 1964 annual meeting of the Baptist Revival Fellowship which constituted a conservative evangelical grouping within the Baptist Union.

There were tentative inklings that the Charismatic road was the way forward. Two years earlier the Baptist Union had its 150th anniversary (created in 1812). There were a number of publications including a new service book entitled *Orders and Prayers for Christian Worship*. It is significant that in the introductory essay written by the General Secretary Ernest Payne (along with Stephen Winward) he characterized the elements of New Testament worship important to the Baptists, but claimed that the Pentecostal dimension involving the use of the spiritual gifts, which would undoubtedly allow the entire congregation to participate more fully, was absent.

Because of the controversial nature of renewal, its radical break with tradition, and not least the profound theological questions raised, it was not even mentioned in the *Baptist Times* until 1971. But for a few at least, the path of renewal appeared to be a viable option for reversing congregational decline. By that time it was evident to those straddling the denominational divide that the Pentecostal experience had to be given a name. Charismatic Renewal was as good as any. The term partly resulted from the coincidence of its rise with the Kennedy era in the United States which was described as the 'charismatic years'. The stronger reason however, denoted caution and reflected the desire to avoid too close an association with classical Pentecostalism which, in the minds of many evangelicals at least, was given to excessive emotionalism.

In a sense the growth of renewal for the Baptists has been self-perpetuating. Success breeds success, and it is not difficult to see why younger Baptist pastors are endeared to renewal. In retrospect Steve Hunt's estimation that 20 per cent of all Baptist churches in Britain could be described as at least sympathetic to the main tenets of renewal is too cautious an approximation although he admits this is hard to verify (Hunt, 1995, p.106). The difficulty of confirmation largely results from the fact that not all congregations have opted for the entire Charismatic package. There has been a certain amount of picking and choosing from what it offers, often determined by the requirements of the congregation. At the same time statistical speculation says little about other important aspects of the life of these churches which might only be mentioned here in passing. These include the skill with which these changes have been introduced, the speed with which ministers have sought change, and the moral depth and spirituality of the leadership in sustaining the numerical increase.

A more realistic appraisal is that the majority of Baptist ministers in Britain who began their ministry from the middle to late 1970s onwards appear to be willing to identify themselves with what they perceive to be the positive attributes of renewal. It has become a central force affecting many, if not the majority, of young ministers under the age of 40. This assessment can be made from an observation of the system which operates at the moment for the settlement or resettlement of students or ministries in their pastorates. A vital part of the process is the completion of a nomination profile by the candidate in which they declare their attitude towards renewal issues. Since prospective ministers will be matched to those most democratic of institutions, the Baptist congregation, it can be deduced that there is, at least potentially, a high level of popular acceptance of renewal. However, this rise of renewal from a fringe position to a central one raises a number of important questions. To what had the Baptist Charismatics owed their success? Could developments be traced with such a straightforward simplicity? Were there no casualties on the way?

Part of the dynamic growth was due to the relationship between Baptist minister and congregation. Contrasts can be made with the Methodist church. Although the Methodists had been there at the beginning of renewal, much weighed against the movement in that particular denomination. The Methodists, short of ministerial manpower, had developed a 'circuit system' whereby one clergyman was frequently responsible for a number of churches. While the congregations were likely to be consulted as to which minister might serve within a circuit, there was neither a permanent nor personal relationship between congregation and minister. A key ingredient in the acceptance and growth of renewal, the dynamic between shepherd and flock, was absent. If a Baptist congregation wanted to go further down the Charismatic road, the minister was often the determining factor.[1]

SOME LITTLE LOCAL DIFFICULTIES

In 1963 the bishop of Woolwich, John Robinson, published his renowned work of theological reflection entitled *Honest to God*, which amounted to a despondent account of the contemporary Church. There was another publication that year, by no means scholarly, but at least as significant. *The Cross and the Switchblade* by John Sherrill made an immeasurable impression. It related the story of David Wilkerson, a Pentecostal pastor working among the violent youth gangs in New York, and told of remarkable conversions. In the USA it had considerable impact upon some established churches, not least of all, the Roman Catholics. It pointed towards the possibility of revival through the Pentecostal experience. In Britain, the book was recommended by the Bishop of Salisbury to the churches of his diocese. The editorial of the *Church of England Newspaper* recognized its impact while wryly noting:

> It is all so different from the genteel Christianity of the suburban church.
>
> (*Church of England Newspaper*, 3 Dec. 1965)

This statement hinted at the fact that what was happening in Britain was very different from what was occurring in California and other parts of the USA. The religious climate in Britain, like the meteorological climate, is much cooler than on the west coast of the USA. This meant that renewal in the Baptist churches, as elsewhere, had no easy passage. Cherished traditions were inevitably questioned, theological touchstones were challenged. There was opposition, accommodation and reconciliation, all of which were indicative of inherent contradictions and dilemmas. It also brought to the surface sensitive issues which had been simmering for some time.

During the growth of renewal in the Baptist denomination the controversies thrown up centred upon ecumenism and the fear by conservatives of what they perceived as the growing impact of liberal attitudes in general, and liberal theology in particular. In their minds, at least, the themes were intricately interwoven.

A principal platform for renewal were the attempts at reconciliation and cooperation between the traditional denominations. This spirit of reconciliation also extended to the Pentecostal churches largely outside of the fold of 'respectable' churches. Typical was Lesslie Newbigin, Bishop of the Church of South India, who brought to attention a strand of world Christianity outside the Protestant, Roman Catholic and Orthodox communities: the Pentecostal churches. Newbigin suggested an open dialogue with them. His message was felt most keenly by those in Britain already sympathetic to the work of the World Council of Churches which the conservatives tended to view with some suspicion.

From the other direction David du Plessis, a skilled ecumenist, broke with Pentecostal tradition by opening channels with the established churches (Hocken, 1986, p.128). Du Plessis (originating from the South African Pentecostal Apostolic Faith Movement) operated within a grander scheme and openly announced a prophecy allegedly given 25 years earlier by the renowned Pentecostal healing evangelist Smith-Wrigglesworth that the established denominations (including the Roman Catholic church) should be brought into the Pentecostal experience in order to precipitate a great revival.

More widely, the ecumenical movement's acceptance of the institutional basis of the existing denominations was an important factor in the growth of renewal. Ecumenism had worked on the basis that the various denominations should establish common doctrinal grounds and interests, and proceed from there, rather than to allow spiritual revival to establish new structures outside of the mainstream churches. In 1964 the umbrella organization for the charismatically inclined established churches, the Fountain Trust, was set up by Michael Harper at All Souls', Langham Place, to pursue and promote the work of renewal on an interdenominational basis. The main concern was to seek an understanding of a common spiritual experience and give the growing movement direction and coherence. Its stated aims were not just to promote the virtues of renewal but also to emphasize the need for revival and the rediscovery of the lost spiritual dimension of the faith: an ecumenical vision of spiritual unity.

In its first few years the Fountain Trust was content to organize small conferences in different parts of the country and, in 1966, published the magazine *Renewal* which still enjoys a wide circulation. The first large scale conference, ecumenical and international in flavour, was held at Surrey University in 1971 to articulate the reasons behind what was understood to be a major move of the Spirit, and broke down Protestant reservations. The conference was described as the 'coming of age of the Charismatic movement in Britain (and elsewhere) and . . . The participation of Roman Catholics was everywhere welcomed' (*Renewal*, Sept. 1971).

The involvement of the Roman Catholics, hitherto seen as beyond redemption by most Protestant denominations, many Baptists among them, was significant. When the matter was discussed in 1972 by the appropriate committee within the Baptist Union, the Advisory Committee on Church Relations, a change of heart emerged, and while not mentioning the Catholics by name hinted at a reconciliation which had previously been unthinkable:

> It was clear that the blanket condemnation is no longer possible of the Charismatic movement. It would be important for us to consider how best to keep in contact with those participating in the movement.
> (The Minute Book of the Baptist Union Advisory Council on Church Relations, 4 Feb. 1972)

In 1977 the Roman Catholic Primate for Belgium, Cardinal Suenens, whom Rome charged with overseeing the Catholic renewal movement, came to Westminister as one of the key speakers. In the same year he led an evangelical mission to Oxford University supporting both renewal and its ecumenical base. On the strength of his contribution the Principal of Regent's Park Baptist College, Westminister, warmly commended renewal to all Baptist ministers (White, 1977).

While the renewal movement created a great deal of ecumenical unity, there were also divisions and a measure of recrimination. The initial response by conservative evangelicals inside and outside of the Baptist Union was predictable given their suspicion of what they interpreted as overzealous and emotional Pentecostalism.

Typical of the initial reaction of the conservative wing was that of the Anglican Philip Edgcumbe Hughes writing in *The Churchman:*

> News that Episcopalians were speaking in tongues was certainly strange. It sounded incongruous. But it was probably attributable to a flirtation under the hot Californian sun with the extravagances of Pentecostalism.
>
> (*Churchman* editorial, Sept. 1992)

However, Hughes, like some other conservative evangelicals, came to see the virtues of renewal. Yet not all were suitably impressed. The ultra-Calvinist wing soon distanced itself. Significantly, the early meetings of the Fountain Trust at Metropolitan Tabernacle, London, a heartland of conservative evangelicalism, were not allowed to continue since they were viewed as stained by links with Roman Catholicism.

Many Baptists were strongly influenced by the most renowned conservative evangelical of the day, Martyn Lloyd Jones at Westminister Chapel, who gave positive support to those aspects of renewal that could promote revival. The danger signal for him was the ecumenism which was interpreted as little more than a cover for the advancing interests of the Church of Rome and evidence of creeping liberalism. In 1966 Lloyd Jones promoted a view which was later to be echoed in Restorationism: all true evangelicals should leave their theologically compromised denominations and form an evangelical fellowship of churches characterized by resistance to ecumenism. Since he did this from the platform of a national conference organized by the Evangelical Alliance the fallout was considerable. The effect on the unity of the Alliance was disastrous and the creation of the British Evangelical Fellowship (BEF) became the alternative for some evangelical churches, a number of Baptists among them. Five years later the BEF was also the haven for many of the 38 churches who jumped ship following the acrimony over a sermon given by Michael Taylor during the 1971 meeting of the Baptist Union Assembly at Westminister Chapel in the course of which he so affirmed Christ's humanity that to many conservatives he was rejecting His divinity.

These more visual and public events hid what was happening at congregational level. At an early stage those moving into the Charismatic mode did not necessarily find life easy. This was a fairly universal phenomenon. Dennis Bennett, whose Charismatic experience is widely attributed as signalling renewal, on Passion Sunday, 3 April 1960, found himself in difficulty with his Episcopalian church in California. When he, as it were, 'came out', resignation was immediately demanded and a pastoral letter banned all tongue-speaking in the diocese.

Although methods of containment found among the Baptists were not quite so draconian, at a congregational level there were difficulties which ensured that the spread of renewal was not an even one. It might be the pastor who felt threatened by more congregational involvement in Sunday services. Hostility to renewal was, then, not only theological, but the result of concern for the repercussions of displaying the charismata in congregations that were otherwise unused to this expressive revolution. A Baptist pastor enquired of that section of the congregation that stood for the first time with their arms raised in praise during his church service 'do you all wish to be excused?'. It was also a metaphor for disobedience; democracy could only be taken so far.

Some Baptist and evangelical churches divided. A number of congregations became so committed to the principles of renewal that it was the more traditional-minded members who were encouraged to leave. On other occasions it was the pastor sympathetic to the cause who was required to depart, or did so of his own accord. Alternatively, a church might accommodate its Charismatic faction in order to retain congregational unity. Several ministers, not unsympathetic towards renewal, objected to the teachings espoused by the more zealous that all those truly born-again should be able to speak in tongues. This gave the impression that other Christians were second class citizens in the Kingdom.

What happened in Scotland was particularly noteworthy. Here the growth of renewal was slow and sporadic. The *Scottish Daily Express* reported a 'Strange new Sect in Scottish kirk . . . [with] a form of worship bordering on the supernatural' (Bebbington, 1983, p.227). The report was all the more curious since there had been pockets of renewal in Scotland for a while. Even in the early 1980s renewal was only making limited progress. The Scottish Baptist Union observed that in some Baptist churches there were 'tensions and problems' especially where healing and the exercise of the other spiritual gifts seemed to be at the expense of Biblical teaching, encouragement and other pastoral concerns.[2]

There was much resistance to renewal. As in Holland and some regions of Germany, the Charismatic movement found it difficult to wash over the barriers of traditional Calvinism. In addition, Church structures in Scotland were traditional and inflexible. The life of the kirk was typically rooted in more settled communities than the more geographically mobile population of south-east England where renewal had advanced so impressively. The conservative nature of Scottish culture also constrained the new movement. The Scots remained suspicious of anything new from the other side of the Atlantic, and even more so from the other side of the border. Scottish worship tended to be a fairly solemn affair particularly in Presbyterianism, and faith a private matter.

Finally, the strong Scottish tradition of expository preaching had seen extensive rejuvenation since 1945 and had partly filled the spiritual vacuum that renewal has satisfied elsewhere. Because of such factors, those within the major denominations in Scotland experiencing a baptism in the Spirit found the public cost of involvement to be too high. This is not to suggest that there have not been success stories. There are some flourishing Baptist Charismatic churches in Scotland's large cities. Nonetheless, those in the more outlying areas seeking a Charismatic congregation may find themselves travelling some distance or, alternatively, seeking the hospitality of a house church.

NEW DIRECTIONS

In 1977 an agenda item of the Consultative Council of the Fountain Trust asked 'The Renewal – Is It Stuck?'. The renewal movement had largely been a great success, however it appeared to have stalled. Two years later a leading figure optimistically suggested that 'The lull at the present time could be seen as the end of the overture before the main opera' (Fountain Trust Council Meeting, 21 Nov. 1979). By this was meant that renewal would continue to spread and that a large scale revival was imminent. In 1979 the Fountain Trust was wound up because it had largely accomplished its job. Its *raison d'être* had gone (Smail, 1980, pp.2–5). However, in the same year the annual report of the Baptist Union provided evidence of further and continuing numerical decline. This was attributed to the reduction in the birth rate and social trends including changing leisure patterns which, among other things, affected Sunday churchgoing.

In 1979 the principal Conservative Evangelical–Charismatic coalition, known as 'Mainstream' organized a series of annual conferences to seek ways of reversing decline and made recommendations for reviving spiritual life and growth within Baptist churches. By 1985 the Charismatics were the dominant faction. Also established in 1979 was Spring Harvest, the annual convention for Charismatic Christians of all denominations in which the Baptists were well represented. In the established denominations and those independent churches, Spring Harvest still enables the Charismatic movement to be dispersed among those not previously of a Charismatic persuasion.

During the same period there was another monumental development, the growth of the major 'house churches', or what was then known as the Restoration movement. Today, what is now referred to as the 'new churches', constitute 14 per cent of all Charismatic churches in Britain. Such churches are now the fastest growing segment of Christianity, in western countries, and in the Third World. In Britain this complex pattern of independent Charismatic churches was to have a profound effect upon the Charismatic Baptists.

To understand the impact upon the Baptists we have to go back to the 1970s. It was against the background of uncertainty, dismay and the division between the Charismatics and traditional evangelicals at that time that the teachings of the most prominent figure in the Restorationist movement, the late Arthur Wallis, began to impinge upon some Baptists involved in renewal. His theme was of revival which had also been emphasized elsewhere in the formative stage of renewal, and even earlier through the evangelizing crusades of Billy Graham.

Wallis, originally from the Brethren, was an early enthusiastic supporter of the Fountain Trust. In 1956 he had already published a study for revival in the well received book *In the Day of Thy Power* (1956). Together with some of his colleagues in the Brethren movement, he held a number of conferences in England's west country to address the need for revival in the light of the perceived spiritual plight of the nation. A familiar theme could be identified in a letter sent to potential attenders at a conference he had organized:

Almighty God has ceased to be a reality in the minds of the mass of His human creatures and in this land a generation is arising which has so little grasp of the significance of any moral standards that one wonders how the present social order can survive apart from a spiritual revival.[3]

In later years Wallis began to argue that Christ intended a Church that was Charismatically renewed but totally freed from any of the restrictions that denominations brought with them:

I see no future for denominations but a glorious future for the body of Christ.

(Wallis, 1981)

Many Restorationists had joined the renewal conventions at the 'Downs' and 'Dales' Bible Weeks in the 1970s. This gave the impression that they were part of the mainstream renewal movement and rubbed shoulders with Baptist Charismatics and others.

There were good reasons why some Baptist Charismatics were attracted to aspects of Restorationism. Some ministers had found that renewal in their churches had begun to dry up. Many in the mainstream denominations appeared to be looking for ever more spiritual depth and 'experience' (Pousson, 1994, p.88). Wallis himself had spoken of many spirit-filled Christians finding themselves with 'post-Charismatic values' and subsequently seeking a greater purpose and articulation of their faith (Wallis, 1981, p.7). Another leading Restorationist suggested that renewal had degenerated into a static, inward-looking middle class lifestyle (Noble, 1982, pp.2–4).

In some areas the house churches appeared to satisfy a latent demand. In Scotland they were initially slow to get off the ground. However, for Baptist churches they were probably a greater challenge even than they were south of the border. These churches gained many of their initial members from the Charismatically inclined in the established denominations, drawing firstly from groups which came together for fellowship. From the late 1970s the rapid growth in these new churches increasingly attracted members from non-churchgoers as well as former members of the main denominations.

The Baptist Union estimated that in Scotland alone, independent Charismatic churches at the beginning of the 1980s numbered some 70 sizeable groups which in terms of membership 'profoundly affected' some Baptist churches.[4] In the mid-1990s the seven largest of these churches could claim between 250 and 450 members. In total there are about 220 independent fellowships. This is higher than the total number of Baptist churches in Scotland of which only approximately 12 of the 160 in total are Charismatic.

Some of the larger Charismatic Baptist fellowships were so inspired by the teachings of the larger house churches that they opted out of the Union altogether embracing Restorationism with vigour. In doing so they spawned congregations which tended to be exclusive and sectarian. Most of these come under the auspices of the largest of the new church networks, New Frontiers. Others, perhaps around a dozen in London, have a dual loyalty to New Frontiers and the Baptist Union with a surprising lack of contradiction.

Other congregations, while having amicable links with New Frontiers, have preserved their autonomy which is a major feature of Baptist ecclesiology and which would be compromised by the Apostolic system of the new churches where some highly respected individuals (Apostles) oversee a string of churches. At the same time the new churches have become more compromising, more adaptable and have suitably modified their hostility to the established denominations. Common ground has been explored and in recent years new church leaders have preached in Baptist churches and seminaries and there are signs of increasing respect. In turn, notable figures in the larger Charismatic Baptist churches regularly share platforms with the new church leaders at principal Charismatic events.

SIGNS AND WONDERS, AND BEYOND

If renewal had peaked in the late 1970s, Restorationism reached its apogee by the middle of the next decade. The enduring issue was that of church growth and possible revival. In the USA the teaching of a former missionary in India, Dr Donald McGavran, of California's Fuller Theological Seminary, was gaining attention. The strategy for church growth he endorsed was not so much an art as a science. He called for concessions to cultural traditions and endorsed the virtues of human psychology and sociology (McGavran, 1970).

Since McGavran taught the possibilities of numerical and spiritual growth without the necessity of churches committing themselves to Charismatic renewal, many evangelicals found the teachings intriguing. By the same token, such ideas were attractive to those who wanted the renewal movement to be reinvigorated but wanted an alternative to Restorationism. The attraction to discerning British Charismatics was the possibility of reaching those whom renewal had not previously touched, particularly the working classes (McBain, 1978). The man to emerge with both an understanding of growth issues and a sensitivity to the renewal movement was the former Director of the Fuller Growth Institute, John Wimber.

The impact of Wimber's teaching and ministry on the renewal movement has been enormous. He has remained the central figure from the early 1980s through to the present day. It has become clear that from the outset Wimber had more to offer than church growth strategies. The so-called Toronto Blessing possibly marks the final episode in a colourful and controversial ministry. A much more detailed treatment of Wimber's ministry is found in Chapter 4 of this book.

Since the Third Wave conference in Britain in 1984, Wimber's specialist interests – whether healing or prophecy – have caught the attention of British Charismatics. His Vineyard churches have been the focus of the Toronto Blessing and British churches, including many Baptists of a Charismatic persuasion, have been involved. Wimber, on this occasion, has kept on the fringe and distances himself from the Toronto Vineyard church at the centre of events. Reading between the lines it seems as if a combination of poor health and a series of mis-judgements on the significance of a variety of Charismatic issues is finally leading to a reduction in his personal authority and hence his following. It is too early to be sure that this is the case. What does appear certain, however, is that the influence of the teaching of Wimber, which has been endorsed by so many Charismatic mainline churches, requires careful and reflective study not only by his critics, but even more so by those on whom he has been most influential.

Baptist Charismatics have been forward, second only to their Anglican cousins, in carrying the so-called Third Wave to the denominations. The key observation is that it is how these churches in the mainline denominations respond to such esoteric movements as the Toronto Blessing which may determine the course of the renewal movement into the twenty-first century.

TALE-ENDERS

It must be self-evident that a movement which had begun from an inauspicious base yet which continues to grow globally must be taken seriously by all Christian churches, both inside and outside the established denominations. This is especially the case when so much of the growth has been in a western church context otherwise characterized by decline. Clearly there have always been many aspects of modern culture involved in renewal; this is even more the case today. In an Anglican report (1981) issued on renewal within its own ranks it was stated that the wider movement could be described as a 'form of christianized existentialism'. John Wimber's ministry highlighted this.

Clearly the Charismatic movement is not the same movement as it was 30 years ago. Some mainline Charismatics believe that the situation today is one where statements of traditionally understood Christian truths have become of less worth than personal testimonies to the state of the art spiritual experience. Hence accuracy of terminology, careful exegesis of Scripture, and even the importance of the role of expository Biblical teachings have all been undermined to one degree or another.

The movement has reached the stage where the flow of Charismatic songs has become more important than the core beliefs of worship. People can be attracted to a Charismatic service for what they 'get out of it', rather than to the act of worship itself. In this ambience of spiritual relativism where another level of experience is proposed for every unresolved problem, renewal has been found to flourish. However, if the movement ends up as a form of inverted narcissism at the expense of evangelism, then the long hoped for revival will tarry.

At its deepest level there are profound weaknesses as well as strengths of the movement. From one perspective it has become increasingly amorphous. Even concepts of God have changed and sometimes been forced to conform to human images. Much was epitomized by the Toronto Blessing. While God could still appear as Loving Father and as Holy Fire, He was equally portrayed as a divine dad full of homely fun, ever ready with a minor miracle for those who know the correct formula.

Such reasons for the success of renewal at the same time indicate grounds for much concern about its ultimate health. The constant emphasis on fresh experience has some value in that the grace of God is always appreciated as new. Yet it can and does seriously impair understanding of the proper place for ethical teaching at the heart of the faith. A greater grasp of the historical story of the Church leading to a greater spirituality would provide a better framework for faith than unsubstantiated claims to extraordinary miracles. The honest lesson of renewal must be that genuine miracles are rare events. Over time some of the more seasoned Charismatics, many in the mainline churches, have become convinced that the incidence of healing miracles claimed by those such as Wimber was exaggerated and that the significance he attached to various phenomena was, at best, a result of that flirtation with the excesses of Pentecostalism under the Californian sun.

In spite of many of its shortcomings, there is positive evidence of a profound spirituality in the lives of many adherents. The 'pluses' of renewal still far outweigh its shortcomings. There is the element of divine surprise seen in the way in which the ecumenical spirit has been able to jump over the barriers of self-defence, ignorance and prejudice. Moreover, the movement has cut across cherished theological traditions and touched those who some would regard as untouchable. The movement which has caused so many unnecessary divisions has also prompted admirable loyalty. The outstanding virtue has been that through the experience of renewal there is a fresh sense of evangelical purpose leading to the planting of new churches as well as reviving established ones.

Answers to questions about the worth of renewal must include not only an appreciation of the weaknesses but also its positive insights for a fresh vision. The process of cross-fertilization, examination and development is probably more likely to happen within the respected Christian traditions rather than outside of them. The need to anchor all that is Charismatic within the established denominations, with their deeper roots, experience and lines of accountability, is imperative. Renewal is as much in need of the accepted patterns of church life as the ongoing life in the churches is in need of the spirit of renewal.

NOTES

1. These insights contrasting Baptist and Methodist renewal were provided by Roger Standing in an interview with Stephen Hunt (5 Sept. 1996). Roger Standing is pastor of West Croydon Baptist church and has been active in Charismatic renewal in both camps.
2. These are comments to be found in a magazine called *Viewpoint* produced by the Scottish Baptist Union. They are undated with no reference to volume or number. We have denoted this edition as Viewpoint #1. Note (4) refers to another edition which we denote as *Viewpoint* #2.
3. From a letter written with Dennis Lillie, quoted in Hocken, 1986, p.33.
4. *Viewpoint* #2, see note (2).

BIBLIOGRAPHY

Agenda of the Fountain Trust Consultative Council Meeting, May 1977.
Baptist Times, Dec. 1971.
D. Barrett, in S. M. Burgess and P. H. Alexander *Dictionary of Pentecostal and Charismatic Movements* (New York: Zonderman, 1988), pp.810–29.
D. W. Bebbington, *Evangelism in Modern Britain: A History from the 1730s to the 1980s* (London: Unwin Hyman, 1983).
P. Brierley, *Christian England: What the 1989 Church Census Revealed* (Marc, Europe, 1993).
Church of England Newspaper, 3 Dec. 1965, p.8.
Fountain Trust Council Meeting, 21 Nov. 1979.
P. D. Hocken, *Streams of Renewal* (Exeter: The Paternoster Press, 1986).

S. Hunt, 'The Anglican Wimberites', *Pneuma: The Journal of the Society for Pentecostal Studies*, vol.17, no.1, Spring, 1995, pp.105–18.

D. McBain, 'The Spirits Call to the Hard Places', *Renewal*, no.42, April/May 1978, pp.28–31.

D. McGavran, *Understanding Church Growth* (Grand Rapids, MI: Eerdmans, 1970).

T. Noble, *Tomorrow Today*, Spring, 1982, pp.2–4.

E. K. Pousson, 'A "Great Century" of Pentecostal/Charismatic Renewal and Missions', *Pneuma: The Journal of the Society for Pentecostal Studies*, vol.16, no.1, Spring, 1994, pp.81–100.

Renewal, no.34, Sept 1971.

T. Smail, *Fountain Trust: A Theological Farewell*, editorial (The Fountain Trust, 1980), pp.2–5.

The Charismatic Movement in the Church of England (C10 Publishing, 1981), p.38.

The Churchman editorial, Sept. 1992.

The Minute Book of the Baptist Union Advisory Council on Church Relations, 4 Feb. 1972.

A. Wallis, *In the Day of Thy Power* (London: CLC, 1956).

A. Wallis, *The Radical Christian* (Eastbourne: Kingsway Publications, 1981).

B. R. White, 'The Ministerial Tightrope', *The Fraternal*, no.180, July 1977.

3 The Nature and Variety of Restorationism and the 'House Church' Movement[1]
Nigel Wright

Anyone who sets out to write on this subject encounters certain immediate technical difficulties. There is the problem of sources. When a movement is still young, objective written sources are in short supply and dependence upon oral tradition, personal observation and acquaintance with short term publications so much the greater. Although the Restoration movement has now been in existence for over 20 years the written sources relating to it are still largely informal in nature.

Secondly, there is the problem of nomenclature. The title of this chapter with its reference to the 'house church movement' is quite misleading despite the fact that it reflects the earlier usage of the movement itself. Some of the groups of churches we here describe are committed to not owning property but to maintaining instead a pilgrim existence. Others have erected some of the most sophisticated and costly church buildings that can be found today. To suggest that all are 'house' churches is therefore far from accurate. The term 'new church' has developed as an alternative and enjoys some favour. It refers to the apparent mushrooming of new, independent groupings of churches outside the historic denominations over the last 20 years. 'New churches', however, would have to include the rapid growth of Afro-Caribbean, African and ethnic congregations in the cities, especially London, over this same period, many of which have their roots in older Pentecostalism or other forms of revivalism which do not directly share the ethos of the movement under consideration. Further, not a few of the churches involved in the house church/new church movement are no more 'new' than they are without regular premises. Rather, they are long-established churches, often with Baptist, Brethren or independent evangelical roots, sharing in the vigour of a new movement. Other possible terms are the adjective 'restorationist' or the noun 'restorationism' which seek to identify the movement according to a cardinal theological concept, namely 'restoration'. Even this term is inadequate, since not all the churches which will be identified necessarily see this concept as their dominant theological characteristic. Despite this, it will emerge as the preferred description in this chapter since it identifies most clearly the specific movement with which we are concerned.

Already, however, a third problem in writing this chapter has emerged, the danger of generalization. Commentators on Charismatic Christianity frequently fail to appreciate the shades and varieties of opinion within it. The phenomenon cannot be understood without an adequate grasp of its polygenetic nature. It is a mistake to view it as exclusively 'fundamentalist' in mindset or theology. As a movement, Restorationism is a variation within the total Charismatic spectrum and is then to be further sub-categorized as a coalition of diverse networks of churches rather than one cohesive whole. As time has passed the differences between the networks of churches of which it is comprised have become more evident and often quite stark. They are both theological and attitudinal in nature, deriving characteristically from the stance, personality or eccentricities of the dominant leaders. Therefore, any one statement about Restorationism is unlikely to be true of all its segments.

A fourth difficulty concerns the state of flux in which the movement finds itself, such that anything written in this chapter may relatively swiftly be out of date. New developments, variations and ironies are always in hand. An example of this is the way the so-called 'Toronto blessing' has reshaped the scene. If the true nature of present phenomena only emerges in their future development, we are to a certain extent still guessing, in this area more than in most.

Having outlined the difficulties of writing anything and the provisionality of any assessment, what actually should be written? What follows comprises an exposition of its dominant theological motifs, a summary of the historical origins of the movement, an examination of its current form, and a reflection upon its future development.

RESTORATIONIST THEOLOGY[2]

Restorationist theology arises out of the Charismatic movement but reaches back to older traditions which it represents in a modern form. Restorationism's controlling insight was that the new wine of charismatic experience, itself gratefully received, required new wineskins if it were not to be dissipated. Otherwise expressed, this means the search for a new way of being the church which escapes from the perceived traditionalism and compromise of denominational religion and which is a recovery of New Testament patterns of church life. In the belief that the status quo is incapable of extensive reform, Restorationism rejects the liberal option of patient reform from within in favour of a radical restoration of the New Testament church from the bottom up.

Seen in this light, the movement can be understood to be within an historically continuous stream of church life, reaching back at least as far as sixteenth century continental Anabaptism, in which the same vision has been kept alive, although variously expressed.[3] The influence of Arthur Wallis in this regard cannot be underestimated, rooted as he was, along with other early leaders, in the Brethren tradition and imbued with an enduring passion for the recovery of New Testament realities. Such an interpretation of the movement is at once a relativizing statement. Restorationism is another example of a persistent phenomenon of church life which is well documented in post-Reformation history and has its counterparts in pre-Reformation movements against the institutionalizing of primitive Christianity. But it is not something unheard of and totally new in the church's history.

The theology of Restoration assumes that there is a point of origin against which the current state of the church may be tested and judged. That point of origin is the New Testament church, which is to be imitated not only in matters pertaining to faith and justification but also in its patterns and forms. Post-Reformation church history is thus understood as a succession of recoveries of lost or neglected truth. Luther recovered the doctrine of justification by faith, Baptists believers' baptism, Wesley assurance of salvation, Christian Brethren New Testament forms of worship and participation, Pentecostals the baptism and gifts of the Spirit, Charismatics the sense of being the Body of Christ, and so on. The present-day Restorationist movement was perceived in the earliest days of its existence as being the extension and possibly the climax of this process.

Of primary importance in the Restoration movement is the recovery of apostolic ministries understood as the concomitant of spiritual gifts. After the recovery of New Testament gifts comes the recovery of New Testament ministries. Clearly, apostleship is not understood as the reconstituting of the original 12, who were marked out as being historically unique by the Resurrection appearances, but as the recovery of a spiritual function in the church in line with the five-fold ministry referred to in Ephesians 4:11. This ministry is understood to be both enduring and foundational, such that churches which lack the benefit of 'apostolic input' are not only missing out but are seriously defective. When joined to a moderated shepherding doctrine, such an approach can lead to an understanding of the church as identical with kingdom, to be organized as a hierarchy through a patriarchal system of authority and submission. This in turn can create a sectarian or even cultic feel to the movement as other churches, even charismatic churches, are regarded as deficient where such hierarchies are lacking or where they are staffed by people who would not be regarded in Restorationism as truly apostolic. Precisely here were found the seeds of tension between the majority of early Restorationists and the historic churches.

The concept that the process of divine restoration may be coming to a climax gave rise to a heightened eschatological awareness which saw Restorationism as potentially writing the last chapter of history. This was accompanied by a decisive rejection of the pessimistic premillenialism in which the majority of the early leaders had been reared in favour of a form of post-millenialism which expected the restoring to the church of its New Testament pattern to be accompanied by a massive and final revival as the immediate prelude to the coming of Christ. As the New Testament spoke of the coming of Christ to a church 'prepared as a bride adorned for her husband' (Rev. 21:2), it was deduced that if the church of the Restoration were to put itself in order along the lines of establishing the hierarchy and entering into submissive relationships, this could itself be the impetus to 'bring back the King' to claim his bride. Restorationism was therefore seen in eschatological and almost apocalyptic terms, creating a sense of urgency which sometimes found expression in a ruthless condemnation of the historic churches as abandoned by God and in consequent proselytizing from them. Characteristic traits of post-millennialist optimism and triumph are also manifest in the broad range of songs and hymns that have emerged from the movement or been preferred by it.

HISTORICAL ORIGINS

Restorationism is a later development of the Charismatic Renewal movement which had begun to make its impact in Britain from the early 1960s. Although the origin of the movement as such must be located within the period 1970–4,[4] the ground out of which it grew was already being prepared under the formative influence of Arthur Wallis (1923–88) in the 1950s.[5] Wallis, together with David Lillie,[6] served as a convenor of three Devon conferences in 1958, 1961 and

1962 concerned with a vision for the restoration of the New Testament church. These conferences were attended by a number of independent, itinerant and increasingly charismatically inclined Bible teachers who were later to be leading figures in or around Restorationism. The decade of Charismatic Renewal, the 1960s, saw the emergence in various places of house churches delighting in a new freedom from traditional practices and restrictions, and the simultaneous movement of more established churches in Charismatic directions. From the flowing together of these streams the movement we are calling Restorationism was to emerge.

In the 1970–4 period emergent leaders in the 'house churches' began to come together in worship gatherings in London. They included John Noble, Gerald Coates, Terry Virgo, George Tarleton, David Mansell and Maurice Smith. At the same time and independently, a Welsh evangelist and former missionary in Guyana, Bryn Jones, was establishing in Bradford a 'community church' destined to be highly influential in that region. In these ways Restorationism began to develop as a conscious movement. Its upward march and distinct tradition may then be traced via a series of Bible Weeks, initially at Capel, then from 1976 at the Great Yorkshire Showground in Harrogate and a parallel event on the Downs near Brighton, which acted as an ideological platform, shop window and magnet for the movement. By means of these events considerable visibility and influence was to come to Restorationism. Many from a quite different church background would attend these events to gain from their vitality and exuberance yet without a full grasp of the growing Restorationist philosophy which lay behind them or, when they did grasp it, with less than complete agreement with it. Yet behind the public events were serious attempts to establish two fundamental realities – 'covenant relationships' and 'apostolic ministries'.

The immediate origins of these concerns are once more to be found in an initiative taken by Arthur Wallis to call a conference together in 1971 to discuss eschatology. In the event this took a different turn. Wallis' fundamental conviction, forged against his theological heritage from the Christian Brethren, was that the coming of Christ was to be greeted, not with the pessimistic decline of church life expected by traditional pre-millenialism[7] but by a gloriously restored church. Unexpectedly, this gave rise to an attempt to hammer out the principles of the restored kingdom which was to be expected as a prelude to the second coming. The conviction grew in those who attended this conference that seven leaders from among them were to be set aside for prophetic or apostolic ministry in the end-time church. They were Arthur Wallis, Peter Lyne, Bryn Jones, David Mansell, Graham Perrins, Hugh Thompson and John Noble. Later this group was increased to 14 with the inclusion of George Tarleton, Gerald Coates, Barney Coombs, Maurice Smith, Ian McCullough, John MacLaughlan and Campbell McAlpine.

To list these names is itself to trace the subsequent development of the movement, although it is of interest to note that certain names, including Terry Virgo and David Tomlinson, are absent. In effect this group was to be a Charismatic leadership for the burgeoning Restorationist movement, which was seen in eschatological terms as the emergence of a spotless Bride fit to welcome the return of the King. The leaders were to be bound together in covenant relationships and in this way were to be the catalysts of a coming together of the Body of Christ, joined and knit together in a way which would supersede the broken and compromised state of the denominational churches. The key element in this restoration was to be the influence of 'apostles', charismatically gifted and proven men [*sic*] who would give leadership and direction to the movement. This is the philosophy which began to find expression in Bible Weeks, celebrations and publications.

The ideological rhetoric masked the fact, however, that covenant relationships were more difficult to forge and sustain than was at first imagined. Accordingly, the wider group of leaders was to divide in 1976 as deeper temperamental difficulties came to the surface. Since then the development of Restorationism has taken place in fragmentation, sometimes in competition, sometimes in newly forged or restored coalitions. Some of the above listed names fell by the wayside, others never truly integrated in the first place, others have been marginalized, and in 1988 Arthur Wallis, whose vision was at the heart of the enterprise, died suddenly, adding to the sense that instead of being the decisive and final chapter in the church's history, Restorationism was simply another episode in the long story. The demise of the Bible Weeks at Capel and Harrogate, the rise of the more mainstream Spring Harvest weeks and of significant centres of renewal in the Anglican tradition, such as Holy Trinity Brompton, and the emergence of other figures in the tradition of charismatic renewal with different and comparatively more catholic values, most notably John Wimber, have added to the relativizing of the movement in importance so that it may now more easily be seen as a virile and creative but by no means decisive and final manifestation for the church. Alongside this more modest place must be set new initiatives which have continued to keep Restorationism at the cutting edge. The Downs Bible Week, at its

inception a southern counterpart to the Dales Week, has developed
into the Stoneleigh Bible Week in the Midlands and attracts large
numbers. More recently a process of 'centring' has been under way
and in particular the Evangelical Alliance under the leadership of Clive
Calver has proven to be an umbrella organization through which
Restorationists might affirm their place in the mainstream of British
evangelical Christianity.

THE MOVEMENT'S PRESENT FORM

In the mid-1990s Restorationism may be seen to be more varied than
ever. In 1985 an influential sociological typology of the movement
was attempted by Andrew Walker which divided it into 'R1' and 'R2'.
In R1 was to be located the axis of churches which lay behind the
then Dales/Downs Bible Weeks, associated in particular with the ministries of Bryn Jones in the North and Terry Virgo in the South. These
were characterized by greater ideological precision and tighter relational structures than the churches in R2, a broader category containing the more loosely federated churches in a variety of networks. The
difficulties of typology have increased immeasurably since this early
attempt, to the point that each Restorationist network ought now more
accurately to be seen as a distinct entity with a particular ethos. My
own attempt assumes a sectarian scale, that is to say, a spectrum drawn
as it were from right to left (but without political connotations) according to the degree of 'sectarian otherness' which the groups of
churches feel about themselves over against the wider church.
    (1) At the far right of the spectrum are two older clusters of house
churches associated with the names of G. W. North and the town,
South Chard. Both of these groups predate the more modern movements, the former distinguished by the somewhat esoteric teachings of
Pastor North and the latter by the practice of baptizing only in the
name of Jesus. Both groups are regarded in some sense as forerunners
by the Restorationist movement and have provided personnel for the
newer churches. A certain mystique and obscurity surrounds both and
neither has proven in the event to be a main player in the unfolding
drama of Restorationism.
    (2) A full description of Restorationism ought to include a refer-
ence to the Bugbrooke Community or Jesus Fellowship in Northamp-
tonshire.[8] In the 1970s an ordinary village Baptist church passed under
the leadership of its lay pastor, Noel Stanton, into Charismatic Re-

newal and then into practising the community of goods in the style of the Anabaptist Hutterites. With large numbers of its members sharing households in a simple lifestyle based on community properties, it has been able to initiate and develop several successful businesses including a major supplier of wholefoods. More recently the community's evangelistic wing, the Jesus Army, has engaged in aggressive and effective street evangelism among the marginalized sections of society. The community is conscious of the historical antecedents to its own positions and has a well thought out, if highly eclectic, theology for its practices.[9] Nevertheless, perceived sectarianism and particularly what have been deemed 'unbrotherly' practices in its evangelism and extension activities, has led to its expulsion successively from the Evangelical Alliance and the Baptist Union. In recent years Noel Stanton has been working hard to re-establish fraternal relationships wherever possible, but the style and aggressiveness of the community clearly pose problems for some. The Jesus Army is highly active in evangelism amongst the poor and styles itself in this regard upon the early Salvation Army, using for this purpose designer flak jackets and an annual conference at Wembley Arena which self-consciously celebrates being 'over the top' in its worship style and intensity. The Jesus Fellowship has a strategy for extension based upon the development of 'community houses' throughout the country. Not surprisingly, the Fellowship's intense style and all-engulfing requirement of commitment lead to occasional allegations of abuse from disillusioned former members.

(3) The 'Basingstoke' group of churches, now sometimes known as 'Salt and Light', developed out of Basingstoke Baptist Church under the leadership of its pastor Barney Coombs. To a greater degree than other Restorationists the group has taken on board the 'discipleship' teaching which emerged from a coalition of American leaders called 'The Fort Lauderdale Five' in the 1970s. This group, comprising Ern Baxter, Bob Mumford, Derek Prince, Don Basham and Charles Simpson, functioned as the American connection for Restorationism in its early days, particularly providing platform ministry for the Bible Weeks before home-grown leaders had grown in confidence sufficiently to provide their own.

. The 'shepherding movement', as it came to be called, stressed the need for every believer to be in a relationship of submission on a one-to-one basis. The resultant church resembled a patriarchal pyramid in which all the male members were to be 'covered' by an authority within the church. Wives and children were of course 'covered' by husbands and parents. It is around this particular teaching that much of the early unease about Restorationism developed, but it was never wholeheartedly embraced in this country as originally taught but usually in an ameliorated form. The Basingstoke circle developed it most consistently and therefore, despite the overtly outward-looking attitude of these churches and the attempt to maintain a foothold especially in the Baptist Union of Great Britain,[10] they have been particularly prone to legalism, a sectarian ethos and an in-house group mentality. This group maintains a strongly patriarchal and confrontational style which, in my experience, is frequently overlooked and underestimated.[11] I am inclined to believe that the methods of this group, although not cultic, are bordering in some respects on the cult-like. More recently Barney Coombs' extensive North American connections have drawn his interest to developing Reconstructionism, a right-wing social and political philosophy developed by R. J. Rushdoony which purports to apply Biblical law to social and economic affairs. The consequences of such a philosophy and its espousal in the British context even by the churches linked with Coombs are as yet far from clear but would be worth careful examination.

(4) The churches associated with Bryn Jones and his brother Keri, formerly based at Bradford but now located more centrally in the Leicester area, have moved from a position of dominance in the movement to an increasingly marginal position. This is in part due to the closure of the shop-window Dales Bible Week in the early 1980s in favour of more in-house events, but more so to the highly independent and individual line pursued by Jones, which makes him a difficult person with whom to sustain an equal partnership. If the early typology of Andrew Walker is maintained, the only network of churches still in R1 is that associated with Jones, formerly called Harvestime and more recently known as Covenant Ministries, although the most recent developments render even this judgement subject to qualification. The late 1980s and early 1990s witnessed a number of significant defections by churches from this group at the same time as it aspired to an American-style upgrading of its resources, including the building of a new headquarters and the associated Covenant College in the Midlands. The separation of the Virgo and Jones networks of churches took place amicably but decisively in the mid-1980s, actualizing what had been perceived for some time as a difference in ethos. Jones has responsibility for some churches in North America and has been influenced by the American scene and partially by prosperity doctrine, a fact which is reflected not least in his ambitious and expensive plans for the movement of which he is at the head. This said, sight should never be lost of Bryn Jones'

working class origins in South Wales and of the radicalizing influence this has had upon him.

Of all the Restoration groups Covenant Ministries is the one which appeared until recently most independent, most negative towards denominational churches and most aloof even from other like-minded churches. But now this judgement must be qualified. In the past two years a marked change of spirit has taken place within this stream towards opening up to the wider church. During the more sectarian years the drive within these churches was towards excellence, partly as an outcome of Jones' American experience. This was expressed in part by an increasing emphasis upon educational attainment with both Bryn Jones and Hugh Thompson, a leading teacher within the movement, gaining Master's Degrees in Peace Studies at Bradford University. Jones then went on to gain his Doctorate while his brother Keri has been conducting doctoral research into the origins of Restorationism. The change in ethos within this group has been accompanied by a more self-critical approach and a willingness to open up previously unquestioned theological issues, not least the status and role of women. More liberal opinion-formers, among them Tim Laarson, Bryn's 'researcher', have advanced a libertarian interpretation of Scripture in this regard against the inherited patriarchalism of the movement. The most significant feature in this is that the new freedom of expression is allowed official forums for debate within the movement as a whole and therefore legitimated. It is possible to interpret this shift of mood within Covenant Ministries as an outcome of the impact of the 'Toronto Blessing'. It is sometimes claimed that one fruit of this wave of religious experience is the breaking down of barriers between previously separated groups. It may be more accurate, however, to understand the new openness of Covenant Ministries as predating the Toronto phenomenon, in which case the opportunity of the phenomenon has been seized with enthusiasm by Bryn as a way of re-entering the mainstream of Charismatic church life, re-legitimating himself there and forming new alliances.

(5) One of the most significant features over the last decade of Restorationism has been the emergence of Terry Virgo and his Brighton-based New Frontiers network as the most important movers in the movement in succession to Bryn Jones. Whereas Jones is an erstwhile Pentecostal and shows some of that movement's aggressive drive, Virgo's own background and conversion were amongst the Baptists and he reflects the more cautious and measured approach of that tradition as well as its generally Reformed theology to which he is strongly

committed. Without being an outstandingly charismatic personality, Virgo's combination of pastoral concern, teaching ability and wise counsel plus his ability to gather and maintain a strong team of leaders around himself has led to the formation of a well organized network of churches relatively free from authoritarianism and sectarianism. This now includes some significant Baptist churches which have in addition been able to maintain their denominational membership, and not only nominally so. In recent years Virgo has developed close links with John Wimber and the Vineyard churches. These have added significantly to the style of church life found in New Frontiers and have contributed towards a more open and expansive attitude towards non-Restorationist churches. In origin New Frontiers is a southern grouping[12] but is moving steadily to become nationwide partly through a strategy of church-planting, as for instance in Manchester, partly through drawing to itself existing churches from an increasingly wide sphere of influence.

(6) A small and sometimes overlooked group of churches has its focal point in the King's Church, Aldershot, and is associated with the names of Derek Brown and Mike Pusey. Most of these churches have developed from a Baptist base embracing Charismatic Renewal and have sought to discover more authoritative forms of church leadership.

(7) Gerald Coates and John Noble are amongst the early figures of Restorationism who have gone on to become leaders of a sizeable group of churches associated with Cobham in Surrey. While Noble has mellowed into a trusted elder statesman, Coates has acquired a reputation as a colourful and controversial extrovert and entrepreneur. He has become one of the best known Restorationist leaders although not always one who is taken with full seriousness in all circles and certainly one who, although an outstanding communicator, would be regarded more as a prophetic preacher than a Biblical expositor, an area where Virgo excels. This axis of churches was the core of what Walker described as R2, a more liberally minded and anarchic stream which has wanted to avoid the tendency towards institutionalization found in other places. Although Coates has remained critical of denominations, there has been a willingness to cooperate with others which has also sought to be affirmative and has found particular expression in the Marches For Jesus and the Dawn 2000 initiative on planting new churches.

(8) The Ichthus Fellowship in South London must be considered as a Restorationist group, although one which has developed quite independently under the remarkable leadership of Roger Forster and has consistently sought, unlike some of the others in their early days of existence, to achieve growth through evangelism rather than transfer.

This group is distinctive by virtue of its theology, which is self-consciously Arminian and Anabaptist; its model of church growth, which is strong on church-planting while seeking to maintain its congregations as part of one large church; its ethos of ministry of women on equal terms with men and appointing women as congregational leaders; and in its ecumenical concern – Roger and Faith Forster have played significant roles within the Evangelical Alliance and Spring Harvest. While the instinct of other groupings has been to establish their own platform and to guard it jealously, Ichthus has involved itself in Spring Harvest, an interdenominational and evangelically pluralist event which, while others have run out of steam or rationale, has gone from strength to strength. Roger Forster possesses one of the most fertile brains of the Restoration movement, is an avid reader of history and theology, and is an able and yet eirenic polemicist.

(9) A ninth grouping[13] is difficult to characterize at all. A large number of community churches remain unaffiliated to any wider network and are all so well integrated with mainstream churches that were it not for the fact of Restorationism they would simply be regarded as healthy and independently-minded congregations. Chief among these is the Sheffield House Church and its daughter congregations under Peter Fenwick, who is widely regarded within and beyond Restorationism as an astute and sane counsellor and a wise father in God. Significantly, however, Fenwick has been sufficiently critical of the Toronto phenomenon to want no longer to be identified as a 'Charismatic'. Although the Toronto experience has brought some of the streams of Restorationism closer together, its overall impact has been to add to the fragmentation of the movement as a whole.

(10) To the extreme left of the spectrum I have chosen to place the churches previously associated with David Tomlinson, based in Brixton, a grouping of churches which now scarcely exists as a distinguishable entity for reasons relating to Tomlinson's progressively divergent career. This has been at points a weathervane for tendencies in the movement as a whole. Himself a product of the W. R. North related churches, Tomlinson became closely linked with Bryn Jones and was clearly and publicly recognized by him as an apostle. By the mid-1980s he had disentangled himself from this connection and moved steadily away from the kind of authoritarianism instinctive to Jones. At the same time his ministry began to take account of considerations largely neglected in the movement as a whole, namely concern for issues of peace, justice, creation and culture. As part of this shift Tomlinson moved with a group of fellow-workers from his former base in the north-east to

live in Brixton and in due course planted a church there. While maintaining a Restorationist perspective Tomlinson came to understand this in a way which is socially radical and liberationist by contrast with the more conservative implications of Jones' authoritarianism. It is within Tomlinson's network of churches that the 'prophetic word' came claiming that the 'house church movement' is over, a word taken to mean not that the new churches should go out of business but that as a movement which distinguishes itself critically from the mainline churches it has no future. God's concern is with all the churches. As an extension of this mood, Tomlinson then gave up his role within the church he had planted in favour of an alternative version of church called 'Holy Joe's', meeting in a pub. He accompanied this with studying for a Master's Degree in Biblical Interpretation at London Bible College. In 1995 he published his book *The Post-Evangelical*[14] in which, without declaring himself an ex-evangelical, he made clear his unease with some aspects of cultural evangelicalism. Currently, Tomlinson is associated with an Anglican Church and there is the possibility of his seeking ordination to the Anglican ministry. In hindsight Tomlinson is vulnerable to being dismissed as an enigma and a maverick, but it is of interest to note that his pathway has taken him from the extreme right to the extreme left of the spectrum as we have constructed it and possibly beyond it altogether.

The diversity of Restorationism should now be plain. Given that in embryo it has been there from the beginning, it is no surprise that the history of the movement gives evidence of the ability of its leaders to disagree strongly. The earliest expectations of an unbreakable covenant relationship binding all together in a way which would transform the face of the church have proven unsustainable. Yet movement has taken place which indicates that a new kind of unity based upon mutual respect and the ability to disagree may well be in the offing for some of the streams and groupings indicated. If this is to be achieved it will be more modest than the original hopes while at the same time more closely akin to the kind of unity-in-coalition being sought among evangelical believers across the historic denominations.

A THEOLOGICAL ASSESSMENT

From the perspective of Christian theology a fruitful way of criticizing Restoration theology would be to concede it broadly in principle and find it inconsistent in practice. The notion that the New Testament provides the final and infallible rule for the manner of the church's life can be argued as a respected tradition of essential Protestantism, particularly its radical wing. The question remains whether in finding its ground of critical reappraisal in Scripture Restorationism has actually drawn the right conclusions. In fact it has tended to find its primary references either in the notion of the restoring of a Davidic kingdom or in the Pauline teaching on submission.[15] On the basis that neither of these points of reference can themselves be properly understood in Christian terms until seen through the lens of Jesus Christ, it is the contention of this chapter that Restorationism has been misleading. The teaching of Jesus stands sharply against some of the teachings and emphases which we have outlined and replaces them with a form of church life which is not hierarchical or only minimally so, which looks to God rather than to his servants and seeing the Lordship of Christ as qualifying and confining their authority, and which sees authority displayed and practised in servanthood rather than domination. At these points the movement is to be regarded as having taken wrong and potentially abusive turns, but the Restorationist impulse which goes back to the sources of the faith in Jesus is itself what leads to these criticisms. Restorationism is therefore in principle right in what it attempts to do, but in practice, at these points, wrong in the conclusions it draws because it is inadequately faithful to its own chief insight.

Here a significant qualification needs to be entered in the light of the previous section. What was outlined early on in this chapter is largely the theological rationale of *early* Restorationism. To understand the present scene it becomes necessary to grasp that the variety of the movement we have described means that not all have accepted or propagated the teaching as expressed and that, more interestingly, some have moved decisively away from it while still being shaped in thought and practice by the tradition from which they have moved.

The reasons for this may be located in part in disillusionment at the early high hopes and aspirations not being fulfilled, incipient differences rising to the surface, and further reflection taking place on what exactly was being claimed in the first place. There may even have been recognition that in practice certain things have proved harmful. Outside influences have also contributed to a shift, such as that of John Wimber, in whom a spiritual vitality that Restorationists would respect is combined with a more open and negotiable ecclesiology.

Most significant, however, must be rated the way in which the New Testament itself, and in particular its witness to Jesus, has brought about a questioning and modification of early teaching. This is most clearly perceived in the pilgrimage of David Tomlinson and is at the root of the break with Bryn Jones. Whereas Jones' instinct would be to understand apostleship in an authoritarian, patriarchal manner and interpret Scripture accordingly, Tomlinson's capacity for self-criticism has led to a reappraisal of such a style in the light of Jesus and his teaching and to a consequent shift. This did not initially mean for him a complete rejection of previous categories, such as apostleship, but their reinterpretation in a non-authoritarian, servanthood direction. The result is not very different from what many other Christians would be happy to affirm concerning their own forms of translocal ministry and this has contributed further to the rapprochement to the mainstream. A similar shift may be traced in other strands of Restorationism, although it must also be understood that the theological journey travelled by the leaders is not always imitated immediately by their followers and might even lead to a change of loyalties and affiliation. We are thus led to conclude that Restorationist theology is in transition. Much of the early extravagance which tended towards sectarianism has faded away and a variety of theological stances is left, the majority of which sit quite happily within the mainstream evangelical coalition of theologies, but some of which, not yet purged from idiosyncrasies, are on its margins.

RESTORATIONISM AND THE DENOMINATIONS

Many Restorationist leaders have been trenchant critics of the denominations while being blind to the fact that they themselves exhibit many of the characteristics of denominationalism. Of course, while a denomination is defined as a legal federation of churches in some form, Restoration churches can imagine themselves to be outside this particular 'trap'. If on the other hand denominations are defined as groups or networks of churches which distinguish themselves self-consciously from other church bodies and display common qualities, practices and a sense of identity, then Restoration churches are as denominational as the rest and possibly more so. This produces several tensions.

The stronger the sense of identity and common purpose to be found among a group of churches, the more likely they are to be effective in corporate mission while at the same time becoming a definite sect or denomination. This is the road taken for some years by the Bryn Jones group. As an alternative, being a denomination can be avoided by loosening formal ties and maximizing the freedom of each local church. This was David Tomlinson's road but it led to the danger of loss of identity and thus of the sense of common endeavour. The Virgo route seems to be to maintain strong relational links between churches but so to straddle denominational structures that they act as a bulwark against the new network itself being seen as a denomination. The other groupings are sufficiently small as yet not to face the issue so acutely.

Future moves are likely to mean that the trend towards diversification continues while a new sense of new church coalition develops simultaneously despite it. The diversification will be manifest at the level of theology and style and will be largely dependent on the new movements with which each grouping chooses to identify itself. Reconstructionism (Coombs) or issues of peace, justice and the integrity of creation (Tomlinson) lead in very different directions, as we have observed (although the Toronto connection has reinforced coalition among some). The most crucial decision to be made will concern whether or not to merge more completely with the evangelical mainstream as it becomes progressively more charismatic and informal. The influence of Restorationism must be seen not only in those bodies which are directly allied to it but also in the ways in which numerous Baptist and Anglican churches in particular have accommodated themselves to or gained consciously or unconsciously from the trends it represents. Between many churches of whatever background there is now very little to choose in practical terms. All of this points to a merging of Restorationists into the mainstream while maintaining a sense of their own distinctiveness. Those groups which resist this tendency will inevitably distinguish themselves more and more surely as denominations in their own right with all the paraphernalia which belongs to this state. As a sign against the excessive institutionalization of the churches, their formality and inflexibility, the movement has nonetheless spoken loudly.

NOTES

.1. This chapter is a revised, updated and partially restructured version of an article which first appeared as 'Restorationism and the "house church" movement' in *Themelios*, vol.16, no.2 (Jan./Feb. 1991), pp.4–8.
2. For a fuller appraisal see my *The Radical Kingdom: Restoration in Theory and Practice* (Eastbourne: Kingsway, 1986); Max Turner, 'Ecclesiology in the Major "Apostolic" Restorationist Churches in the United Kingdom', *Vox Evangelica*, vol.XIX, 1989, pp.83–108; Andrew Walker, 'The Theology

of the "Restoration" House Churches' in David Martin and Peter Mullen (eds), *Strange Gifts: A Guide to Charismatic Renewal* (Oxford: Blackwell, 1984), pp. 208–16.

3. Cf. D. F. Dumbaugh, *The Believers' Church: The History and Character of Radical Protestantism* (London and New York: Macmillan, 1968). An influential although historically debatable work in this regard is E. H. Broadbent, *The Pilgrim Church* (London: Pickering and Inglis, 1931).

4. The origins of the movement are most fully documented by Andrew Walker in *Restoring the Kingdom: The Radical Christianity of the House Church Movement* (London: Hodder and Stoughton, 1985; rev. edn 1988), and Peter Hocken, *Streams of Renewal: The Origins and Early Development of the Charismatic Movement in Great Britain* (Exeter: Paternoster, 1986). See also Stanley M. Burgess and Gary B. McGee, *Dictionary of Pentecostal and Charismatic Movements* (Grand Rapids, MI: Zondervan, 1988) and Nigel S. Scotland, *Charismatics in the Next Millennium* (London: Hodder and Stoughton, 1995) which, despite its title, is largely about the last 30 years.

5. Wallis later supplied an early rationale of all that Restorationism stood for in his book *The Radical Christian* (Eastbourne: Kingsway, 1981).

6. Cf. D. Lillie *Beyond Charisma* (Exeter: Paternoster, 1981).

7. Pre-millenialism is the belief that Christ will return to this world and will then establish on earth a thousand-year reign of justice and peace.

8. See Chapter 6 in this book by Keith Newell.

9. See Simon Cooper and Mike Farrant, *Fire in our Hearts: The Story of the Jesus Fellowship* (Eastbourne: Kingsway, 1991).

10. At least two leaders within this stream, Stephen Thomas and Mike Beaumont, are ministers of the Baptist Union of Great Britain whose accreditation is maintained through their being nominally attached to the circuit of Baptist churches in Oxfordshire in which Thomas began his pastoral career in 1974.

11. In the original article of which this chapter is a revision I placed the Basingstoke group in fourth position in the spectrum I developed. I have now placed it third and so have repositioned it in relation to Covenant Ministries. This reflects the changes in Covenant Ministries but on reflection this could have been its position with equal accuracy in the original article.

12. This was reflected in the group's first name, 'Coastlands'.

13. In my original article I placed this group in tenth position. The progressive shifts undertaken by David Tomlinson and outlined under (10) make it clear why this change is necessary.

14. David Tomlinson, *The Post-Evangelical* (London: Triangle, 1995).

15. An example of this approach is Ron Trudinger, *Built to Last* (Eastbourne: Kingsway, 1982).

4 'Doing the Stuff': The Vineyard Connection

Stephen Hunt

From the outside St Jude's (not the real name) is an insignificant looking church in a sleepy suburb of London. The vicar had attended John Wimber's MC510 course on church growth strategy at Fuller Seminary in California and brought the ministry back to his dwindling congregation that numbered fewer than 40. The choir master left in protest against the Charismatic choruses introduced, and took the choir with him. In ten years the church had grown to a membership of well over 400. It may have had something to do with the vicar leading the Charismatic faction of his congregation around the parish boundary shouting 'out Satan out'. More realistically it may reflect the overwhelming attraction of Wimber's Charismatic package.

People are drawn to St Jude's from miles around. Apart from the structure of the building there is little to suggest that it is Anglican. In fact, inside it looks like any large Charismatic church which could be found practically anywhere. Large pennants proclaiming that 'Jesus heals' hang from the pillars. The altar is primarily where the 'worship team' place their guitars when not in use. There are three services on a Sunday. A traditional one at 8.30 a.m. to placate the Bishop, which few attend. The other two are very Charismatic affairs where Anglican liturgy only occasionally surfaces and where glossolalia is a familiar part of the worship. After the evening service the Holy Spirit is evoked to fall on the congregation. Some will hold their hands out expectantly. Others will begin to tremble. A few will claim healings, perhaps deliverance. A minority of parishioners, rather disturbed by the proceedings, take their leave.

THE DYNAMICS OF VINEYARD

According to its own sources John Wimber's Vineyard Ministry International (VMI) has a worldwide membership somewhere in the region of 50,000 spread across as many as 550 independent churches (Vineyard, various leaflets). It is, by any criterion, one of the great Charismatic success stories. In its earliest stages what became known as the Toronto Blessing appeared to be spread through channels directly, or indirectly, associated with Vineyard (Hunt, 1995a, pp. 264–6). The significance of this particular strand of the Charismatic movement was highlighted in the way that this supposed move of God became associated with the Vineyard church in Toronto which also provided a focus for events as they unfolded. While the 'Blessing' has not significantly added to its membership it has firmly put the Vineyard organization on the world map. At the same time it has confirmed that the VMI has many of the ingredients necessary for a prosperous Charismatic church. This is not only in terms of its own numerical growth, but also the way that its ideas and strategies have been adopted by other Charismatic churches in very different cultural contexts. One only has to consider the extraordinary impact Vineyard has made not just upon the New Church scene in Britain, but upon Charismatics in the Anglican church which the arrival of the Toronto Blessing merely confirmed.

This chapter is concerned with providing at least some of the answers to why Vineyard has been so attractive in the Charismatic marketplace. It largely identifies the success of Vineyard as derived from the construction of a worldview which brings together a mixture of this-worldly and other-worldly components. The theological framework which has emerged is extraordinarily well designed to confront the challenges of modernity in simultaneously counteracting and embracing rationalizing and pluralist forces. Collectively, they merge to provide a meaningful and action-orientated, 'fundamentalist' belief system which emphasizes the immanence of the supernatural realm and the reality of the struggle with demonic forces. In doing so Vineyard offers an attractive product appealing to a fairly specific membership.

The Association of Vineyard Churches was established in 1986 and has subsequently flourished to become a fully-fledged international organization. There should be no hesitation in seeing the Vineyard as a 'movement' in its own right. Since the early 1980s it has expanded from five congregations in California to approximately 300 in the USA, although over half of them are still on the west coast. Vineyard itself estimates that there are some 10,000 churches across the USA and Canada directly connected with the organization with varying degrees of alignment. Most display an emphasis upon the 'signs and wonders' ministry which has became the hallmark of Vineyard from its inception. Indeed, it was precisely because of such alleged 'power encounters' with the supernatural that many conservative churches became attracted to what Vineyard had to offer (Perrin, 1989, pp.73, 85).

The name of John Wimber is practically synonymous with the Vineyard organization. Initially he was a successful Californian rock and jazz musician, composer and record producer before his conversion and apparently profound ecstatic spiritual experience in 1963 at the age of 29. Always gifted with communication skills, he has referred to himself as a 'pre-hippie hippie' (Springer, 1985, p.29). After heading a Quaker church in Yorba Linda, California, Wimber broke away in 1978 to establish his own church, the Vineyard Fellowship, in Anaheim. At the turn of the decade it appeared to be merely one of a cluster of rapidly growing independent 'boom' Californian churches.

Until 1995 Wimber remained the senior pastor at the original church in Anaheim which now boasts a congregation of over 5000. Even after a run of serious illnesses his role in the larger organization remains, as once described, rather like 'an apostle or a Bishop' (Parrott and Perrin, 1991, p. 31). The personal charisma which he projects is beyond dispute although he does not, in any sense, come across as the leader of a cult with an undisputed mastery over the rank and file membership.

Nevertheless, 'charisma', in the sociological sense, is itself an important resource for any religious collective in providing a focus of allegiance and source of motivation for its membership. Located in the modern context of an entrepreneurial culture there is an extra dimension. In the spiritual marketplace 'enterprise' religion has encouraged the charismatic *persona*, the superperformer who is always seen to succeed and overcome adverse circumstances (Roberts, 1992). In Vineyard's case, it is congruent with an overt triumphantalism espoused by an organization dedicated to continued church growth and 'taking the ground' from the forces of darkness.

There is always, however, the danger of putting too much emphasis upon the personal magnetism of single individuals. The sociological understanding of charisma locates it very firmly within a cultural ambience and, where applicable, prevailing theological constructs as well (Weber, 1947). The success of Vineyard, and the wider Third Wave movement in which it is embedded, is at least partly due to the cultivation of a worldview and a wider, distinct theological framework with a profound dualism which tends to divide the world neatly into that which is of God and that which is of Satan. Above all, Vineyard sees itself at the 'cutting edge' of what God is supposed to be doing at the end of the twentieth century.

THE CONSTRUCTION OF A WORLDVIEW

To a large degree notions of 'spiritual' consumerism and marketing derive from the work of Peter Berger for whom secularization practically equals the pluralization of religious belief. Competition arises in the religious marketplace through the existence of competing worldviews or 'plausibility structures'. Religions are also compelled to compete and conflict with each other for the allegiance of their clientele. The pluralist situation is above all, according to Berger, a 'market situation', and as allegiance is voluntary it is, by definition, less certain (Berger, 1967).

Ever since Berger's contribution, surveys of religious involvement have tended to focus on the demand side, attributing developments to the shifting needs, perceptions, and circumstances of religious consumers. More stringent applications of market metaphors have been associated with the work of Iannaccone where religion has to be marketed and supplied on the one hand and on the other demanded and consumed (Iannaccone, 1992).

To simply suggest that there has to be some disposition towards the theology of a religious group which an individual joins, and which makes sense to that person, is obviously true, but needs qualification (Lynch, 1978, p.314). Religious movements will appeal to those who seek a distinct ideological worldview located in a 'cosmology'. In the pluralist context this can be regarded as a resource which can be mobilized for organizational growth. In the spiritual marketplace, therefore, religious groups are likely to include attractive ideologies in their recruitment strategies. It may also be the case that modernity itself generates a specific need. Contemporary religions can offer entrepreneurially induced fundamentalist worldviews that advance cognitive security in an ever-changing world in which certainties are continually undermined (Warner, 1993, p.1068).

The acceptance of the certitude associated with religious fundamentalism is usually part of the process of personal change. For instance, converts to traditional Pentecostalism are expected to embrace a fairly closed cognitive organization of belief by those churches they join. There is, however, another level to consider. The personal cognitive shift experienced at conversion is structured, and perhaps exploited, by religious movements. This is conducted with a certain rigidity of belief formation necessary to motivate and support radical attitudinal or behavioural alteration in terms of the movement's goals and priorities (Gerlach and Hine, 1970, pp.160–1). This is important in understanding the dynamics of successful religious movements like Vineyard which offers a comprehensive, meaningful and fundamentalist worldview.

At this point it is necessary to appraise Vineyard's teachings as rooted in the wider theology and accompanying church-growth strategies espoused at Fuller Seminary, where Wimber had taught since 1975. Historically, Fuller had sought to bridge the gap between American fundamentalism and the more liberal mainline denominations, a division that had created a great deal of theological mud-slinging in US churches (Marsden, 1987).

The liberal element endorsed by Fuller attempted to bring the Church into the modern age with the assertion that by 'making the gospel relevant to modern man' converts might be gained. A core aspect of this teaching is that it is necessary to allow concessions to cultural and social settings when spreading the gospel. Reactionary fundamentalism, in contrast, had stubbornly refused to compromise with the world, but in doing so tended to become insular and failed in the evangelizing endeavour. Fuller (and arguably Wimber) attempted to bridge these two divergent, and apparently irreconcilable, views. At the same time Fuller was sensitive to the need to reverse what was perceived as a damaging and counterproductive worldview derived from the Enlightenment which stripped modernity of much of its supernatural perceptions. This involved a further dimension: rediscovering the reality of God's power.

The self-assigned mission of making the gospel appropriate to the contemporary world might seem to negate the view that Vineyard is in any meaningful sense 'fundamentalist'. To a large extent this apparent contradiction is removed in Martyn Percy's work on fundamentalism which, importantly, focuses upon Wimber's teaching (Percy, 1996). There is no room here to detail Percy's significant contribution. Nonetheless, we can derive from it several key points. Fundamentalism is decidedly more than 'a cognitive reality' as sometimes suggested (Barr, 1978). Neither is it primarily a reaction 'against many of the mixed offerings of modernity' (Marty, 1987, pp.299–300). Rather, it is a 'multifaceted reality', a complex and systematic worldview involving claims to a unique interpretation of scripture brought to bear for its own legitimation (Percy, 1995, p.85).

Notions of divine power are also an important part of the equation. Charismatic fundamentalists, like traditional evangelicals, hold to the absolute authority of the word of God, but also emphasize the value of personal and collective 'experiences' of God's power (Percy, 1995, p.87). Scriptural references are then read into these experiences and serve as an unambiguous confirmation for both individuals and the group to which they belong. Nowhere does this appear to be more applicable than in the case of the Third Wave movement where belonging is to be at the forefront of what God is understood to be doing in and through the Church today.

Vineyard, according to Wimber, is merely 'a small piece in a large pie in which God is working wonders' (quoted in Perrin, 1989, p.42). However, it appears that through the Vineyard organization He works with more vigour and there is a deeper experience of His power. This is not to suggest that this amounts to a clear sectarian element whereby 'we have the truth and all others are in error'. Yet, there are built-in notions of supremacy and self-enforcing 'sacred canopies' that concur with Percy's understanding of fundamentalism.

The Third Wave movement, notably through Peter Wagner's influence at Fuller, brings its own theological construct involving a clear historical appraisal of the Christian Church believed to be caught up in the perceived eschatological theatre of the twentieth century. Wagner designated the 'First Wave' as the rise of classical Pentecostalism. After centuries of complacency and spiritual powerlessness the Church, through this movement, was emerging with vigour, displaying a greater measure of the power of the Holy Spirit, and manifesting a 'truer' understanding of its historical role.

The Second Wave, according to Wagner, constituted a major working of the Holy Spirit among evangelicals from the early 1960s in the form of the Charismatic Renewal movement. This evidently brought many mainline churches into line with the will and purpose of God. Wagner identified the Third Wave as originating around 1980, typified by Vineyard which attempted to bridge the gap between Charismatics, classical Pentecostals and conservative evangelicals in the last gasp proselytizing endeavour before the Second Coming of Christ (Wagner, 1986). According to Wagner each of the twentieth century waves of the Holy Spirit was believed to bring an outpouring of revival so that by 1987 277 million people (or 17.5 per cent of the World's Christians) had been 'born-again' into the dynamic 'core' of the Church and charged with the necessary 'power' for evangelism.

THE IMPERATIVE OF POWER

The emphasis upon the discernible and demonstrative active power of God is not unique to Vineyard. Jim Beckford, among others, has drawn our attention to the extensive return of concepts of 'power' to contemporary religion (Beckford, 1983). Similarly, McGuire has suggested that to a great degree this preoccupation may be the most important consideration for understanding the complex link between modern religion and other spheres of life at all levels: individual, societal and global (McGuire, 1983).

In a sense there is nothing new here. Concepts of power in religion have always reflected the underlying problem of 'legitimation' of values, beliefs and ideologies which function as symbols held to be meaningful by those who accept the exercise of power as legitimate (Kokosalakis, 1985). This renewed, contemporary, emphasis on supernatural power, however, might be imperative in the light of relentless secularization, scepticism and the subjective relativism of human knowledge particularly in the context of globalization. In other words, the demonstration of divine power in particular, brings the necessary 'proof' to unbelievers, while verifying the faith of those who do believe. In the modern world, however, it becomes indispensable.

In *A Rumour of Angels*, Peter Berger (1969) contended that the supernatural (as a meaningful reality) was absent or at least remote from the horizons in the modern era. Western man appears to have practically lost the capacity to comprehend the experience and expressions of the transcendental. Those whose worldviews exist in 'nooks and crannies' of fundamentalism need constant reinforcement of beliefs, of the continuing evidence of the supernatural. Renewed experiences of that world are to be expected, and beyond that, consumed. Religious movements need the constant affirmation of their beliefs by others in a relentless attempt to avoid cognitive dissonance.

Clearly, a theme running through Wimber's work is power; it includes constant references to 'power healing' and 'power evangelism'. Power is an attractive part of supply-side Christianity. God's power is a resource to be mobilized in the precarious marketplace of Charismatic Christianity. Through such public displays of God's power Wimber provides an uncompromising response to the modern doubters and answers in no uncertain terms the question of how God acts today. This is why theologically, the Third Wave strand of neo-Pentecostalism, of which Wimber is a leading exponent, has ushered in one of the most consequential theological developments of the last two decades. Above all, it concerns itself with the emphasis upon evidence of the miraculous 'signs and wonders' and 'spiritual warfare', and the relationship both have to church growth. Sociologically, its significance is that, on the one hand, the theological component apparently embraces a world-rejecting orthodoxy as a response to the challenges of the secular world, while on the other, there is a discernible cognitive reasoning and set of rationally-orientated strategies embraced by the movement which is undoubtedly anchored in precisely the same secularity.

Wimber's own notable theological contribution is the weight placed upon the 'Kingdom'. He contends that while the Kingdom of God will be ushered in, in full, with Christ's Second Coming supernatural manifestations can, in some measure, break through in the here and now if God is given room by believers. The impact of 'Kingdom theology' upon the wider Renewal movement has been phenomenal. For Wimber the Kingdom of God is a realm of power which overthrows the controlling power of Satan. Here is the recurring theme of God dynamically intervening throughout history with 'signs and wonders' and supernatural manifestations.

Wimber's theology is certainly radical since it insists that the Church must harness God's power if it is to be rescued from its impotence and numerical decline. It is necessary, he ventures, to rediscover a mighty, immediate and accessible God who could be 'experienced' as a constant and continuing reality. Wimber's main emphasis, therefore, has been upon what he himself refers to as 'Doing the Stuff'. The 'stuff' is short for 'the stuff in God's book', or 'the stuff which Jesus did'; proclaiming the Kingdom, healing the sick and casting out demons (Lawrence, 1990, p.35). This endeavour has given Wimber a high profile, since it has amounted to an attempt to restore and 'live out' the acts and commands of Christ through the experience of the Holy Spirit. From this framework Wimber advanced the concept of 'divine appointment' which means an appointed time at which God reveals His power to an individual or group through the Spiritual Gifts, or other supernatural phenomena.

Partly, the notion of divine appointments is derived from George Eldon Ladd's influential Kingdom theology where the dualist struggle between the forces of good and evil were bound to result in the evidence of supernatural phenomena.[1] Yet, there is more than a theological undertone here. Convinced Wimberites such as John White are more renowned for their work in Christian psychiatry circles than their theological offerings. White has brought analytical science to bear upon human emotions and their relationship to the coming of the Holy Spirit in times of revival. This includes a look at the behavioural manifestations in the great revivals of the past including those of Wesley, Whitfield and Edwards (White, 1988).

White argues that the Holy Spirit brings signs and wonders, healings, miracles and other manifestations under specific conditions if people are open to them. In my interpretation this is not, strictly speaking, an attempt to manipulate hidden supernatural forces as some kind of metaphysical causality. Rather, the foremost consideration is in creating those psychological and sociological conditions which allow the Spirit of God to work, although God Himself is not said to be restricted by them.

Creating the psychological medium conducive to producing supernatural occurrences was an important component of the classes held on Wimber's MC510 course on church growth at Fuller. As an integral part of their studies students were taught that manifestations displayed by individuals were the workings of the Holy Spirit active under a distinct and predictable human environment. This not only involved the historical accounts of conditions in which the Holy Spirit was evident, but a clinical study of the physical and psychological manifestations of His possession. These include fluttering eyelids, changing complexion and weeping. Accompanying this was an exposition of what each particular phenomenon meant (White, 1987). Students were also presented with the opportunity of applying the theoretical basis of the course almost under laboratory conditions. Hence, there were attempts at divine healing, and later exorcisms, when the Holy Spirit was evoked within what appeared to be a scientific remit.[2]

HOW THE DEVIL GETS HIS DUE

It is important to acknowledge that Wimber's emphasis upon supernatural power is located in a strong dualist theology. In a secular world, and in the marketplace of theodicies, the forces of darkness have their place. Whereas liberal and modernist Christian thinkers have tended to reduce 'Satan' and the 'demonic' to merely symbolic status for evil, Charismatics in much the same way as conservative evangelicals have clung to the concept of evil as a malevolent personal spiritual force.

Perhaps more than Charismatics previously allowed, the teachings developed at Fuller have tended to create a dualist perception of the world: good and evil, the divine and the demonic, in very stark terms. The natural and material world, which is understood by the Third Wave to be the primary focus of western consciousness, is played down. Again, profoundly influencing Wimber at Fuller was George Eldon Ladd. From him Wimber gained not only his understanding of the Kingdom of God and its immanent nature, but also the view that the world was under the domination of Satan who was the cause of human bondage to sickness, demons and death.

There were other influences on Wimber at Fuller that came to inform his theological dualism. These are significant since they seem to indicate that the limits of evangelism in the developing world were due to the forces of evil. At the same time, these influences legitimated a kind of 'reversed colonization' by which syncretic forms of Christianity, or even non-Christian beliefs, from the underdeveloped world have become increasingly respectable in the west.

Among those inspiring Wimber at Fuller were C. H. Kraft, director of anthropology and intercultural communication, and the Dean and Professor P. G. Hiebert. Both seemed to suggest that western man had lost a supernatural worldview which made proselytizing difficult. Moreover, that the lesson of evangelizing in the Third World was the actual reality of the struggle with demonic powers which hindered evangelism (Kraft 1989; Hiebert, 1982); in short, that the pagan deities were tangible spiritual entities. Arguably, both men were convinced by the views of classical Pentecostal and Charismatic students, especially from the Third World, where pagan gods and ancestral spirits tended to be literally perceived as demonic forces.

C. P. Wagner, who had taken over from McGavran in the Church Growth chair at Fuller, also made a significant contribution in this area. While Wimber has distanced himself from some of the theological strands espoused by Wagner they have had a profound effect upon the wider Charismatic scene and are worth mentioning here. In Wagner's account satanic forces had brought a rebellion against God which subsequently brought degrees of demonic power and wickedness in the spiritual hierarchy to specific geographical areas, a notion that was to give way to that of territorial spirits (Wagner, 1989). Since the early 1980s interest has grown in the subject to such an extent that vague and esoteric scriptural references have been moulded into an intricate theology of spiritual warfare that sometimes looks like a sophisticated version of the board game Dungeons and Dragons.

Here the action-orientated belief system truly comes alive. To overcome these demonic forces it is first necessary to ascertain or 'discern' the 'spiritual atmosphere', a procedure sometimes referred to as spiritual mapping. The extent to which demonic powers can continue to hold an area in 'bondage' is believed to be directly related to the commitment to intercessory prayer of Christians in the territory ('prayer warriors') in combating the dark forces (Wagner and Pennoyer, 1990).

This tendency of the Third Wave movement to veer towards extreme dualist positions can be accounted for in two ways. Firstly, perception of a real or imagined opposition, spiritual, or otherwise, is a strong motivating force and therefore a principal attraction of any social movement (Gerlach and Hine, 1970, pp.23–4). The fact that the opposition is 'supernatural' has a special appeal. Secondly, Satan and his kingdom come to have certain characteristics that enhance the Charismatic worldview in much the same way that certain perceptions of God lend themselves to Charismatic themes. At times Satan and the demonic become the embodiment for whatever blocks collective and individual advance in this world. It provides, for instance, an explanation for the lack of church growth:

> Three years ago, there were approximately eight Vineyard churches in the Los Angeles city area. Since then, there's been a ferocious backlash of the enemy. Most of those churches are now closed down.
> (Wimber, 1993)

Here Satan is clearly blamed for when things go wrong and appears to get far more than his due. This is a familiar tendency of the more fundamentalist type of religious group (Bruce, 1984). There is no reflection on the failures of church-growth strategy, individual responsibility, or mention of the wider social factors which would not allow or sustain Vineyard congregations. The organization retains its integrity.

EQUIPPING THE MIDDLE CLASS SAINTS

Understanding organization dynamics is not the only way of accounting for the success of a religious group. It must also be attractive to particular social groups. This is especially the case within the religious marketplace of the modern world.

A vital part of Vineyard's strategy of church growth is the attempt to make Christianity relevant to 'where people are', in short, to allow considerable concessions to cultural background and historical traditions whatever they may be (Duin, 1988). However, there does seem to be, in terms of social composition, a rather restricted membership. An integral part of Vineyard's evangelizing strategy is that of the 'homogeneous unit principle', that is, people will be attracted to churches which comprise those of the same background as themselves. Nonetheless, not all social groups have been attracted into the fold. The middle classes are overrepresented. This appears to be the case on both sides of the Atlantic. In the USA, Perrin showed that Vineyard members tended to be highly educated, economically secure, with an overrepresentation of people in management or the professions. The survey indicated that 74 per cent were aged between 23 and 42 years old, with the membership comprising 59 per cent females and 41 per cent males (Perrin, 1989, pp.90–100). This is, to some extent mirrored in Britain.

Although previously observed in Anglican evangelical circles the six day 'Third Wave' conference held in October 1984 was the first occasion that the British Christian public had encountered Wimber's ministry on a large scale. The intensity of the phenomena encountered: weeping, visions, prophecy and intense physical shakings (the 'Wimber wombles'), which followed when Wimber evoked the Holy Spirit, took even the most seasoned Charismatics by surprise. Almost as surprising was that the great bulk of representatives attending the conference were middle class.

The conference was held at the Methodist Central Hall, Westminster, at the invitation of leading British Charismatics. Mana Ministries, which had made the invitation to Wimber, felt obliged to send out questionnaires to ascertain the success of the conference. The findings were outlined in an unpublished report.[3] Notwithstanding the fact that the conference was London-orientated, there seems to have been a profound disappointment that working class areas were clearly underrepresented. The lack of delegates from inner London was noted in the report with the comment:

> One may ask if the signs and wonders ministry might have any effect on the evangelism of this kind of area. Is the Charismatic movement (whether in a Renewal, Restoration or Wimber package) predominantly white skinned, white collar and wealthy? . . . Is Charismatic Renewal confined to those already Christian? Has it promoted evangelism in areas hitherto untouched?

The very low figure for the traditional Pentecostals was interpreted to be a result of 'cultural problems', that is, the lower class background of the membership, and the historical distrust of the mainstream denominations; or, alternatively, that Pentecostal churches already had what Wimber was offering. The report asked:

> Are traditional Pentecostals and the black churches more culturally suited to the 'working classes' and Wimber more 'middle-class'?

What is the attraction to the middle classes? In answering this question we must tread with care and avoid crude economic reduction. Observers of the modern religious marketplace have suggested that there are 'customers' or 'seekers', not just of religious 'truths', but of religious expressions that suit their lifestyles. In fact, the term 'seeker' appears to be practically synonymous with a quest for a personally satisfying life, whether at a philosophical level of 'meaningfulness' and theodicy, or at practical level with enhanced material benefits, for example, success, power and creativity (Straus, 1979, p.161).

From the beginning the success of Vineyard partly stemmed from the concessions it made to modernity, its attempt to be 'relevant to modern man'. At one level there should not be too much of a surprise here. The greater difficulty is to ascertain whether, on the one hand, there are consciously selected themes utilized as a 'resource' in order to be attractive to the middle classes, or on the other, a simple adaptation by Charismatics to the relentless wave of secularity which had been there from an early stage (Quebedeaux, 1974).

Certainly, the teachings of Vineyard had initially found fertile ground in California where the evangelical Charismatic churches were characteristically presented in a kind of counter-cultural style, or at least very informally. It therefore appeared particularly attractive to the young and sections of the middle classes, especially the so-called 'baby-boomers' (Roof, 1994, pp.182–3). Although there was never a direct link with the Jesus Movement of the early 1970s there is sufficient evidence to suggest a certain cultural continuity (*Christianity Today*, 29 Jan. 1971). In most Vineyard churches there is an emphasis on casual dress, contemporary music, and spontaneity in worship. The informality is also reflected in the meetings which are often held in buildings such as school halls, warehouses, or rented churches which do not actually belong to the Vineyard organization.

Mauss and Perrin's study (1992) of Vineyard in the USA provides some of the empirical evidence of its attraction to baby-boomers although they tend to play down the significance of fundamentalism. Their account utilizes a theoretical framework largely derived from the work of Kelly who contended that the success of conservative churches lay in simultaneously offering 'Strictness' and 'Social Strength'. The former denotes the absoluteness of the religious belief alongside the insistence on conformity and fanaticism (which sociologically is more associated with sectarianism, lower class movements including classical Pentecostalism). Social strength means more than a sense of belonging to a community but provides members with an ardour that 'catches up their lives in a surge of significance and purpose' through commitment and discipline (Kelly, 1972, p.51).

Mauss and Perrin separate the variables of social strength and strictness as different wares in the spiritual marketplace. Those 'customers' seeking the psychic security of certainty, and the assurance of knowing and obeying God's will in all aspects of life, are predominantly attracted to 'strictness'. Here the 'customer' seeking the attraction that comes from collective sacrifice and participation will 'buy into' a 'strong' evangelical religion that offers prospects both for community solidarity as a worthy religion and for the future growth of that enterprise through conversions. In short, belonging to a successful church caught up in a significant tide of evangelism, without a great commitment to the church itself.

Vineyard has come to develop a universally applied two-fold strategy. Firstly, to plant its own churches internationally. Secondly, to serve and service other churches through ministry based on 'signs and wonders' and 'equipping the saints'. Certainly, this appears to be an honest endeavour to support other churches outside of the organization. Vineyard teams pay visits to Charismatic churches as a matter of course, or when support is requested. Typically, these are mini-conferences amounting to revamped versions of the ministry of emotional healing first seen at the 1984 Third Wave conference.

Here is another considerable concession to modernity that has a strong middle class appeal. What we may be looking at then is a distinct emphasis upon different aspects of psychotherapy albeit given a spiritual gloss and encapsulated within a fundamentalist framework of 'power'. Typical was the three day conference 'The Blessing' (not to be confused with the Toronto Blessing that followed some 18 months later). This essentially concentrated upon emotional healing by the cultivation of positive thinking and unselfish attitudes towards others in order to bring spiritual blessing upon the individual believer.

There was much here which might be attractive to the middle classes. From one perspective there is a great deal of literature to suggest that it is this social class which is attracted to alternative forms of healing because of its general dissatisfaction with orthodox medicine. This is not fully substantiated, however. Indeed, McGuire shows Charismatics appear to be more favourably disposed towards orthodox medicine while also seeking the 'spiritual' or 'inner healing' alternative (McGuire, 1988).

To explain the attraction of such therapeutic techniques we have to look elsewhere. Above all the preoccupation with such healing is that it enhances middle class lifestyles and reflects cultural preferences.

Certainly, one cultural attribute that attracts the middle classes to the new religions, particularly those with a healing theme, is the moral evaluation and self-expression of achievement-orientation, the constant pursuit of human potential and self-improvement in all aspects of life (Buckley and Galanter, 1979). One of the key attractions that the new religions offer the adherent is the promise of being successful by unlocking alleged spiritual powers dominant in the individual that can be used for his or her ultimate worldly potential. Hence, in some new religious movements 'salvation' is typically perceived in terms of personal achievement and overcoming problems generated by the modern world through a heightened awareness of one's own ability.

The emotional healing techniques offered by neo-Pentecostalism to its middle class cohorts might be the adoption of a 'spiritualized', inward-looking, psychotherapeutic technique marking a shift away from the virtues of suffering to a more positive and optimistic emphasis upon 'growth' (Favazza, 1982). Here there are strong parallels with the modern secular ideas of healing as a continuing process 'within'. Spiritual development, therefore, becomes more associated with overcoming wrong thoughts, beliefs and images about the individuals themselves accompanied by notions of renewing the mind.

This may all seem rather narcissistic. However, among Charismatics this is not the secular self-indulgence identified by some writers (Lasch, 1970). Rather, the aim of Charismatics, particularly through the strategies offered by emotional healing, is to enter into a more complete spiritual, rather than worldly life (Fitcher, 1975, p.128). Hence, the emphasis by Wimberites upon the necessity of releasing believers from the 'bondages' of past hurts for the purpose of spiritual development (White and Blau, 1985).

Within the framework of 'equipping the saints' the middle class concerns with continual personal growth and fulfilment of spiritual potential are given a contrasting, but dynamic interpretation. While Wimber himself has been critical of Charismatics because they have overindulged in the spiritual gifts at the expense of evangelism (Wimber, 1985, p.32) he does encourage their cultivation and fosters an expectation that the believer will go through a process of periodic 'fillings-up' by the Holy Spirit. There is a marked contrast here between the earlier Pentecostal/Charismatic teaching of the Baptism in the Spirit as a one-time event in favour of the 'empowering' of the Holy Spirit as part of the ongoing process of spiritual development.

Church-growth strategies and individual empowerment are themes subsequently woven together. By suitably equipping the saints, through

freeing them from emotional 'hang-ups', the kingdom of God can be
advanced by evangelism so that the walls of the demonic kingdom are
brought tumbling down. It is at this point that we are reminded of the
work of Jim Beckford (1983) concerning what he terms New Religious Healing Movements (NRHM). The attraction of many such new
religions lies in their ability to fuse notions of cosmic power and individual empowerment. He or she in no uncertain terms is empowered
through harnessing spiritual power. The capacity or potential for self-
realization and self-expression can be released or unblocked within a
wider transcendental framework and cosmic drama.

This emphasis upon healing may partly explain why Wimber's ministry has been so attractive to Anglican Charismatics.[4] This is not to
say that there are not other considerations in explaining the apparent
curious contradiction where the church of State and the Establishment
can accommodate a faction that is thoroughgoing in its evangelicalism
and even millenarian in tone. They are different parts of the equation.
The development of personal contacts between leading Anglican
Charismatics and Wimber, the expectancy of further spiritual refreshing, the debate with conservative evangelicals on the question of 'how
does God communicate today', all paved the way for the impact of
Vineyard (Hunt, 1995b). However, for at least two decades the healing ministry among Anglican clergy, Charismatic and otherwise, has
gained a higher profile.

There also appears to have been a latent demand within the congregations for healing. Wimber's ministry was an attractive proposition.
In contrast, the traditional American healing evangelist is rather too
brash for the Anglican palate. It is scarcely conceivable that parishioners
would feel comfortable with the likes of Benny Hinn or Morris Cerullo.
In Anglican circles, at least, Wimber had truly met the middle classes
'where they are' and the model he left of his ministry turns up in the
most obscure rural parish. This does not mean, however, that indulgence in more genteel forms of emotional healing excludes the average
Charismatic from the rollercoaster ride associated with Vineyard.

AT THE 'CUTTING EDGE'

There is always something going on at the Vineyard and those churches
influenced by it. Being at the 'cutting-edge' of what God is doing
means that members must constantly be on the edge of their seats.
New revelations and the rediscovery of 'truths' are perennially on the

agenda. The preoccupation with healing and deliverance, prophecy, and territorial spirits, have all passed through the prism of Vineyard into the wider Charismatic movement. To be at the cutting edge is to be where the action is; 'that means us, stand up!'.

The emphasis upon all things prophetic has been particularly significant. Since the late 1980s this 'gift' of the Spirit was singled out for special attention and cultivated in Charismatic churches, albeit with a large degree of confusion. The great initiates were the Kansas City Prophets. One member, Paul Cain, was at this time very close to Wimber. In fact, it was believed that Cain was on a divine mission to seek him out (Pytches, 1990). Cain prophesied a world revival in October 1991 beginning in England. For that purpose tens of thousands of Charismatics convened in a specially organized conference in London's East End. This turned out to be a farce which led to elaborate attempts to explain why revival had not occurred.

Another Kansas City Prophet, Mike Bickle, laid claim to a panoramic view of the purposes of God in the next generation which included the outpouring of the Holy Spirit in an unprecedented manner as a prelude to the coming of Christ. Vineyard, it was prophesied, would have a special role to play when some of its members would acquire extra-special supernatural qualities. Wimber was to distance himself from events, but his credibility was seriously damaged. The Vineyard story, however, continues.

On Pentecost Sunday in 1994 something curious happened at St Jude's during the confirmation service. At the altar rail the Bishop laid hands upon those kneeling down. More than anyone else he was surprised to see them fall over 'slain in the Spirit', laughing and crying. The vicar, discerning that this was a moment of great spiritual significance, evoked the Holy Spirit to fall upon the congregation. Some members of the congregation just sat and wept, others fell into the aisles. The cucumber sandwiches and tea planned for after the confirmations were cancelled. The Toronto Blessing had arrived.

NOTES

1. Ladd's work was sometimes literally passed around in brown paper bags in British Charismatic churches, particularly Baptist, before Wimber appeared on the scene.

2. In 1986 the course was cancelled by Fuller on the grounds that its Biblical justification was slim and Wimber's emphasis on the miraculous was theologically unbalanced.
3. I am grateful to Douglas McBain for granting permission to quote from the report. Lewis' study of those receiving prayer for inner-healing at Vineyard conferences in the mid-1980s broadly concurs with this picture. There were found to be more women than men, more of those with a higher rather than lower social class background, and derived from the better educated sections of the general population (Lewis, 1989).
4. The 1984 Third Wave Conference Report showed the Anglicans to be over-represented as shown in the table below.

Denomination	%
Anglican	42.5
Baptists	25.5
House churches	16.0
Pentecostals	4.0
Evangelicals	3.5
Methodists	2.0
Roman Catholics & others	8.5

Note that totals do not tally due to rounding.

Significantly, the leader of the Vineyard organization in Britain is an ex-Anglican cleric. Three others head-up independent Vineyard churches.

Baptist Charismatics and many of the 'new' churches also have strong links with Vineyard. The Kingdom theology of Wimber dovetailed well with Restorationism which also stressed the millenarian theme of building the Kingdom on earth. Similarly, Wimber's view of Church history is not that different from British Restorationism which maintains that the Holy Spirit was 'lost from' or neglected by the Church since the time of the Apostles, but had been 'restored' in the Last Days and clearly marks a close parallel with a major tenet of Restorationist post-millennialism (Wright, 1991, p.20).

Wimber has also heavily influenced specialist deliverance ministries which have taken his teachings on the demonic to 'his furthest conclusions' (McBain, 1987, p.186). The most notable has been Ellel Ministries which has brought media attention to its annual conferences through the attempted mass deliverance of Christians.

BIBLIOGRAPHY

J. Barr, *Fundamentalism* (Philadelphia: Westminster Press, 1978).
J. Beckford, 'Holistic Imagery and Ethics in New Religious Healing Movements', *Social Compass*, vol.31, no.2/3, 1983, pp.259–72. See also Beckford's

'The World Images of New Religious Healing Movements' in Jones, R. (ed.), *Sickness and Sectarianism* (Aldershot: Gower, 1984) pp.72–93.

J. Beckford, 'The Restoration of "Power" to the Sociology of Religion', *Sociological Analysis*, vol.44, no.1, 1983, pp.11–32.

P. Berger, *The Sacred Canopy: Elements of a Sociological Theory of Religion* (New York: Doubleday, 1967).

P. Berger, *A Rumour of Angels* (Harmondsworth: Penguin, 1969).

S. Bruce, *Firm in the Faith* (Aldershot: Gower: 1984).

P. Buckley and M. Galanter, 'Mystical Experience, Spiritual Knowledge, and Contemporary Ecstasy', *British Journal of Medical Psychiatry*, vol.52, 1979, pp.218–19.

J. Duin, 'Signs and Wonders in New Orleans', *Christianity Today*, 21 Nov. 1988, pp.26–7.

R. Favazza, 'Modern Christian Healing of Mental Illness', *American Journal of Psychiatry*, vol.136, no.6, June 1982, pp.728–35.

J. Fitcher, *The Catholic Cult of the Paraclete* (New York: Sheed & Ward, 1975).

L. Gerlach and V. Hine, *People, Power and Change. Movements of Social Transformation* (Indianapolis, IN: Bobs-Merril, 1970).

P. G. Hiebert, 'The Flaw of the Excluded Middle', *Missionology: An International Review*, vol.X, no.1, Jan. 1982, pp.35–47.

S. Hunt (1995a), '"The Toronto Blessing": A Rumour of Angels?', *Journal of Contemporary Religion*, vol.10, no.3, 1995, pp.257–71.

S. Hunt (1995b), 'The Anglican Wimberites', *Pnuema, The Journal for the Society of Pentecostal Studies*, vol.17, no.1, Spring, 1995, pp.105–18.

L. R. Iannaccone, 'Religious Markets and the Economics of Religion', *Social Compass*, vol.39, no.1, 1992, pp.123–31.

D. Kelly, *Why Conservative Churches are Growing* (New York: Harper & Row, 1972).

N. Kokosalakis, 'Legitimation, Power and Religion in Modern Society', *Sociological Analysis*, vol.46, no.4, 1985, pp.367–76.

N. Kraft, *Christianity with Power: Your Worldview and Your Experience of the Supernatural* (Ann Arbor, MI: Vine Books, 1989).

C. Lasch, 'Collective Narcissism', *New York Review of Books*, 30 Sept. 1970.

P. Lawrence, *The Hotline* (Eastbourne: Kingsway, 1990).

D. C. Lewis, *Healing: Fiction, Fantasy, or Fact?* (London: Hodder & Stoughton, 1989).

R. R. Lynch, 'Towards a Theory of Conversion and Commitment to the Occult', in Richardson, J. T. (ed.), *Conversion Careers: In and Out of the New Religions* (Beverley Hills: Sage, 1978), pp.91–112.

G. M. Marsden, *Reforming Fundamentalism: Fuller Seminary and the New Evangelicalism* (Grand Rapids, MI: Eerdinas Publishing, 1987).

M. Marty 'Fundamentalism Reborn', *Religion and Republic* (Boston: Beacon Press, 1987).

A. L. Mauss and R. D. Perrin. 'Saints and Seriousness', *Review of Religious Research*, vol.34, 1992, pp.176–8.

D. McBain, *Discerning the Spirits* (Basingstoke: Marshall Pickering, 1987).

M. McGuire, 'Words of Power: Personal Empowerment and Healing', *Culture, Medicine and Psychiatry*, vol.7, 1983, pp.221–40.

M. McGuire, *Ritual Healing in Suburban America* (New Brunswick, NJ: Rutgers University Press, 1988).

L. Parrott and R. D. Perrin, 'The New Denominations', *Christianity Today*, 11 March 1991, pp.29–33.

M. Percy, 'Fundamentalism: A Problem for Phenomenology?', *Journal of Contemporary Religion*, vol.10, no.1, 1995, pp.83–91.

M. Percy, *Words, Wonders and Power: Understanding Contemporary Christian Fundamentalism and Revivalism* (London: SPCK, 1996).

R. D. Perrin, *Signs and Wonders: The Growth of Vineyard Fellowship*, Unpublished Ph.D. Thesis (Washington: Washington State University, 1989).

D. Pytches, *Some Said It Thundered* (London: Hodder & Stoughton, 1990).

R. Quebedeaux, *The Young Evangelists* (New York: Harper & Row, 1974).

R. H. Roberts, 'Religion and the "Enterprise Culture": The British Experience and the Thatcher Era (1979–1990)', *Social Compass*, vol.39, no.1, 1992, pp.15–33.

W. C. Roof, *Towards the Year 2000: Religion in the 90's* (London: Sage, 1994).

P. Springer, *Power Encounter Among Christians in the Western World* (San Francisco: Harper & Row, 1985).

R. A. Straus, 'Religious Conversion as a Personal and Collective Accomplishment', *Sociological Analysis*, vol.40, no.2, 1979, pp.158–65.

P. Wagner, 'Theology of the Third Wave', *Christian Life*, Jan. 1986.

P. Wagner (ed.), *Territorial Spirits* (Chichester: Sovereign Press, 1989).

P. Wagner and F. D. Pennoyer, *Wrestling with Dark Angels: Towards a Deeper Understanding of the Supernatural Forces in Spiritual Warfare* (Ventura, CA: Regents Books, 1990).

T. M. Warner, 'Dealing with Territorial Demons in The Power Encounter and World Evangelism', Church Growth Lecture (Fuller Seminary School of Mission, 1988).

R. S. Warner, 'Work in Progress Towards a New Paradigm for the Sociological Study of Religion in the United States', *American Journal of Sociology*, vol.98, no.5, 1993, pp.1044–93.

M. Weber, *The Theory of Social and Economic Organization* (Oxford: Oxford University Press, 1947), p.328.

J. White, *When the Spirit Comes with Power: Signs and Wonders Among God's People* (Grove, IL: Intervarsity Press, 1987).

J. White, 'A Look Inside', *First Fruits*, July/Aug. 1988.

J. White and K. Blau, *Healing the Wounded* (Leicester: Intervarsity Press, 1988).

J. Wimber, 'John Wimber Calls it Power Evangelism', *Charisma*, Sept. 1985, pp.41–3.

J. Wimber, 'The Christian Life as Warfare', *Equipping the Saints*, vol.7, no.1, Winter, 1993, p.6.

N. Wright, 'Restorationism and the "House Church" Movement', *Themelios*, vol.16, no.2, Jan./Feb. 1991, pp.4–8.

R. Wuthnow, *The Consciousness Reformation* (Berkeley: University of California Press, 1976).

5 The Toronto Blessing: Charismatic Evangelical Global Warming

Philip Richter

It has been described as 'like getting drunk without the hangover', as 'ecstasy without the need of drugs'. The 'Toronto Blessing' is a form of religious experience characterized by many unusual physical phenomena – such as bodily weakness and falling to the ground; shaking, trembling and convulsive bodily movements; uncontrollable laughter or wailing and inconsolable weeping; apparent drunkenness; animal sounds; and intense physical activity (Richter, 1995, pp.6–8, 16) – as well as being accompanied by such things as a heightened sense of the presence of God; 'prophetic' insights into the future; 'prophetic' announcements from God; visions; and 'out of the body' mystical experiences. Although centred outside the mainstream churches, especially within the 'House Church' or 'New Church' movement, Vineyard churches and the older Pentecostal churches, the Toronto Blessing has also, to a lesser extent, affected churches within mainstream denominations, especially, but not exclusively, those with previous Charismatic leanings. This chapter will concentrate on Charismatic evangelical churches. As the name implies, the Blessing has been popularly linked with the Airport Vineyard Church in Toronto at which it 'broke out' in January 1994. In fact similar phenomena were already sporadically seen during Charismatic Renewal in the 1970s and within John Wimber's international 'power ministry' in the 1980s (Richter, 1995, p.11; Hunt, 1995, p.260). Devotees have also claimed historical precedents from eighteenth and nineteenth century Protestant revivals (MacNutt, 1994, p.2; Roberts, 1994, p.119; Chevreau, 1994, p.77) and Christian mysticism (MacNutt, 1994, pp.18, 35, 88). There is, however, in the case of alleged historical parallels, no guarantee that like is being compared with like (Kent, 1995, pp.93–8). The Toronto Blessing is claimed to surpass recent similar phenomena in terms of its wide geographical spread (to at least 34 countries)[1], its frequency and its intensity.

In December 1995 the Airport Vineyard Church parted company with the Association of Vineyard Churches (AVC), following the AVC's withdrawal of their endorsement on the grounds that the Toronto church 'had chosen not to minister within the framework of values and ministry style of the Association' (AVC (UK) Press Statement, 13 December 1995). The Church is now called Toronto Airport Christian Fellowship. In sociological terms, the Toronto church and its parent body had chosen somewhat different ways of resolving the dilemmas facing any Charismatic movement. The AVC, for instance, was concerned that wider society might be alienated by the 'exotic' phenomena given free rein at Toronto and preferred to have a reputation as 'evangelists', rather than 'roarers' or 'shakers' (AVC Board Report on the Current Renewal, September/October 1994). It also appears to have been sensitive to the danger that the Toronto church might be mistaken for a cult, given its openness to extra-Biblical manifestations (such as animal noises), and the degree of 'hype' and manipulation involved in its services (Todd Hunter (AVC National Coordinator, USA) letter, 13 December 1995)[2]. Vineyard Church, on the other hand, according to the AVC, believed that 'one can't and should not administrate or pastor renewal for fear of quenching the work of the Holy Spirit' (Todd Hunter letter, 13 December 1995).

One of the most salient features of the Toronto Blessing has been the number of 'pilgrimages' that have taken place to Toronto or other Blessing 'epicentres'. In this chapter I shall, firstly, focus on the nature of these pilgrimages, then attempt to account for people's investment of time, energy and money in the Blessing, and, finally, analyse ways in which the Blessing has increasingly been framed in global terms.

THE NATURE OF THE PILGRIMAGE

Airport Vineyard has come to be known as a 'charismatic "mecca"' (Hunt, 1995, p.262). By June 1995 over 300,000 different people had attended Airport Vineyard Church in Toronto[3] to witness at first hand the extraordinary Charismatic phenomena that have come to be known as the 'Toronto Blessing'. On average Airport Vineyard Church has hosted over 800 people per night since the Blessing first manifested itself. Up to 20 per cent of those attending are clergy professionals and ten per cent of the attendance comes from the UK. It is estimated that 12 per cent of visitors are drawn from other Vineyard churches,

28 per cent from 'non-denominational churches' and the remainder from over 35 other Catholic and Protestant denominations (Poloma WWW, 1995). In November 1994 the Church had to move to larger premises to accommodate their visitors. Pilgrims have been flocking to Airport Church from all over the world (Chevreau, 1994, pp.17,18).

Although Toronto has been the main pilgrimage venue for those seeking to immerse themselves in the Blessing, there have also been more accessible local epicentres of pilgrimage. In the UK churches such as Queen's Road Baptist Church, Wimbledon, Holy Trinity Brompton (HTB) and Sunderland Christian Centre have attracted large crowds, often visitors from other churches curious about the Blessing. The Blessing arrived at HTB in May 1994 and was to attract over 2000 people per Sunday through its doors at its peak. Pilgrims may well visit both Toronto and local venues: Dave Roberts, author of *The 'Toronto' Blessing*, reports that 'in Toronto God took care of my pride, in Sunderland God broke my heart' (Roberts, 1994, p.58).

Devotees of the Toronto Blessing have already begun to describe this as a *pilgrimage* to Toronto (Fearon, 1994, p.145). Ironically, evangelicals have traditionally distanced themselves from the practice of pilgrimage, seeing it as a Roman Catholic custom. There are annual evangelical gatherings which take on some of the feel of a pilgrimage, such as Spring Harvest, Easter People and Keswick Convention, but these are generally much more speaker-oriented. Although pilgrimage is unusual in the evangelical setting (Neville, 1987) and the practice is not claimed to be directly 'Biblical', the pilgrimage has become an important feature of the Toronto Blessing. Its legitimacy has been underpinned by reminders that pilgrimages have been associated with previous revivals (Fearon, 1994, p.214). The Azusa Street revival (1906), central to the birth of modern Pentecostalism, similarly drew 'huge numbers of people .. from all over the world' who then took revival back to their own churches (Chevreau, 1994, p.198): the Toronto pilgrimage was 'exactly the same story again' (Chevreau, 1994, p.199). Interestingly, Dave Roberts draws a parallel between Toronto and another major site of Christian pilgrimage – Jerusalem – and suggests that going to Toronto should be seen in the light of the disciples who 'tarried in Jerusalem' after the Resurrection (Roberts, 1994, p.145).

Pilgrimage is a slippery term to define. Chris Park cites *Collins English Dictionary* (1979) which defines pilgrimage as 'a journey to a shrine or other sacred place' (Park, 1994, p.258). John Eade and Michael Sallnow, on the other hand, dismiss attempts to arrive at uniform definitions of pilgrimage: their post-modern 'new agenda in pilgrimage studies' involves deconstructing 'the very category of "pilgrimage" into historically and culturally specific behaviours and meanings' (Eade and Sallnow, 1991, p.3). This chapter will follow Eade and Sallnow and seek to explore some of the specific dimensions of the pilgrimage which has become such an important feature of the Toronto Blessing.

The Blessing has become known as the *Toronto* Blessing because its followers believe that it is found in 'major concentration' (MacNutt, 1994, p.2) at Airport Vineyard, Toronto. The God of the Charismatics is above all an immanent God who acts in the world and in this case has chosen to act powerfully at Toronto. Although Airport Vineyard is a special locale for the manifestation of the divine, it is of course not the only place where the universal God can be found (Kim WWW, 1995). The sacred focus at Toronto is primarily place- rather than person-centred: the leaders at Toronto have not become cult figures. It is true that within the Toronto Blessing movement as a whole such figures as Rodney Howard Browne have by some been treated as dynamically holy people but their ministry is not based at Toronto. Devotees describe Airport Vineyard as somewhere that is 'awesome' or 'special' (Roberts, 1994, p.68). This has nothing to do with any intrinsic sacredness attaching to the terrain on which it is built. It is, for instance, unlike the pilgrimage to Ballyvourney that Sean Dunne described in *The Tablet* (17 June 1995, p.773): 'a holy place where something very old and deep was contained'. Pilgrims are constantly surprised by Airport Vineyard's dismal location, in an industrial estate at the end of the runway of Toronto's Pearson Airport. The church, which has a café attached, is a plain, square room, seating about 500. This is no ancient cathedral exuding holiness from its stones; this is a modern, utilitarian 'comically-improbable' (Fearon, 1994, p.91) building. The Blessing did not originate there: similar phenomena had been associated with the international evangelism of Rodney Howard Browne, himself influenced by the Word of Faith movement, and, before that, with John Wimber's 'power ministry' in the mid-1980s (Richter, 1995, pp.8–11; Smail, 1995, p.156); Randy Clark the 'initiator of the outbreak' at Toronto Vineyard had himself been profoundly influenced by Howard Browne (Chevreau, 1994, pp.24–5). Airport Vineyard has become a 'sacred' venue of pilgrimage simply because the Blessing is believed to have been focused and intensified there.

Whilst at Toronto pilgrims generally attend as many meetings as they are able. Renewal meetings are held in the evenings, Tuesday to Sunday. The Renewal meetings include up to one hour of 'worship' (mostly singing), testimonies for about half-an-hour from those who have already received the Blessing, talks (of between 20 to 40 minutes' duration), and 'ministry time' – opportunities for individuals to 'receive prayer', which typically leads to the experience of the Blessing (ministry time typically lasts at least two hours). Conversation and further prayer take place in the café that is part of the church. Some meetings, on weekday mornings, are intended to be just for pastors.

Many pilgrims go to Toronto with an experimental, non-committal 'wait and see' attitude. Mike Turrigiano tells how the Holy Spirit spoke to him: 'Here's the chance, Mike. Check it out. What have you got to lose?' (Chevreau, 1994, p.202). Some will go because it has become a popular thing to do and they do not want to risk being left out; Eleanor Mumford admitted: 'I went because I've never been slow to go to a party! I heard that there were things going on and I was mad to get there and see' (Holy Trinity Brompton, 29 May 1994). Pilgrims usually have some preformed expectations about the experiences that await them at Toronto, based on what they have already heard or begun to experience at their home churches. As Glenn Bowman's perceptive analysis of Jerusalem pilgrimage concludes: 'It is at the sites whence the pilgrims set out on their searches for the centre that pilgrims learn what they desire to find' (Bowman, 1991, pp.120, 121; cf. Reader and Walter, 1993, p.241). Personal change had already been prophesied for Dave Roberts before he set off for Toronto (Roberts, 1994, p.67), although the nature of this change only became clear at Airport Vineyard (p.71). Norman Moss, Pastor of Queen's Road Baptist Church, Wimbledon, went to Toronto after similar phenomena had started to occur in his own church: 'he figured that they had four months more experience, from which he was anxious to benefit' (Fearon, 1994, pp.127, 128).

Although many pilgrims have already witnessed or experienced the Blessing after it has been 'catalytically transferred' (Chevreau, 1994, pp.19, 151, 152) from Toronto by previous returnees, pilgrims speak of wanting to 'experience *firsthand* the moving of the Holy Spirit' (Chevreau, 1994, p.167 – my italics). One might object that experience of the Holy Spirit, if genuine, is always firsthand and that it is hardly necessary to cross the Atlantic to receive it! Devotees of the Blessing seem, however, to be operating with a quasi-materialistic notion of the activity of God's Spirit, which enables them to think in terms of different levels of exposure. The experience of the Blessing is often described as being like having an electric current pass through one's body. Like electricity, the Blessing can come in different strengths. The attraction of Airport Vineyard is that it is possible for pilgrims to receive what they term an intense 'jump start' to enhance their *'daily infilling of the Spirit'* (Chevreau, 1994, p.167). Whatever the precise social mechanisms at work[4] it is clear that pilgrims to Toronto typically feel extraordinarily and intensely aware of the Spirit's activity whilst they are there; they often experience profound personal change in a very short time-span (Kim WWW, 1995); and they descend to a rather different plane when they catch the flight home! Ideally, something of their pilgrimage experience survives the journey home and has a continuing impact on their personal lives and own churches, indeed this is one of the aims of the pilgrimage: Ken Gott of Sunderland Christian Centre reports that he went to Toronto with the express intention of '[tasting] revival and refreshing and [taking] it back with me' (Roberts, 1994, p.55).

In common with other pilgrimage sites a variety of expectations (Reader and Walter, 1993, pp.8–10), sometimes mutually conflicting, is brought to Toronto, and its associated epicentres. As Eade and Sallnow point out: a pilgrimage shrine can be 'an arena for the interplay of a variety of imported perceptions and understandings, in some cases finely differentiated from one another, in others radically polarized' (Eade and Sallnow, 1991, p.10). In the case of Toronto Blessing pilgrimage there is an interplay between at least two different discourses: the *pilgrims' expectations*, which chiefly revolve around experiencing the unusual phenomena themselves and receiving various forms of healing, and the *church leadership's expectations*, which, whilst they encompass many of the pilgrims' expectations, are less phenomena-centred and more focused on the redemptive power of the Cross of Christ. The transcendent discourse of officialdom (Eade and Sallnow, 1991, p.15) attempts to correct the more pragmatic discourse of the ordinary pilgrim. I shall now look at each set of expectations in turn.

The ordinary pilgrim, as at many pilgrimage sites, is led to expect that miracles will occur; these may be physical, emotional or spiritual (Percy, 1995, p.6). Physical healing may be as modest as the disappearance of a skin rash (Chevreau, 1994, p.180) or as impressive as the recovery of sight (Roberts, 1994, pp.72–4; Chevreau, 1994, pp.146–8). In one especially graphic account of recovery from dyslexia a 13 year old girl described how she had been conscious that 'angels had done brain surgery' on her (Chevreau, 1994, p.171). A good deal of emotional healing is also reported by pilgrims. Sarah X sensed a 'deep healing' in her heart, 'relating all the way back to childhood' (Chevreau, 1994, p.162). Kim Gentes came away 'feeling that God had really done some major changes in [his] life dealing with [his] childhood and [his] father' (Kim WWW, 1995). For Lois Gott 'the residual emotional pain from the loss of her child [which had been stillborn] began to dissolve' at Toronto (Roberts, 1994, pp.70, 71). Pilgrims expect miracles when they go on Toronto Blessing pilgrimage, but they also expect to receive the Blessing itself. Kim Gentes was initially disappointed to find that, by the end of his second day at Toronto, he had merely received 'healing for past situations'; 'I was really looking for God to visit me with something else', he confessed (Kim WWW, 1995) – this occurred the following day. If pilgrims fail to receive the physical phenomena associated with the Blessing, for any reason, this can cause them great disappointment, although worship leaders have been quick to reassure people that they can be powerfully blessed even if they remain 'physically untouched' (Roberts, 1994, pp.139–41).

The expectations of the church leadership, on the other hand, partly reproduce those of ordinary pilgrims, but also transcend those expectations. Pastors and other leaders have offered explicit or implicit correctives to the ordinary pilgrim's expectations. John Wimber, International Director and founder of the Vineyard churches, has tried to shift the focus away from physical phenomena to 'preach[ing] the gospel to the lost' (*Church Times* 30 September 1994); 'meetings ought to be characterised by messages that are Christ-centred . . ., as opposed to phenomena-centred' (Roberts, 1994, p.122). Wimber has warned that churches must not lose sight of 'Christ's substitutionary death on the Cross, and our subsequent new life as publicly expressed in baptism' (*Alpha* magazine, August 1994, p.5). Dave Roberts, editor of the leading Christian monthly magazine, *Alpha*, was glad to find 'Christ-exalting worship' and 'a deeply moving sermon about the cross' at Toronto (Roberts, 1994, p.71), having feared something much more superficial. Graham Cray, Principal of Ridley Hall Theological College, Cambridge, has advised Toronto Blessing devotees against 'shopping in a religious supermarket, when [they] should be serving in a spiritual soup kitchen!' (Fearon, 1994, p.235). John Arnott, Senior Pastor of Airport Vineyard, Toronto, tells how his church has tried to shift the focus off the physical manifestations 'and appreciate rather the inward work of grace and empowering that is always the result' (Chevreau, 1994, p.viii). Norman Moss, Pastor of Queen's Road Baptist Church, has been keen to 'put something on the fire whilst God is moving in this way'; he has encouraged intercession and evangelism, ensuring that there is always a presentation of the gospel at each Queen's Road meeting. In these and other ways the church leadership have been offering correctives to the more pragmatic, present-centred, sometimes narcissistic expectations of ordinary pilgrims. Narcissism can be transformed in a religious context and lead to outer commitments (Roof, 1993, p.170; Neitz, 1987); but, as yet, there is little evidence that the church leadership's version of the Toronto Blessing has taken the high ground (W. Porter, 1995, p.126).

A COSTLY INVESTMENT

One of the most startling things about the Toronto pilgrimage is its cost, both to individuals and sponsoring churches. Unlike the Islamic *hajj*, there is no obligation to go to Toronto. It has, however, become 'the thing to do' in many Charismatic and evangelical churches. Norman Moss' advice to church members is: 'Fine, if you can afford it, go' (Fearon, 1994, p.128). Sometimes individuals and their families have met the cost; in other cases their churches have sponsored their visits; £3500 was raised by Sunderland Christian Centre to send their pastor and his wife and the church youth leader. The total money invested by British individuals and churches in the Toronto pilgrimage, up to July 1995, can be estimated at over £24m (see Table 5.1).

Pilgrims are unlikely to have invested their money and their annual leave without weighing up the likely return on their investment: in this case, more intense contact with the Blessing and its associated benefits. God is expected to 'honour' their sacrifice of money and time and to make their visit spiritually worthwhile. Not for nothing have pilgrimage sites been described as 'stock exchanges of the religious economy', mediating 'intensive sacred commerce' (Eade and Sallnow, 1991, pp. 24, 5). Interestingly, some sociologists of religion have taken such language at face value and have recently begun to use models borrowed from the world of economics to understand the behaviour of churches and 'religious consumers'. Their approach has come to be known as the 'new paradigm' for the sociological study of religion (Warner, 1993). One prominent proponent of the new paradigm, Laurence Iannaccone, claims that 'the logic of economics and even its language are powerful tools for the social-scientific study of religion' (Iannaccone, 1992, p.123). In particular, rational choice theory has been a preferred tool. This theory presupposes that people treat religion in the same way that they treat other objects of choice: they weigh up costs and benefits and act in a way that is intended to maximize their net benefits. Our analysis of the Toronto pilgrimage therefore needs to take into account the fact that 'religion is advertised and marketed, pro-

Table 5.1   *Estimated cost in £ sterling of the Toronto pilgrimage (based on an exchange rate of 2.13 Canadian dollars to the £)*

Costs		£
Return flight from UK to Toronto[1]		590
Expenditure in Toronto per day:		
Accomodation[2]	34	
Meals	10	
Free-will offerings	2	
Total	46	
Expenditure in Toronto for a 5-night stay		230
Total cost per person[3]		820
Total cost for 30,000 UK pilgrims		24,600,000

[1] American Airlines October 1995 price, including taxes and security. This could be cut if ticket bought at bucket shop
[2] Price based on Airport Vineyard information sheet for bed and breakfast hotel accomodation
[3] Excluding other spending money

duced and consumed, demanded and supplied' (Iannaccone, 1992, p.123); why do its followers see it as a good investment?

Vineyard may well have been seeking to preserve its share of the Charismatic market, as Martyn Percy has hinted (Percy, 1995, pp.17–19). This is not to imply that Vineyard has been able to totally 'guide' the Blessing: by its very nature, ecstatic religious experience of this kind resists control. Neither is this necessarily a conscious strategy on the part of all Vineyard leaders. Use of the new paradigm here is not intended to cast doubt on the motives of Vineyard, which itself would talk in terms of 'saving souls' rather than 'winning markets'. Nevertheless, however worthy their motives, Vineyard is not immune from the commercial dynamics that today even affect religion. One should, incidentally, not underestimate the financial benefits reported to be accruing to Airport Vineyard Toronto as a result of (ten per cent) commission payments from hotels recommended to pilgrims.

There has been a persistent tendency for commentators to attribute the Toronto Blessing to the effects of pre-millennial tension (PMT) – people's deep anxieties at approaching the end of the millennium (Roof, 1993, p.156). Martyn Percy surmises that 'the "Toronto Blessing" is . . . a sign of "Pre-Millennial Tension", the well documented history of religious paranoia and hysteria that accompanies the end of each millennium' (Percy, Chapter 10 of this book and 1995, p.20; Hunt, 1995, p.267; Fearon, 1994, p.37). This is an untestable claim and an inadequate explanation for the Toronto Blessing: millions of people are probably suffering from pre-millennial tension, but relatively few of them have turned to the Blessing. Parallels have been drawn between the Blessing and the Great Awakenings in US religious history. Roger Finke and Laurence Iannaccone have plausibly argued that the Great Awakenings should be understood in relation to supply-side shifts in the religious market in early America: in fact these 'were nothing more – or less – than successful marketing campaigns of upstart evangelical Protestants' in a newly deregulated market (Finke and Iannaccone, 1993, p.29). The Toronto Blessing, similarly, can be understood as an attempt to capture world markets, or at least to preserve market share in a religious economy which, in the west, is relatively static. There is nothing new, for US churches at least, to find themselves in an 'open market' where they must compete for religious consumers: Stephen Warner traces this back to the disestablishment of North American churches in the late colonial era (Warner, 1993, p.1050; Finke and Iannaccone, 1993, p.29). It is not without significance that Queen's Road Baptist Church advertises its Sunday Services on the back of till receipts at Safeway's Wimbledon store. The normal commercial price for advertising on these till receipts is approximately £475 per 120,000 + VAT.

Modern cities offer fertile conditions for churches keen to succeed in the religious marketplace. Toronto is no exception and can be expected to 'provide resources and conditions conducive to religious mobilization' (Warner, 1993, p.1056). There is evidence that, at least, subconsciously, the leadership of Airport Vineyard Toronto had for some time nursed desires to be an international centre 'from which many are sent out to the nations, on all continents' (prophecies by Marc Dupont, May 1992 and July 1993 – cited in Chevreau, 1994, pp.28–35).

Airport Vineyard and other churches which have become epicentres of the Blessing have a product that is marketable in late twentieth century societies. Emotional and other forms of healing associated with the Blessing have a ready market, as many New Religious Movements know (Robbins, 1988, pp.122–7) – although many of the claimed cures are unverifiable and middle class western in nature (Percy, 1995, p.6). In fact the Toronto Blessing may be more effective than many secular alternatives and this may enable it to steal a march on some of its competitors (Percy, 1995, p.9). Its closest secular rival is probably primal scream therapy; a non-Christian psychotherapist has remarked of the Blessing that 'she and her colleagues would "give their right arm" to see in their surgeries what was happening in . . . church building[s]' (*Renewal* magazine, November 1994, p.27). Part of the Vineyard movement's marketability lies in its attractiveness to needing and hurting people (Chevreau, 1994, p.196). It has also proved particularly successful in appealing to 'baby-boomers' (Perrin and Mauss, 1991), attracted maybe by its marrying together of psychology and faith (Roof, 1993, p.165; Hunt, 1995, pp.264–5), although much of its growth has been amongst those previously committed to other churches.

Experience-based religion is also well marketable. This helps to explain the attraction of Vineyard churches (Hunt, 1995, p.265). It also helps to account for the popularity of the Blessing within those and other churches. The Toronto Blessing experience has been compared to a 'ferocious white-knuckle ride' (Fearon, 1994, p.208). Like Alton Towers theme park, the Toronto Blessing Movement can capitalize on consumers' demands for thrills and spills! Martyn Percy has drawn attention to ways in which Charismatic churches have mimicked the 'rave culture' (Percy, 1995, p.8). A church that sounds exciting and attractive and definitely non-boring is likely to perform well in the religious market, particularly if it can also offer the reassurance of dogmatic certainty (Percy, 1995, p.17). Interestingly, the name of Airport Vineyard may have helped in its success. When I cited the name to an International Directory Enquiries assistant recently his response was: 'Good Lord. Is that the name of a church? I might go there myself!': the name 'Vineyard' was well chosen! The form taken by the Blessing (for instance, spiritual drunkenness) fits with changing approaches to bodily disinhibition in late capitalist society: consumerist society has supplanted erstwhile more ascetic Protestant work ethic attitudes. Pastors teach that recipients of the Blessing should not be 'afraid to come for more and more and more': like the material abundance of consumer society the Blessing is not in short supply! (Richter, 1995, pp.24–7).

It is likely then that the churches involved have done their homework and are aware of what the market wants and have chosen accordingly from their religious repertoire. It is even conceivable that churches in which the Toronto Blessing originated have consciously induced the phenomena. Stephen Hunt has drawn attention to the influence of course MC510 which John Wimber led for a short while in the early 1980s at Fuller Seminary. Students were taught how to create the most fertile sociological and psychological environments within which the Spirit of God might work. Furthermore, they learnt how 'the apparent manifestations of the Holy Spirit in the emotional and physiological states of believers . . . could be induced' (Hunt, Chapter 4, this book and 1995, p.264). As John Wesley commented on similar phenomena, here we may have 'the end without the [true] means' (*John Wesley's Journal*, 17 January 1739). This is not to suggest that the Toronto Blessing has been deliberately manufactured along these lines in every church in which it has appeared. Some churches will have merely copied the methods of others or simply stumbled across the Blessing.

Whatever the original motives and hopes the Toronto Blessing does not appear to have dramatically expanded churches' market share or resulted in many new conversions; indeed it is typically referred to as a time of 'refreshing' rather than 'revival'. At most, it has helped churches to retain their precarious share of the market (Richter, 1995, pp.19–21), or, to adopt a metaphor from the broadcasting business, to 'hold their audience' (Percy, 1995, p.17). One of the attractions of Charismatic churches has been their offer of a direct, unmediated and unpredictable encounter with a God who is anything but dead. Periodically, as that encounter itself tends to become familiar and predictable, fresh innovation and excitement is needed. The novelty of the Toronto Blessing has been a means both of retaining members and of adjusting to shifts in (religious) consumer preferences (Richter, 1995, pp.19–21). In many respects the Toronto Blessing is a somewhat older product (Richter, 1995, p.11) 'relaunched on a existing market, but with some subtle re-profiling' (Percy, 1995, p.19). Within the churches involved it has, however, been a fairly successful product. Although it may turn out to have been ephemeral, pilgrims to Toronto are certainly currently still prepared to invest their time and money in what is on offer.

For church leaders themselves the Blessing has often provided an invaluable opportunity to resolve a religious mid-life crisis, to radically re-evaluate the course of their ministries and to rediscover their Charismatic roots. Leaders may hope to reverse the tendency of all organizations (the church not excepted) to lose their Charismatic dynamism and to become staid, bureaucratic and conformed to modern society. This may be a vain hope – ironically, the Blessing also depends a great deal on modern communications technology and reflects the pragmatic 'functional rationality' that dominates western societies: 'if it works, trust it!' (Richter, 1995, pp.21–3). Margaret Poloma, a sociologist writing from within the Toronto Blessing movement, has warned that the 'Charismatic moment' of Toronto Airport Vineyard may itself ultimately prove vulnerable to the forces of institutionalization. In particular, Poloma suggests that it may not be able to deal successfully with what Thomas O'Dea has called the 'dilemma of delimitation': 'TAV is at risk of falling into the trap of delimitation by focusing on the conservative fringes of Christianity and in reining in charisma to please this potential constituency' (Poloma, 1995).

Much of the behaviour associated with the Blessing might appear to the onlooker to be quite irrational. I have attempted to demonstrate that, on the contrary, there is a good deal of economic rationality built into this movement. It can be seen as a viable strategy to hold on to their share of the religious market. It would not be the first time that phenomena similar to the Toronto Blessing have been mobilized to increase market share in the religious economy (Finke and Stark, 1992, pp.92–3, 95). Of course there is no guarantee that consumers will automatically be attracted to new products in the religious marketplace, however ostensibly marketable these goods may be. Modern consumers are also notoriously fickle. Although it throws important new light on the Toronto Blessing phenomenon, my analysis here has been predominantly 'supply-side' oriented and does not pretend to be an exhaustive account. Elsewhere I have examined a number of the social influences that help to construct the Toronto Blessing as a desirable product for at least some religious consumers (Richter, 1995).

A GLOBAL PHENOMENON

One further salient feature about the Toronto pilgrimage is that it is global in nature. Airport Vineyard has not merely amplified previously sporadic phenomena; it has helped to spread them worldwide. Whilst the Charismatic movement has been international in its scope mass international pilgrimage of this order is an important new feature. Pilgrims are travelling from literally all over the world and the Blessing is being increasingly framed in global terms. Wes Campbell, pastor of New Life Vineyard in Kelowna, BC, Canada, has claimed that 'This is for the world. The Church is being refreshed and visited for the world' (Riss WWW, 1995). Why should the Blessing be perceived as something for the whole planet? Why should pilgrims be attracted from all over the world?

One reason for the worldwide nature of the Toronto pilgrimage is the relative ease and availability of transatlantic air travel: the cost has actually declined in real terms and highly competitive fares are on offer at so-called 'bucket shops'. If people had been able to travel to

Azusa Street in 1906 in such comfort and in such large numbers perhaps then they would have talked of the Azusa Street Blessing! In fact
comparatively few people visited Asuza Street from other continents
and word was spread as much by correspondence as by personal visits
(Bloch-Hoell, 1964, pp.202, 203, nn. 201, 211, 216). Relatively cheap
transatlantic air travel evidently offers religious producers fresh opportunities (Finke and Iannaccone, 1993, p.39) and the chance to think in
terms of capturing global markets.

Mass air transport is, however, simply part and parcel of a much
more profound phenomenon – the advent of Globalization. In the remainder of this chapter I shall argue that one needs to see the Toronto
pilgrimage in the light of emergent globalization theory. Globalization
is best defined as that process 'that binds the population of the world
into a single society' (Albrow, 1993, p.248). Increasingly people are
beginning to perceive themselves as inhabitants of a 'global village',
linked together by mass communications (Robertson, 1992, p.184).
Computer users are used to 'surfing' the World Wide Web and ordinary mortals are no longer amazed to receive live pictures on their
televisions from the other side of the globe or even outer space. Social
relations have been 'disembedded' from local contexts (Giddens, 1991):
we can maintain relationships by phone, fax or e-mail with people we
might never or hardly ever meet as part of a 'virtual community'. Some
of the most important problems facing politicians are no longer national
issues but human issues, affecting the future viability of the planet: for
instance, measures to control pollution and to reduce reliance on nuclear weapons have potential implications for the whole globe. People
are now starting to think of themselves as part of a 'worldwide society':
'their lives are influenced directly by events and processes that are
happening far beyond state boundaries' (Albrow, 1995, p.3). This is
epitomized in the operations of what are now called 'transnational
companies', firms that transcend national boundaries and interests (Eade,
1994, p.3).

The seeds of globalization are by no means new. Ancient Greek
philosophy already sought to encompass all human beings within its
frame of reference. Christianity saw itself as a religion potentially for
all humanity (for example, Acts 2:6–13; 10:35; 17:26; Ephesians 3:14).
Pilgrimage, often to sites in other countries, helped to raise awareness
of 'the wider community of human beings' (Albrow, 1995, p.17). Eade
and Sallnow note that the pilgrimage is arguably 'the ritual context
par excellence in which a world religion strives to realize its defining
transcultural universalism' (Eade and Sallnow, 1991, p.4). What is termed

globalization is the latest stage in a long process of development (Robertson, 1992, pp.58, 183–4). It is only now, however, that the world has shrunk so dramatically (Albrow, 1995, p.3; Robertson, 1992, pp.52, 54, 182) and distant happenings and local life are able to directly affect each other (Giddens, 1995, p.25). The world of religion is by no means sheltered or insulated from processes of globalization. Until recently it has been commonplace within the sociology of religion to categorize it as belonging to the 'private', rather than 'public', sphere of life – on the margins, rather than at the heart of social change. Globalization has rendered the public/private dichotomy redundant. The 'private' world of the family, with which religion has long been associated, has been transformed by modern telecommunications: the home has become a 'cultural site, an arena of discretionary consumption, wired to receive global messages' (Albrow, 1995, p.20).

It would be possible for churches to react against globalization and to simply reflect more particularistic and nationalistic concerns. Christians are not immune to the 'Little Englander' mentality epitomized so well in the famous newspaper placard: 'Storms in the Channel – Continent isolated' (Eade, 1994, p.3). This is less likely to be true of the churches involved in the Toronto Blessing. Charismatic evangelical churches draw disproportionately large numbers of professional people (including teachers and members of the 'caring professions'), middle managers and graduates, particularly from the sciences (Walker, 1989, p.196; Richter, 1996, n. 65). Preliminary findings from Margaret Poloma's survey of visitors to Toronto Airport Church indicate that most are college graduates (Poloma WWW, 1995). Such people may well already be used to telecommunicating with people all over the globe in their workplace. The churches of the Toronto Blessing also contain significant numbers of global cosmopolitans: members of the 'rootless managerial and financial élites' (Giddens, 1995, p.25) of multinational corporations, ever on the move as their company dictates (Eade, 1994, p.3). Globalization is already part and parcel of the daily lives of many members of Charismatic evangelical churches; this is likely to be particularly true of those who take up lay leadership positions within their churches. Rather than provoking a Little Englander counter-reaction, processes of globalization have stimulated churches to 'think global' and to utilize mass communications to the full.

The Vineyard movement, of which Airport Vineyard Church is a member, has been keen to frame its mission in global terms. Other more mainstream Christian churches have of course traditionally laid claim to having a mission to the world, channelled through their various overseas missionary societies. Some have sought the establishment of the Kingdom of God on earth, inspired by universalist values. But in the world at large globalist values are increasingly superseding universalist values: 'the fate of humanity and the earth' are central concerns, rather than more abstract principles of social justice, liberty and equality (Albrow, 1995, p.6). Charismatic evangelical churches are perhaps best attuned to this shift in values, with their focus on psychological and spiritual integrity, rather than social justice campaigns. The global consciousness of mainstream churches has in any case been limited by their tendency to operate as relatively independent national units – as, for instance, the Church of *England*, or the *British* Methodist Conference.

The Vineyard movement's target is to have 2000 Vineyards by the year 2000 in 29 countries (John Wimber 'The State of the Vineyard', talk at AVC International Pastors' Conference, 25 July 1995). Airport Vineyard Senior Pastor, John Arnott, referred to the 'world-wide reach and impact' of the Blessing (Open letter, 12 December 1995). Richard Riss in his insider's account of the history of the Toronto Blessing (Riss WWW, 1995) repeatedly refers to the global impact of the Blessing, mediated through 'over 550 Vineyard churches *worldwide*': the Blessing had brought 'new anointing to many people in mainline denominational and non-denominational churches *throughout the world*'; a videotape called *The Laugh Heard Round the World* had documented 'Rodney Howard Browne's influence (which) soon reached *worldwide* proportions'; by August 1994, the *worldwide reach* of the revival was already recognized in *Time, Christian Week,* and *The Toronto Star*; Riss reports John Arnott's comment that: 'The angels party whenever one sinner repents, and there are thousands coming to Jesus every day *throughout the world*' (Riss WWW, 1995 – my italics). Other churches have also described the Blessing in global terms: *Alpha* magazine headlined its December 1994 interview with Rodney Howard Browne as 'Exclusive! Meet the man behind global renewal'. Clive Jones, speaking at the Methodist Easter People gathering at Torquay in April 1995, testified that in the Blessing God was 'moving across the nations, not simply this nation' (*Methodist Recorder*, 27 April 1995, p.10).

The global dissemination of the Toronto Blessing (Albrow, 1996) has been facilitated not only by familiar evangelical and Charismatic media such as tele-evangelism (Hadden, 1993), books and videos, but also by pages on that epitome of global communications, the World Wide Web (Poloma, 1995) – a user-friendly, multimedia and interactive network for computers. For instance, the reader with access to the

World Wide Web will find substantial amounts of information via the following sites:

http://205.147.212.2/BlessingsPage/
http://groke.beckman.uiuc.edu/Vineyard/
http://www.grmi.org/TAV/
http://www.grmi.org/new-wine/

The http://groke.beckman.uiuc.edu/Vineyard/ site is operated by Champaign Vineyard, Urbana, Illinois, and includes more general information about Vineyard churches worldwide. Conveniently, it also gives access to user-statistics: as well as the USA there are some 43 other countries listed as active 'client domains'; usage has been highest by the US, the UK, Canada, Australia and Sweden (in that order). Between 15 February 1995 and 26 June 1995 at least 711 requests had been received for *Lifelines* pages called 'When the Spirit comes with power', specifically dealing with the Blessing. 2827 requests had been made for the opening (index) page of Bill Jackson's paper about the Blessing – 'What in the world is happening to us – a biblical perspective'. By December 1995 nearly 1000 people per day were visiting the site. At least some of the followers of the Toronto Blessing have not been slow to exploit the potential of the World Wide Web: 'fishing for Christ' (Mark 1:17) has already begun to take on new dimensions on the Internet!

It has been a boon for researchers to have relatively easy access to Vineyard documents and discussions via the Web. The reply by Senior Airport Vineyard Pastor, John Arnott, to John Wimber at the time of the split between the Association of Vineyard Churches and the Toronto church looks to continuing 'discussions in media and cyberspace'(@http://www.grmi.org/TAV/release.html).

One index of the relative popularity of the Internet amongst Vineyard members is the number of US e-mail (electronic mail) addresses listed in the Vineyard e-mail Directory – 284 (@http://groke.beckman.uiuc.edu:80/AVC/Email/addresses.html). By comparison, the United Methodist Church e-mail Directory lists just 104 US addresses (@http://www.holli.com/~dmullens/umsource/a.html). The United Methodist Church has a US membership of over nine million. Precise figures for overall Vineyard membership are not published, but with approximately 400 Vineyards in the USA and Canada, the total is unlikely to exceed 200,000. Vineyard use of the Internet is clearly disproportionate to the size of its membership. The Vineyard Churches World-Wide e-mail Directory also comprises e-mail addresses in Australia, Canada, Chile,

Costa Rica, England & GB, Netherlands, New Zealand, Norway, South Africa and Sweden (http://groke.beckman.uiuc.edu:80/AVC/Email/ addresses.html – as at 16 August 1995).

Globalization can mean homogenization. Its critics have spoken in terms of US commercial and cultural hegemony. One of the attractions of McDonald's restaurants is that you can be sure of enjoying fundamentally the same product wherever you may be in the world. Paradoxically, at the same time, diversity and fragmentation are also features of globalization, 'permitting individuals to make an increasingly personalized choice from among the diverse cultural resources available to them' (Albrow, 1995, p.19; Robertson, 1992, p.172); this is reflected, for instance, in the greater diversity of culinary traditions espoused by British consumers. Equally, there are claims to distinctive identities: for instance, '"fundamentalism within limits" makes globalization work' (Robertson, 1992, p.180; Beyer, 1994, pp.90–3). To what extent is the Toronto Blessing part of a process of homogenization, or, alternatively, greater diversity?

The Blessing could be interpreted as a process of 'McTorontoization'[5] (!), aiming to export a virtually identical product all over the world. Wisely, perhaps, an American city did not become the pilgrimage centre; this might help to allay fears of American cultural imperialism. Marc Dupont, a member of the pastoral team at Airport Vineyard, has pointed out that the whole world can be reached from Toronto:

> Toronto is, according to the United Nations, the most ethnically diverse city in the world. It's a great city for something to be birthed in because it can be a sending-out place.
>
> (*Alpha*, September 1994, 'Prayer & Revival' supplement, p.3)

There is evidence that consumers from different countries and cultures are expected to consume fundamentally the same product or, at most, variations on a common theme. Inhibited Britons are expected to become just as uninhibited as their North American cousins. Kim Gentes reported that 'it was very interesting . . . to see so many conservative British flopping all over and laughing hysterically' at Toronto (Kim WWW, 1995). The Blessing is evidently able to transcend national and cultural stereotypes. As Colin Dye, senior pastor at Kensington Temple remarked: 'if the Holy Spirit is a gentleman, he's not an English gentleman' (Fearon, 1994, p.139).

Equally, however, as globalization theorists would expect, there is some evidence of diversity alongside the homogenization. Not every local church has been happy to take on board the full paraphernalia of the Blessing. Some, for instance have criticized the barnyard animal and other zoological noises associated in some cases with the Blessing (Richter, 1995, p.14). The Toronto Blessing is a sedate, well-ordered phenomenon at some churches; elsewhere it can be chaotic and bizarre. Although the evidence is at present sparse, one can predict a certain amount of growing syncretism between the Blessing and local cultures, if the phenomenon persists. Syncretism is not unknown in the types of church affected by the Toronto Blessing: Martyn Percy cites the example of syncretism between shamanism and Pentecostalism in some Korean churches (Percy, 1995, p.15). Stanley Porter suggests that at least some proponents of the Toronto Blessing are working with an 'open canon' of scripture, 'subject to expansion (and potentially subtraction)' (Porter, 1995, p.60). The substantial numerical growth within Charismatic and evangelical churches in recent decades has been achieved partly by 'church growth' strategies which include McGavran's principle of evangelizing people within whatever 'homogeneous unit' they happen to belong to (McGavran, 1970, p.198). These homogeneous units may be constructed on the basis of various kinds of difference – for instance, tribal, racial, class, income, educational, and the like. Church growth proponents have tried to discover those things in particular cultures through which the meaning of the gospel can best be conveyed – without compromising the integrity of the Christian gospel. Holy Trinity Brompton, one of the main centres of the Toronto Blessing in Britain, has successfully pioneered what are known as *Alpha* courses, now run in over 1200 churches throughout Britain – 15-session, non-threatening introductions to the Christian faith designed for non-Christians and new-Christians. As Sandy Millar, vicar of Holy Trinity explains: 'stripping the gospel down to its bare essentials, it makes Christianity accessible to men and women of today's culture' (HTB in FOCUS *Alpha* News, April 1995, p.2). One of its highlights is a weekend away focusing on the experience of the Holy Spirit. As part of the *Alpha* course those attending are assigned to small groups, comprising people of similar age and background. This emphasis on 'meeting people where they are', in homogeneous units, is likely to promote local adaptations of the Toronto Blessing.

. Within the much wider context of Christian churches in general the Toronto Blessing can be seen as adding yet greater diversity to the religious scene and to be part of the inexhaustible variety characterizing religion in a global and 'free' market (Warner, 1993, p.1055). Ironically, one suspects the predominantly homogenizing tendencies of the Toronto Blessing may tend to preclude the churches involved from exploring and appropriating other more indigenous Christian traditions. The future vitality of churches may depend on their openness to 'the culture of the people' (Roof, 1993, p.159). In Britain Michael Mitton, himself writing from a Charismatic background, has recently urged churches to reappreciate the value of Celtic Christianity. He believes that the 'early Celtic church was the nearest thing we get in our Christian history to a complete expression of faith in this country' (Mitton, 1995, p.2). It is unlikely that churches preoccupied with the Toronto Blessing will, for the time being, take his words to heart.

Globalization contains other paradoxes as well as the contrary trends towards homogeneity and diversity. On the one hand, the time–space compression associated with globalization means that people have easier access to more people and more places; on the other hand, given their frenetic pace of life, their contacts have become more superficial and ephemeral (Albrow, 1995, p.16). The Toronto Blessing pilgrimage and experience may well prove to have a relatively short life-span as people move on to the next Charismatic 'craze'. It is probably not without significance that Airport Church is located very close to Pearson International Airport. Mass air travel is relatively easy and cheap, but local terrestrial travel to and from airports is frequently irksome. Here lies another paradox: globalization entails disembedding from place, yet the physical location of Airport Church may actually be important. Furthermore, whilst opportunities to scour the world for the best of everything have increased, paradoxically 'the best, by definition, can be found in just one place in the world' (Albrow, 1995, p.16). For the time being, at least, Charismatic evangelicals are finding 'the best' at Airport Vineyard Church, Toronto and are prepared to undertake pilgrimage there.

In the meantime, the pilgrimage to Toronto performs at least two vital functions for those involved. Firstly, it offers the Blessing and the churches involved worldwide legitimation. 'If people are flocking to Toronto from all quarters of the world this must surely be of God'. 'People would not waste their time travelling half way around the world if this was not the work of God'. Global pilgrimage to witness the Toronto phenomena at first hand has given the Vineyard churches, and particularly Airport Vineyard, new prominence and credibility within Charismatic evangelical circles. Secondly, and more subtly, the Toronto Blessing itself, it has been plausibly argued, may be a psychosomatic response to the failure of Charismatic Renewal to become a truly universal phenomenon with an appeal to the wider world: 'the laughter and accompanying barking may be psychosomatic responses to deeply

embedded traumas about the failure of Charismatic Renewal and revivalism to move from being a particular belief to a universal one'
(Percy, 1995, p.19; Richter, 1995, pp.32–3). Ironically, given that the
Toronto Blessing's appeal is largely to the already committed, it is
unlikely to set the world on fire!

NOTES

1. 'Toronto Airport Vineyard Facts & Figures' @ http://www.grmi.org/TAV/
   facts.html
2. Available @http://groke.beckman.uiuc.edu:80/AVC/TAVhunter.html
3. Source: Correspondence with Steve Long, Airport Vineyard Administrator,
   28 June 1995.
4. See, for instance, Turner and Turner's (1978) analysis of pilgrimage as
   liminal, anti-structural and egalitarian – and Reader and Walter's critique
   (1993) – or Tuan's (1984) modelling of pilgrimage in terms of the pilgrims being 'out of (ordinary) place'.
5. cf. Globalization as *McDonaldization*. Ironically one of the Toronto Blessing's reported successes took place at a branch of McDonalds (see World
   Wide Web @ http://205.147.212.2/BlessingsPage/macminis.html (sic)).

BIBLIOGRAPHY

M. Albrow, 'Globalization', in W. Outhwaite and T. Bottomore (eds), *The
Blackwell Dictionary of Twentieth Century Social Thought* (Cambridge, MA:
Blackwell, 1993) pp.248–9.

M. Albrow, 'Globalization', in R. J. Brym (ed.), *New Society: Sociology for
the 21st Century* (Toronto: Harcourt Brace, 1995) chapter 15, pp.1–25.

M. Albrow, *The Global Age* (Cambridge: Polity, 1996) (forthcoming).

P. Beyer, *Religion and Globalization* (London: Sage, 1994).

N. Bloch-Hoell, *The Pentecostal Movement* (London: Allen & Unwin, 1964).

G. Bowman, 'Christian ideology and the image of a holy land: the place of
Jerusalem pilgrimage in the various Christianities', in J. Eade and M. J.
Sallnow (eds), 1991, pp.98–121.

G. Chevreau, *Catch the Fire: The Toronto Blessing, an experience of renewal
and revival* (London: Marshall Pickering, 1994).

J. Eade, 'The Global Context for Ministry', in P. Richter (ed.), *Social Analysis for Prophets* (Aston: Aston Training Scheme, 1994), chapter 12.

J. Eade and M. J. Sallnow (eds), *Contesting the Sacred: The Anthropology of
Christian Pilgrimage* (London: Routledge, 1991).

M. Fearon, *A Breath of Fresh Air* (Guildford: Eagle, 1994).

R. Finke and L. R. Iannaccone, 'Supply-Side Explanations for Religious Change', in W. C. Roof (ed.), 1993, pp.27–39.

R. Finke and R. Stark, *The Churching of America, 1776–1990: Winners and Losers in Our Religious Economy* (New Brunswick, NJ: Rutgers University Press, 1992).

A. Giddens, *Modernity and Self-Identity: Self and Society in the Late Modern Age* (Cambridge: Polity, 1991).

A. Giddens, 'Government's last gasp?', *The Observer*, 9 July 1995, p.25.

J. K. Hadden, 'The Rise and Fall of American Televangelism', in W. C. Roof (ed.), 1993, pp.113–30.

S. Hunt, 'The "Toronto Blessing": A Rumour of Angels?', *Journal of Contemporary Religion*, 10, 3 (1995) 257–71.

L. R. Iannaccone, 'Religious Markets and the Economics of Religion', *Social Compass*, 39, 1 (1992) 123–31.

J. Kent, 'Have we been here before? – A Historian looks at the Toronto Blessing', in S. E. Porter and P. J. Richter (eds), 1995, pp.85–102.

Kim WWW, 1995 – Kim Anthony Gentes @ http://205.147.212.2/BlessingsPage/Kim1.html

F. MacNutt, *Overcome by the Spirit* (Guildford: Eagle, 1994 – originally published 1990, new prologue, 1994).

D. McGavran, *Understanding Church Growth* (Grand Rapids, MI: Eerdmans, 1970).

M. Mitton, *Restoring the Woven Cord: Strands of Celtic Christianity for the Church Today* (London: Darton, Longman & Todd, 1995).

R. Murphy, 'Risen with Healing in His Wings: An Exploration of the Psychology of the Toronto Blessing', in S. E. Porter and P. J. Richter (eds), 1995, pp. 65–84.

M. J. Neitz, *Charisma and Community: A Study of Religious Commitment within the Charismatic Renewal* (Oxford: Transaction Books, 1987).

G. K. Neville, *Kinship and Pilgrimage: Rituals of Reunion in American Protestant Culture* (New York and Oxford: University Press, 1987).

C. C. Park, *Sacred Worlds: An Introduction to Geography and Religion* (London: Routledge, 1994).

M. Percy, 'Sociological and Theological Perspectives on Christian Charismatic Healing Ministries, with Special Reference to "The Toronto Blessing"', paper given at The Annual Meeting of Contemporary and New Age Religion Conference on 13 May 1995.

R. D. Perrin and A. L. Mauss, 'Saints and Seekers: Sources of Recruitment to the Vineyard Christian Fellowship', *Review of Religious Research*, 33 (1991) 97–111.

M. Poloma, 'Charisma and Institutions: A Sociological Account of the "Toronto Blessing"', paper presented at Society for the Scientific Study of Religion meeting, St Louis, October 1995; available on Toronto Airport Vineyard World Wide Web site @ http://www.grmi.org/TAV/poloma.html

Poloma WWW, 1995, letter to John Wimber @ http://www.grmi.org/TAV/margaret.html

S. E. Porter, 'Shaking the Biblical Foundations?: The Biblical Basis for the Toronto Blessing', in S. E. Porter and P. J. Richter (eds), 1995, pp.37–64.

S. E. Porter and P. J. Richter (eds), *The Toronto Blessing – or Is It?* (London: Darton, Longman & Todd, 1995).

W. J. Porter, 'The Worship of the Toronto Blessing?', in S. E. Porter and P. J. Richter (eds), 1995, pp.103–29.

I. Reader and T. Walter (eds), *Pilgrimage in Popular Culture* (London: Macmillan, 1993).

P. J. Richter, 'God is not a Gentleman!: The Sociology of the Toronto Blessing', in S. E. Porter and P. J. Richter (eds), 1995, pp. 4–36.

P. J. Richter, 'Charismatic Mysticism – a Sociological Analysis of the "Toronto Blessing"', in S. E. Porter (ed.), *The Nature of Religious Language* (Sheffield: Sheffield Academic Press, 1996).

Riss WWW, 1995 – Richard Riss' History @ http://www.grmi.org/Richard_Riss/history.html

T. Robbins, 'Cults, Converts and Charisma: The Sociology of New Religious Movements', *Current Sociology*, 36, 1 (1988) whole issue.

D. Roberts, *The 'Toronto Blessing'* (Eastbourne: Kingsway, 1994).

R. Robertson, *Globalization: Social Theory and Global Culture* (London: Sage, 1992).

W. C. Roof (ed.), *Religion in the Nineties* (London: Sage, 1993 – *The Annals of the American Academy of Political and Social Science*, 527, May 1993).

W. C. Roof, 'Toward the Year 2000: Reconstruction of Religious Space', in W. C. Roof (ed.), 1993, pp. 155–70.

D. E. Sherkat, 'Embedding Religious Choices: Integrating Preferences and Social Constraints into Rational Choice Theories of Religious Behavior', in L. A. Young, *Rational Choice Theory and Religion: Summary and Assessment* (London: Routledge, 1995).

T. A. Smail, A. Walker and N. Wright, *Charismatic Renewal* (London: SPCK, 1995).

Y. F. Tuan, 'In place, out of place', *Geoscience & Man*, 24 (1984) 3–10.

V. W. Turner and E. Turner, *Image and Pilgrimage in Christian Culture: Anthropological Perspectives* (Oxford: Basil Blackwell, 1978).

A. Walker, *Restoring the Kingdom: The Radical Christianity of the House Church Movement* (London: Hodder & Stoughton, 1989).

S. R. Warner, 'Work in Progress toward a New Paradigm for the Sociological Study of Religion in the United States', *AJS*, 98, 5 (1993) 1044–93.

6 Charismatic Communitarianism and the Jesus Fellowship
Keith Newell[1]

Community living has deep roots in the Charismatic movement. For over 30 years, some people have held the conviction that collective life would provide a deeper expression of their faith and charismatic experience.

Probably the earliest, and certainly the most significant, attempt to establish a thoroughgoing community was that established by the Episcopalian priest Graham Pulkingham at the Church of the Redeemer, Houston, Texas. In 1965, five families and a number of single individuals came together to form extended family units which in 1966 took on communal identity. Pulkingham's ministry in a poorer part of the city attracted a number of Christians committed to ministering to the needy (Harper, 1973; Pulkingham, 1973, 1974). Some caught a vision of community ministry in which the resources of finances, time and personal lives were shared so that a declining parish could be charismatically renewed and the socially disadvantaged more effectively reached.

From 1966 to 1972 the community grew from an initial 33 to around 450 members in 32 households, acting as a model for communitarian renewal in other American churches. The community life was also for export. In 1972 Pulkingham moved his household to Coventry, England, to establish a similar parish project which, through the Fountain Trust, aroused interest among clergy. The Houston experience inspired other communal projects in Britain, some of which have gone down in the annals of Charismatic history: the Fisherfolk who from 1973 to 1976 encouraged renewal of worship and the creative arts (Pulkingham and Harper, 1974), the Post Green community in Dorset (Lees and Hinton, 1978), and the Community of Celebration in the Isle of Cumbrae, Scotland (Durran, 1986). The most enduring and certainly the most successful has been the New Creation Christian Community, the communal core of the Jesus Fellowship, which – though drawing on concepts from the Redeemer experiment – developed independently

120

(Cooper and Farrant, 1991). This chapter is primarily concerned with its evolution.

DEFINING CHARISMATIC COMMUNITY

Sociology has historically been concerned with natural, indigenous community, but since the 1960s with the advent of counter-cultural communes (Coates *et al.*, 1995) sociologists have also studied intentional groupings (e.g. Rigby, 1974). We are concerned here with intentional communities within the Charismatic movement – which is not, of course, to deny the importance of monastic and other Christian communities both down the ages and today.[2] The non-Christian communes of the 1960s reflected a search for alternative life-styles and/or a longing to re-establish social bonds eroded by social and geographical mobility and the impersonal nature of the contemporary world.

The Charismatic community shares some broad social aspects with the secular commune. The mode of social interaction tends to be cohesive rather than, as in much of modern society, fragmented and individualistic. Although the contact the participant has with outside society can vary considerably – spatially and qualitatively – the variables of community living are distinctive. They tend toward the affective, ascriptive, mutual, constant and uniform patterns. They constitute *gemeinschaft*, not *gesselschaft*.

In familial terms, however, the Charismatic community is different from most secular communes, indeed from the monastic community. Charismatic community is based on a nuclear family which takes into its home a number of single people or, alternatively, a larger household which includes a number of such families. The household is the distinguishing feature of Charismatic communalism. Numerous other groups and churches use the word 'community', but do not fit this model because of the absence of extended family living. Spiritually, this redefinition of familial ties is seen as central to the kingdom of God, the 'new family' becoming a place of healing, fulfilment and ministry, a place on which the power of the Holy Spirit rests. In this model, a number of such households are grouped together to form the community base of the church or fellowship, this bigger unit organizing worship and outreach. Other interlocking devices include a pastoral leadership to oversee the development of the group, and joint economic and distributive mechanisms.

In the modern world at least, intentional communities are notoriously short-lived, with only a very few of those established in the 1960s surviving into the 1990s. Such communes tend to create their own internal tensions and contradictions. The greatest visions and aspirations cannot compensate for the difficulties either generated by the community itself, or in its relationships with the outside world. We can mention two of the most important here, which are interconnected. First, the problem of establishing aims and priorities above and beyond the initial vision. Second, the problem of the succession of leadership after the first generation.

To explore the first difficulty, we can return to the example of the Church of the Redeemer. Despite the original vision, in the community left behind in Britain by Pulkingham there was disagreement among the elders whether the nascent community should service traditional forms of evangelical outreach or whether the community itself should be the focus of ministry to the needy in its own 'rule of life'. On the second dilemma we do not have an exact fit, but the point is still relevant. Religious groups tend to lose their momentum, unity and vision when the leader and the first generation either dies or moves on. Pulkingham left behind key workers to influence the British participants, but they were not able to inspire the same level of commitment or establish a modus operandi that could be a basis for parish renewal, and ultimately the community disintegrated.

THE NEW CREATION CHRISTIAN COMMUNITY

The New Creation Christian Community (NCCC), comprising one third of the total Jesus Fellowship (JF) membership, displays some of these contradictions and tensions, and others besides. It has had a controversial history, yet may be deemed successful, both in sociological terms of maintaining the community over time and in terms of its Christian goals – significant numerical growth, ministry to members of the underclass, and acceptance within the New Church movement. It ranks as one of the largest communities in Europe, charismatic or otherwise.

The JF developed totally independently of what was happening within the denominational churches. Under the leadership of the pastor, Noel Stanton (who still holds this position), a number of Charismatics gathered at Bugbrooke Baptist Chapel, near Northampton, in 1969. At this point there were some similarities with the Jesus Movement in

California (Palms, 1971). For the first three years the group that met at the chapel to participate in Charismatic life included bikers, drug-users, hippies and others who lived through the counter-culture. Very diverse people joined in the years that followed, including a number of evangelicals from Oxford, and to a lesser extent Cambridge, University.

A pattern of community formation similar to that at Houston began to take place. At this stage the Bugbrooke fellowship was no different from what are now termed the 'new churches'. In 1973, however, having read about the events at the Church of the Redeemer, they decided to create a similar kind of household-based community. This seemed to them a natural development of what they were already experiencing. They bought their first community residence, the former rectory of Bugbrooke's Anglican church, which they originally called Jesus Fellowship Hall and later renamed New Creation Hall. Several members of the fellowship moved into the building, which became the fellowship's new focus. This was the first experience most had had of a communal lifestyle. Not only did the building require major repairs, but interpersonal conflicts had to be resolved and a common spirit built up. Commitment to one another entailed the sharing of possessions, and new roles intended to reflect simplicity and brotherly love.

The combination of pioneering and discovery, the friendships formed in the renovation of the property into a place where members could belong and live together, all contributed to a cohesive base being formed, which could expand into other properties nearby. In 1976 a farm at Nether Heyford was bought and by 1979 several other large houses had been purchased in the surrounding villages to accommodate the growing Charismatic corps which had reached 350 in total.

COMMUNITY LIFE

From 1979 the NCCC, the communal side of JF, grew from ten houses in the villages around Bugbrooke to, in 1996, 60 large houses and 20 smaller ones over the whole of the UK. From six to 35 people live in a house, though a few larger properties have up to 60 residents. There is a simple lifestyle with no television or radio, nor many other things that the modern world would generally consider necessities. Food, clothing and household goods are purchased through the Food Distribution Centre based at the Hall where goods are bought wholesale and then distributed to each house as the weekly order is sent in. In 1996 JF comprised around 800 NCCC residents (including children) and overall 2500 adherents, a much more general term that includes children and regular worshippers who are not part of the residential community.

Domestic consumption reflects JF's understanding of the basic values of the kingdom of God: a new society of simplicity and equality.[3] Identity is less private and competitive, and more communal. JF is committed to mutual openness (cp 1 John). The fellowship believes other brethren, as fellow members are termed, have a truer assessment of the individual than he or she would have him or herself. Openness to others means listening to what the brethren are saying about you, which is intended to remove self-deception and foster the ability to learn. Hardness of heart, impermeability and barriers around the self are intended to melt away as the new person grows to full fulfilment, maturity and spiritual strength. This kind of social interaction varies from household to household, but JF claims that it is uncoerced, unstructured, relaxed and normal in the sense that these are all components of the everyday round of activities.[4] This is not just a matter of spiritual growth but of growth in the community, the two being virtually synonymous. This kind of brotherhood,[5] may well prove to be the missing piece of the jigsaw of Charismatic church growth (Jesus Fellowship Church, 1991).

JF integrates new friends and members into family units where the individual becomes the focus of attention. This contrasts with many evangelical churches where the message may be doctrinally correct and the atmosphere (new songs, dance, drama) may be enlivening, but daily, let alone hourly, support for the new contact is not available. Certainly to stay with the JF means to be included in a household where personal needs and well-being are taken seriously.

If the 'new friend' warms to this kind of welcome, then he or she is drawn into and offered membership. For some this may involve community membership. Before embarking on full community membership there is a probationary period of two years, which extends at least up to the age of 21, during which time they are associate members of the Community Trust Fund. During the probationary period the prospective member's income is placed in the common purse and any capital assets he or she may hold are loaned to the Trust. In many cases new members have no assets or even have debts which the Trust pays off. At the end of the probationary period any assets they have are contributed to the Trust Fund and entered into a legal register against their name. If a person leaves the community then he/she is eligible for this capital to be refunded.[6]

Many are drawn into JF through its Jesus Army activities. Jesus Army is the outreach/evangelistic arm of the fellowship and resembles the recruiting strategies of other large new churches such as Ichthus or New Frontiers. Street evangelism, double-decker coaches, tent campaigns and celebration rallies which appeal to the contemporary rave culture can produce contacts who are subsequently welcomed into a household for follow-up and absorption into further church activities. These 'new friends' are welcomed to meetings, visit houses and are offered friendship.

Critics have charged that JF preys on the vulnerable, cuts them off from their natural family, takes advantage of emotional dependency and conforms the recruit to a rigid legalism that damages the personality. It is not my purpose in this chapter to adjudicate such charges. We may note that any evangelistic group that uses friendship to minister to needy people is liable to such accusations. Any Christian group that *ignores* the vulnerable is liable, of course, to the counter-accusation that it is not taking seriously Christ's charge to minister to the poor, the needy and the outcast.

COVENANT

JF places strong emphasis on the covenant bond. Converts are baptized if not already baptized as believers and then there is the option of making covenant. Many don't at this stage, wanting time to consider the implications of this level of membership. Covenant ratifies the close commitment to the fellowship and brotherhood that should have been established as the new member spends time around a community house. In fact most new members are now not community-based – they live in their own accommodation and participate in congregational or house-based meetings.

Other leaders of Charismatic communities have compared the kind of commitment needed to maintain this covenant bond as on a par with marriage. In theory at least, the love and involvement with one another is of such strength and depth that it leads to a similar undertaking as a marriage. Where there is affection and fulfilment this kind of vow can provide stability and security and removes the transience known in other Charismatic fellowships. Where these are absent, persuasion into covenant can be a straitjacket that stifles individual freedom. If legalism – a code of rules that leads to strictures over failure – creeps in, members will sooner or later want to leave.

Making covenant signifies commitment to one another in maintaining and extending the followship. The intention is that it is for life, though JF is aware that people can change their responses as they grow older and accommodates to this. Covenant is intended to express the social relationships that derive from being born again into a new family as sons and daughters of God. Covenant provides a framework for belonging, expressing personhood without being rejected, exploring relationships, in fact much of what marriage can offer at the emotional and interpersonal level. JF covenant members pledge to:

- uphold the pure Biblical faith
- be loyal to the brotherhood church
- consecrate their whole being in service to God
- love each other in social equality, simplicity and righteousness
- accept suffering for Christ's sake and face opposition without retaliation
- accept wisdom and help from other members of the church with mutual correction, confession of faults, forgiveness and reconciliation
- unite with each other in the full bond of unity in Christ with an intention that this should be a lifelong pledge.

(Jesus Fellowship Church 1995; Flame leaflet no.12)

Covenant exists to provide full blown discipleship for those who are disillusioned with watered down Christianity and require something to give their lives to. JF would be embarrassed if they could not live out to the full what they see as Biblical teaching. However, they recognize that not all find it appropriate to respond in the same way so JF provides different styles of covenant membership with different levels of commitment. These are summarized as follows (Flame leaflet no.1):

- *Style 1 covenant members* have been baptized by immersion, have undertaken covenant, and live in their own home. They are equivalent to members of the new churches who have their own jobs and participate in various non-church as well as church activities.
- *Style 2 covenant members* resemble style 1, except they enter into a closer identification with the JF 'kingdom' culture in terms of time, finances and service. They retain their own house and lifestyle but live a life of simplicity, discipleship and sharing.
- *Style 3 covenant members* live in NCCC households, sharing all wealth, possessions and income.
- *Style 4 covenant members* resemble style 1 except they live at a distance from a congregation and cannot regularly participate in meetings.

As their circumstances change, members often change their style of membership rather than leave outright.

HOUSEHOLDS

Those resident in a community house comprise the household, along with those who live outside who are attached to it. Though the household is the basic unit of JF, the congregation is the focus for meetings. The local congregation consists of several households (residents and non-residents) plus worshippers who do not feel they belong to any household.

Style 3 members – those who live in an NCCC community house – have a routine and lifestyle different from those who live outside. Everything is put in the common purse[7] and the ambition is to overcome egotistical aspirations for the good of all. This means staffing the ministries of the church, being available to others in the house for companionship and support, and being willing to work for the house common purse either through outside employment or in one of the community's businesses. Members have to want to lay aside personal interests and accept a common purpose. Practically speaking all households conform to set patterns of consumption and activities to which the members are obliged to adapt. This is justified in terms of the scriptural injunction to forsake self so that individuality melds with others and a new identity is found in conjunction with the brethren.

Each household is led by several elders (always male) and other young men are apprenticed to them as junior leaders, known as 'leading serving brothers'. A senior leader in one household will oversee a cluster of households in one geographic region. For example the senior leader in Milton Keynes will also 'cover' – provide spiritual headship and direction for – the households in Oxford, Banbury and Luton.

The household is the place where pastoring, or 'shepherding', takes place – a practice now considerably diluted in other new churches. The apparent need for this is that more and more members are being recruited from the underclass, including those who are homeless, unemployed, drug and alcohol abusers – young people who have suffered emotional damage and have grown up in abusive and dysfunctional families. The function of a structure of authority, along with mature adults and peers in the household, is to offer rehabilitation and reparenting. The household restores family to those who have lost it, and is intended to bring emotional healing and personal growth.

The interesting empirical question is the extent to which this is actually fulfilled. For many JF is just one stage in a transient lifestyle. Some stay in their houses and initially respond enthusiastically, often being baptized and taking covenant. But not everyone can adapt to community living or to the wider fellowship practices, and a number leave. The annual drop-out rate of baptized (non-covenant, non-community) members is 30 per cent, but of established community members it is less than 10 per cent.[8] Thus the greater drop-out rate is among the styles of membership with fewer demands; the high profile Jesus Army activities succeed in recruiting a somewhat transient population in addition to new members drawn from other churches and second generation members.

It could be argued that the private, nuclear family does not have the resources to attempt such ministries – only within a community house are there the personnel and interworkings that permit such interventions. In addition, JF businesses provide occupational rehabilitation. JF does not, however, see itself primarily as a social work agency and any healing that takes place is in the context of building up a church. Where necessary social and medical agencies are involved.

Underwriting all this is a theology of the new creation. The act of regeneration brings the individual into a spiritual family that incorporates and transcends the biological family. This new kingdom family consists of mothers, brothers and sisters and men older in age who provide, among other things, a spiritual fathering function. The basic role within the fellowship is that performed by being in a brotherhood (for example, brother–brother, sister–brother) and within this conjugality exist the kin ties of marriage, uncle, grandmother and so on.

These familial relationships within the household are cohesive and all-embracing. There exists the possibility of the spiritual family taking precedence over a member's natural kin who may not be members of the fellowship and who live at a distance. At some stage each member needs to resolve his or her ties to natural kin and the fellowship. For example community members may be discouraged from spending Christmas (which is not celebrated) with their families. 'All we say is that we don't want family visits to interfere with normal church activity'.[9] Anti-cultists have claimed such practices break up the natural family. JF, on the other hand, has argued that many relationships with parents have been strengthened and that JF encourages (and indeed pays for) community members to visit relatives – including visits overseas if parents live abroad.

To move into a community house requires many adaptations and a willingness to expose one's life to a varied set of people. Spatially there is less privacy for the single person since bedrooms are shared. My experience is that it is a spartan existence, most possessions having been divested except for clothes which are kept in a chest of drawers adjoining the bed. Married couples have more possessions, and a room to themselves with separate rooms for children. Meals are taken together in the dining room, and the lounge is like a common room. Except for the bedrooms all areas of the house are common space, for mingling with other residents and entertaining guests.

Community living brings constant contact with fellow residents, often structured around church meetings. Tuesday evening is agape, the covenant meal together where weekly study sheets are discussed, there is plenty of worship and solidarity is reaffirmed. Wednesday evening is servant groups, with small bands numbering four to 12 coming together for nurture, evangelism or prayer, often house-based. On Saturday evenings, when there is not a main church celebration, house groups engage in worship and exhortation. This round of meetings provides a framework to which a member can be oriented. Mealtimes are also fairly structured, not a free for all, but an ordered time of table fellowship with sharing of news and a welcome for guests. JF believes wholeheartedly in getting together round the meal table, sharing hearts, relaxing and being family together.

This kind of setting has particular effects on marriage. The marriage relationship becomes more open to others, in the sense that much of it is lived out in conjunction with the other house residents. There is thus a private face of marriage, maintained in the couple's own quarters, and the public face which is represented in the common areas. Singles can be included in the marriage relationship in that they may make emotional demands on one or other of the spouses. Marriage is seen as a ministering relationship in which human warmth and Christian fellowship is offered to the others in the house, providing spiritual parenting for those who are emotionally damaged.

Healthy marriage and parenthood is strongly encouraged. Marriage is seen as a covenant relationship, 'first with Jesus then with one another and always for the sake of furthering ministry and function within the church group' (Flame leaflet no.8). Children are seen as finding security in the 'discipline and instruction of the Lord' offered by committed, loving parents. Where problems in child-raising occur, support and advice is on hand from fellow residents in the community house. Research at the Redeemer community has found normal maturation

and educational development among its children, but I am not aware
of any comparable research in JF.

All the children go to state schools. Early on, JF, unlike some new
churches, decided that it did not have the resources to run its own
school. Children play with the children of other household members.
Adults nurture the children of single parents. Older brothers may take
a same gender youth under their wing and act as a role model, involving them in house chores and work in the businesses.

There is particular teaching concerning males and females, each having
a specific social and spiritual role. Men and women are expected to
dress differently. Female dress is simple and modest with an emphasis
on non-sensuality, for example, no make-up. Gender roles are strictly
segregated. There is a strong emphasis on 'healthy manhood', expressed
in the range of employment conducted by the fellowship. The aim is
to recreate the gender identities of scripture with parallel occupational
patterns so that the young grow up unspoilt by the temptations of the
secular world. Of course, the only way a group can be assured it is
keeping to Biblical gender roles is to live in a pre-industrial world. As
we shall see in the next section, JF businesses entail largely unskilled
work, some of it on the land, though JF does not have an overtly anti-
industrial ideology and women take leading roles in its businesses.

JF is the only new church stream that advocates and practices celibacy for those called to it, claiming it leads to a full life for single
people. There are couples and celibates, male and female, and JF claims
both as high callings. A main justification for celibacy, following St
Paul, is that it frees a member for ministry, particularly in the unsocial
hours that Jesus Army campaigning requires. Critics have maintained
that JF teaches celibacy as a better or higher way and that single brothers
and sisters are pressurized into the vow, though I have not myself
seen any evidence of this.

A prospective celibate must be over 21 and enters a probationary
year before undertaking the commitment, which is assumed to be for
life. Celibacy is regarded as seriously as the ordinances of a monastic
order, and is sealed with a vow. Celibates have their own meetings for
support and to discuss lessons learned. Forgoing marriage means that
brotherhood relationships become more important, with personal fulfilment
having its locus in a same gender environment. The notion of brotherhood anyway means that those of the same gender will spend a lot of
time together relaxing in the lounge during an evening when there are
no meetings and sitting at a same gender table during mealtimes, occasions which I have observed can be times of natural good fun.

ECONOMIC ASPECTS

As people moved into the Northampton area to be associated with the JF vision, the initial pattern of community financing was sacrificial giving from earnings and savings. But as savings ran out, and with jobs less easy to obtain because of relocation and mismatch of skills, a new means of generating corporate income became a necessity – especially if the goals of buying new houses and providing for the unemployed and less well off were to be realized. JF decided to follow Paul's example of 'tent-making', supporting their own ministries through their own work. So in the mid-1970s financing through business ventures became a priority, all of the businesses being within a few miles of Northampton. In 1976 a farm at nearby Nether Heyford was purchased both as a focus for brotherhood and as a means of support. Some of the farm produce provided in kind for the houses springing up in the area, the rest being taken to market. An orchard was planted at New Creation Hall; later the Food Distribution Centre was located there providing employment for several members.

During this same period Noel Stanton's stationery business in Northampton was sold and the premises utilized for a jeans and health food shop – the beginnings of House of Goodness. A builder's yard in Towcester purchased originally to service NCCC house maintenance came to offer goods to the public, so bringing into being Towcester Building Supplies, while the house maintenance team developed into Skaino Services. An old lorry left at the farm was used for haulage. These businesses all grew during the 1980s and, although they have had harder times during the recession of the 1990s, still employ over 250 members.

This growth and viability was possible in part because members were willing to abandon (sometimes lucrative) outside careers and make their skills and labour available for the common good. Those who joined in later years were willing to be apprenticed into the existing businesses. This is not to say that all were highly skilled. But with the infrastructure of NCCC-owned land and houses needing renovation, many learned on the job. Newly learnt skills could in turn be marketed to outside society. Skaino, for example, now provides building, plumbing, painting, heating, vehicle repairs and gardening. This kind of firm is particularly suited to the working class male youths attracted by JF, who are thus given skills training and vocational rehabilitation.[10] Reflecting their egalitarian ideal, all community owned businesses are cooperatives and all are paid the same wage. There is regular paid employment for resident covenant members, who are given preference over non-residents.

Besides Skaino Services and Towcester Building Services, House of Goodness embraces farming, wholesale and retail wholefoods. As of 1996, there are two farms, the original at Nether Heyford and a later purchase near Rugby. The wholefood operation, Goodness Foods Wholesale, is based in a large warehouse in Daventry. In Northampton and Rugby there are outdoor wear shops which go by the name of White and Bishop. Medical, legal and architectural practices are run by members of the community but not owned by the fellowship.

Nowadays there is a well developed economy for the alternative new creation society. A career structure, training opportunities and ethical wealth creation are carried on in a climate of sharing, mutual aid and support. The aim is to extend the practices of brotherhood and sisterhood into working for the common good and to provide a non-alienating experience of work. Instead of life being compartmentalized, work, residence and spare time pursuits can be integrated. In-house businesses protect members from isolation in a secular workplace and from alienation, and provide the possibility of working alongside their own brethren rather than non-Christians.[11] There is also flexibility. Members can take time off for evangelism and church-planting, activities which are themselves financed by gifts from the businesses. The businesses are owned and controlled by the community through the Trustees, to whom they are accountable: a group of senior members monitors performance, spending and use of assets, and looks for new ventures.

NCCC operates separately from the church side of JF in regard to finances. As a fellowship JF runs the normal programmes of any other new church – evangelism through street work, marquee campaigns, local initiatives, church-planting, renewal weekends and celebrations. A separate charitable trust deals with these expenses and is financed through members' donations. The businesses, community houses and assets (such as vehicles) are administered through a non-charitable trust fund with trustees accountable to its members. All members are on an equal footing and none has special financial privileges or incentives. The senior pastor, Noel Stanton, has the same standard of living as other residential members and shares his life and house (the farm) with all manner of people.

SOME ISSUES IN COMMUNAL LIVING

Survival and persistence

Communes and other intentional communities, both secular and Christian, are known for their transience. Communities with a clear ideological or spiritual orientation tend to survive longer (Rigby, 1974; Coates *et al.*, 1995), but – excepting traditional monastic orders – even these often last only a generation. JF's initial founders, motivated by spiritual adventure and the 1970s' interest in alternatives, are now middle-aged and are looking to a new generation to instil a similar pioneering spirit into the movement. Whether, and if so how, they manage this transition to the second generation is surely the next chapter of their story, yet to be written. Noel Stanton's profile, however, is fairly low, suggesting that the eventual transfer of power may be relatively painless.

The survival of JF from 1974 to the present (1996), a relatively long time for a 1970s commune, has rested on multifarious elements. Unity of purpose and commitment has overridden conflict which in other groups has torn people apart and led to dissolution. Early on, the JF held together by a customized community theology which was passionately held though not widely known. Concepts such as Zion, brotherhood, kingdom and servant hearts held them together as they went through difficult times that included disaffection from within and criticism from without. In addition, there exists a clear structure, roles and organization reflected in organized leadership, agreed role performance in the houses and an ability to adapt to changing social situations. This is no hippy, do-your-own-thing commune that falls apart at the first whiff of dissension.

One key to persistence has been adaptability, particularly the decision in the late 1980s to become more open and to relate to other new churches, representing a desire to move beyond sectarianism to become a stream within new church Charismaticism (cp Walker, 1985). At the time of writing, JF appears stable, with numbers holding up well and a community resolved and hardworking, serving a growing penumbra of non-residents.

Egalitarianism

Communes, in their search for freedom and equality, have dissolved when leadership and direction were rejected. Traditional monastic orders, by contrast, maintain a rigid rule of poverty, chastity and obedience within – or alongside – the strict hierarchy of a historic church which may, however, lack both vitality and consensus. The social order of the monastic community is pre-ordained, and the individual must fit into it. The extent to which JF combines Spirit, consensus and structure has been hotly debated, with charges of authoritarianism and lack of democracy.

In the JF theology, everyone is equal on the basis of participating in the Kingdom, for all have the same spiritual status as sons and daughters of God. Consequently all are servants and overseers of one another, brothers and sisters in the same family. At the organizational level, of course, there are within the community different functions, particularly concerning leadership, headship and occupation. 'Elder', 'domestic sister', 'leading serving brother' all signify different ministries. The theology follows St Paul's model of the church as a body with different functioning parts, none of which can legitimately claim superiority over the others.

Decision making is hierarchic, with a group of senior leaders (once called the Covering Authority) setting the direction for the whole church, which devolves down to decision making at the regional and household level. There is strong emphasis on headship of male leaders at all levels, with the spiritual injunction for all members to submit to and obey all those placed over them.[12]

Within this community or *gemeinshaft* there is an interlocking and mutuality where leadership does not dominate to the extent that a member is unable to relate freely and make opportunities for ministry. This is reflected in the same wage being paid in the businesses, rejecting the worldly idea of demarcation and differential, and introducing onto the shopfloor the practice of brotherhood. In a community, however, in which spirituality is valued and materialism criticized, there is always the possibility that society's status hierarchy based on income can be replaced by a status hierarchy based on spirituality.

It has been claimed that members of new religious movements, having cut off contact with the outside world, may find it difficult to leave the movement. Barker (1989), however, has demonstrated that many New Religious Movement members become dissatisfied and leave within a year or two. That a considerable proportion of the JF community has been there for ten to 15 years notwithstanding its relatively open nature suggests that they are content with decision making and have no major reason to disagree with its modus operandi. How then is dissidence handled? Day to day disputes are resolved in the community house, the house elders having to deal with local and internal issues, and their success in this is one reason for the community's persistence. However, a small number of residents and a large number of non-residents do leave. Questions have been raised by anti-cultists concerning participation and the way members are treated. My personal view is that JF would have fewer people leave if information were disseminated in a more inclusive manner and if members were given more explanations. A key question dividing those who stay and those who leave is whether authority can be reconciled with equality.

Evolution and development

Cooper and Farrant (1991) helpfully identify different stages of fellowship growth and maintenance. The 1960s Charismatic movement provided spiritual power, and the early 1970s counter-culture provided a focus for outreach, giving an impetus for an emergent culture which dissociated JF from secular culture to provide a new social arrangement in which it could work out kingdom values and attract the unconverted.

The next stage was to embody this culture in community living. The Church of the Redeemer, Houston, provided a model that harnessed human potential to serve church ministries. JF saw how it could work for them and houses were bought in the Bugbrooke locality between 1973 and 1979. This removed them from social distractions to forge their new way of living, welding every area of life (except the education of their children) into a common whole.

The New Creation culture was in part devised to attract and hold bikers and others not typically reached by the churches. It took some years, however, for the community to develop to the extent that this goal could be sustained. By then JF felt strong enough to undertake evangelism in urban areas, and households were big enough to absorb newcomers from the streets who might be both disturbed and disturbing. The farm is the most successful example of this, housing around 30 mainly working class and underclass young people.

The community had grown without outside opposition, and strong bonds had formed. From 1980 to 1986, however, these foundations were tested by criticisms from both the secular world and other Christians. Members were unsettled, and had to re-evaluate their commitment. In such a situation, groups can introvert into defensive sectarianism or respond and adapt, and JF seems to have adapted. In this fraught period, with allegations from anti-cultists and attention to the way members fared, fatalities, failures and family issues led to adverse publicity. The community survived, though numerical growth was small, but the basic structures remained in place; profitable businesses were started.

In 1987 the Jesus Army was formed and immediately JF found its profile in major UK cities rose.[13] This coincided with greater openness to other churches and the entry of the church into mainstream new church life, particularly in worship in which features from Wimber's Vineyard and most recently the Toronto Blessing have been in evidence. Instead of retreating into sectarianism and becoming isolated from other evangelicals,[14] they accommodated themselves with wider Charismatic developments and thereby adapted.

Identification with the wider Charismatic movement meant better protection from attacks from outside the churches. The dominant ideology of the 1980s included secularism, individualism, privatism, even the non-existence of society, hardly the ideal climate for the JF notion of community. It is not easy to disengage from the rest of a society whose ideologies of individualism, materialism and the nuclear family percolate through from friends, relatives and other contacts in the outside world.

Adaptation has been the pattern from 1990 to 1996, and has worked in terms of accelerated growth of adherents and more recognition by other churches. The most significant development in these years has been the broadening of the membership so that now community residents form less than one third of the church. This may reflect a general cultural tendency against commitment to institutions. It has certainly introduced a new dynamic into the church/community relationship, and presumably if this trend continues it will dilute the uniqueness of JF as a residential communal alternative and total way of life. Also of major importance since 1984 has been the opportunity for members to change their membership style without having to leave the church, thus reducing the all-or-nothing dilemma felt by those whose circumstances had changed.

The anthropologist Victor Turner (1974) has pointed to the importance of relationships of social equality, but has argued that they can exist only temporarily and in ritual form – they cannot govern everyday life. He shows that attempts to institutionalize a new and entire society based on equality have all, within a relatively short time, either (like many hippie communes) collapsed or (like the medieval Franciscans) developed hierarchies of power and status. It may be that JF's most radical element – materially egalitarian but structured communal living – will continue to involve a decreasing proportion of overall membership, leaving JF as just another new church, with a largely non-residential membership and an emphasis on ministry to the poor. But of course only time will tell.

As with any significant social experiment, from an outsider's perspective contradictions abound: an ideology of brotherhood and equality coexisting with a clear structure of authority, a male language of brotherhood and fatherhood yet a membership that is half female, the attempt to retain Biblical roles in a complex late industrial society, the tension for married residents between commitment to spouse and commitment to the community, the sexuality of celibates, residents' relationships with family and friends outside the community, the community's use of secular culture (for example, raves) in evangelism. From an insider's perspective, however, the perspective of the new creation, these may not be contradictions at all and may simply illustrate the secular viewpoint of the outsider and the critic.

NOTES

1. The author writes as a participant in more than one of the communities described, periodically over 25 years. Acknowledgement is made to Mike Farrant and John Campbell for their comments on drafts of this chapter.
2. The National Association of Christian Communities and Networks represents a wide range of groups and produces an up-to-date directory.
3. Although JF history is documented up until 1991 (Cooper and Farrant, 1991) a full set of teachings has yet to be published. There is a comprehensive set of leaflets, called Flame leaflets, that cover key doctrines and practices. 'Living in the New Creation' (JF Church, 1991) is the clearest statement of JF doctrines, as taught to members; it originated in study notes for the weekly agape and comprises study books for new members.
4. This kind of social psychology based on open, trusting relationships is similar to that of a healthy marriage; see for example Berger and Kellner (1964). Walter (1995) has suggested that the caring mutual surveillance offered by Charismatic house groups may be attractive precisely because many do not experience such relationships within marriage. This level of surveillance may also, of course, be resented, both in marriage and in religious groups.
5. Brotherhood is a generic term denoting the quality of relationship for both male and female.
6. Personal communication from John Campbell, senior leader and JF communications officer.
7. For the Biblical basis and history of the common purse, see Saxby (1987).
8. Personal communication from John Campbell.

9. John Campbell.
10. General William Booth (1890), founder of the Salvation Army, also had a vision of healthy work on the land for the sinners the Army rescued from the corruption of industrial England. The chief difference in that Booth envisaged this not in rural England but in the colonies.
11. Bruce (1984) has noted how living in this kind of totally integrated Christian world can function to exclude alternative definitions of reality and enables certain religious groups to keep their members 'firm in the faith'.
12. Many other Charismatic churches emphasize male headship. Walter (1990) notes that these churches, like JF, are unusual in attracting at least as many men as women.
13. Religious groups that respond to crisis by renewing their evangelistic efforts have received much discussion by sociologists, psychologists and church historians following Festinger's work on cognitive dissonance. In essence his thesis argues that the arrival of converts assures existing members that they are, after all, on the right track. See Festinger (1964), Festinger *et al.* (1956), Gager (1975).
14. JF is not, however, a member of the Evangelical Alliance.

BIBLIOGRAPHY

Barker, E. (1989) *New Religious Movements*, London: HMSO.
Barker, M.K. and Beall, P. (1980) *The Folk Arts in Renewal*, London: Hodder.
Berger, P. and Kellner, H. (1964) 'Marriage and the Construction of Reality', *Diogenes*, 46: 1–25.
Booth, W. (1890) *In Darkest England and the Way Out*, London: Salvation Army.
Bruce, S. (1984) *Firm in the Faith*, Aldershot: Gower.
Coates, C. *et al.* (1995) *Diggers and Dreamers, 96–97: The Guide to Cooperative Living*, Winslow (Bucks): Edge of Time.
Cooper, S. and Farrant, M. (1991) *Fire in Our Hearts*, Eastbourne: Kingsway.
Durran, M. (1986) *The Wind at the Door*, Eastbourne: Kingsway.
Festinger, L. (1964) *Conflict, Decision & Dissonance*, London: Tavistock.
Festinger, L. *et al.* (1956) *When Prophecy Fails*, San Francisco: Harper.
Flame leaflets (1992), Nether Heyford: JF Church.
    No. 1 *Come and Belong to the JF Family*
    No. 8 *Married for Jesus. Marriage and Parenthood.*
    No. 12 *A Covenant People.*
Gager, J. (1975) *Kingdom & Community*, Englewood Cliffs: Prentice Hall.
Harper, M. (1973) *A New Way of Living*, London: Hodder.
Jesus Fellowship Church (1991) *Living in the New Creation: Study Books 1–11*, Nether Heyford (unpublished)
Jesus Fellowship Church (1995) *Church Alive*, Nether Heyford.
Lees, F. and Hinton, J. (1978) *Love is Our Home*, London: Hodder.
Palms, R. (1971) *The Jesus Kids*, London: SCM.
Pulkingham, B. and Harper, J. (1974) *Sound of Living Waters*, London: Hodder.

Pulkingham, G. (1973) *Gathered for the Power*, London: Hodder.
Pulkingham, G. (1974) *They Left Their Nets*, London: Hodder.
Rigby, A. (1974) *Alternative Realities*, London: Routledge.
Saxby, T. (1987) *Pilgrims of a Common Life*, Scottdale, PA: Herald.
Turner, V. (1974) *The Ritual Process*, Harmondsworth: Penguin.
Walker, A. (1985) *Restoring the Kingdom*, London: Hodder.
Walter, T. (1990) 'Why Are Most Churchgoers Women? A literature review'
Vox Evangelica, 20: 73–90
Walter, T. (1995) 'Being Known: Mutual Surveillance in the House Group'
Archives des Sciences Sociales des Religions, 89: 1–14.

7 'On or Off the Bus': Identity, Belonging and Schism. A Case Study of a Neo-Pentecostal House Church

Paul Chambers

> 'Now you're either on the bus or off the bus. If you're on the bus, and you get left behind, then you'll find it again. If you're off the bus in the first place then it won't make a damn.' And nobody had to have it spelled out for them. Everything was becoming allegorical, understood by the group mind, and especially this: 'You're either on the bus . . . or off the bus.'
>
> (Tom Wolfe; *The Electric Kool-Aid Acid Test.* 1968, p.74)

Despite the current high profile of neo-Pentecostalism within the church, the internal life of the Charismatic house church remains largely an unknown quantity. Attention tends to concentrate on the easily visible: ecstatic forms of worship, the remarkable growth rates of many Charismatic congregations and the often highly critical revelations of people leaving these groups. These revelations almost inevitably dwell on the high levels of control over individuals, often seen as an abuse of power, by the group in question. The recent media reportage of events in Sheffield with the Nine O'Clock Service is a good example of both these strands. In recent years there has been a move towards a more open profile on the part of the house churches generally but in many cases the public rhetoric of the leaders of these groups is, on closer investigation, not altogether an accurate reflection of what is happening on the ground. With a few exceptions, what has been written about the internal dynamics of these groups comes from theological sources.

The purpose of this chapter is to present a sociological analysis of the social dynamics operating within a neo-Pentecostal house church operating in South Wales during the 1970s and 1980s, and the schismatic processes that led up to its establishment and eventual demise. This chapter began its life as a paper presented to the University of Wales Sociology Colloquium at Gregynog in the spring of 1995. Originally, this study sought to illustrate how religious success can quickly turn into failure by looking at a series of events in a small Welsh town. It deals with how the presence of pre-existing social networks operates to facilitate recruitment or, in their absence, to inhibit it and also examines the structural constraints and strains within a group that might lead to schism. Central to this study is the question of identity in both its social and cultural forms, how this can lead to the creation and maintenance of distinct boundaries and the whole idea of being 'on the bus or off the bus'. Questions of power and control within Charismatic house churches and their distinctive control mechanisms are also addressed, particularly within the context of individual and corporate identity. Newly available interview material also throws fresh light on similar processes operating within other neo-Pentecostal groups operating in South Wales. Throughout, such existing theoretical insights as might prove illuminating to the data at hand are also incorporated. The original data is in some part autobiographical, reflecting my own participation in some of the events recorded. These reflections on my own experience were augmented by detailed conversations with many of the original participants and some of the material is a matter of public record. The insights and comments of the local clergy have also proved useful in gaining an outsider's view of what were often quite bitter local controversies associated with neo-Pentecostal activities.

Pontnewydd is a medium sized town situated in South Wales. Formerly the local market town it is now better known for its large industrial estate, which is home to a number of diverse manufacturing enterprises. The town now supports 21 churches and chapels as well as a Kingdom Hall, a Spiritualist Church and a Mormon congregation. There is no formal Jewish or Muslim presence. The town is unusual for its size in that it supports three chapels representing established Pentecostal sects and in recent years three neo-Pentecostal congregations have also been established and are operating with varying degrees of success. All three traditional Pentecostal congregations are long established in the town. During the early 1970s, two of these congregations, belonging to the Assemblies of God and the Apostolic Church, were few in number and largely comprised working class adherents. The third congregation, Libanus, associated with the Elim Pentecostal Church, was numerically larger and drew in roughly equal parts from both the working and middle classes. At the time, Pontnewydd could be said to have had a larger concentration of Pentecostal adherents than was typical of other towns in the locale. Libanus stands out as atypical of this period in that while other congregations in the town were struggling merely to maintain numbers, Libanus was successfully recruiting new members, many of them previously unchurched. As such, it was seen locally as *the* model of a successful church, and within their own denomination, as one of its most successful congregations in the field of evangelism.

This image was shattered in the early 1980s by a high profile schism within the congregation and the subsequent establishment of the first neo-Pentecostal congregation in the town. These events and their effects resonated through the town throughout the rest of the decade and beyond and coloured the subsequent chequered history of neo-Pentecostalism within the locality. These effects and the well documented controversies associated with subsequent events were not restricted to the town's religious community, eventually coming to the notice, briefly, of the national media.

The present state of the churches and chapels is not good. At best most are barely able to maintain numbers and in the case of the Libanus, it is now in marked decline. In order to understand the nature of neo-Pentecostalism in the Pontnewydd context we need first to consider the failure of Libanus, a church in the traditional Pentecostal mould and the subsequent establishment of the town's first neo-Pentecostal grouping out of the ashes of this work.

In 1973 a young innovative minister was appointed to the full time pastorship of Libanus, inheriting a church that had been only moderately successful in recruitment. His arrival coincided with the beginnings of a process of polarization within the congregation which was to work itself out fully over the next seven years. At this time the congregation was not dissimilar to that described by David Clark in his study of religious activity in the suburb of Oakcroft (Clark, 1970–1). Clark's study looked at class-based tensions within two Methodist congregations, and Pentecostalism shares many characteristics with Methodism. Both had been primarily working class denominations affected by the growing material prosperity of the late 1950s and 1960s. This had led to a growing middle class presence within congregations, opening up the possibility of tensions reflecting differing class-based orientations. Clark utilizes Robert Merton's categories of the *local* and *cosmopolitan* (Merton, 1957) to differentiate, on the basis of social and geographical mobility, between traditionally working class worshippers and the new middle class adherents. This distinction can be usefully employed in the Pontnewydd material, although I prefer to use the terms *traditionalist* and *innovationist*, as better reflecting the way that both theological and lifestyle differences were filtered through and mediated by class differences within the congregation.

On the one side there was a category of persons, termed traditionalists, representing the older long established members who often had antecedental family connections with the chapel. The prime movers in this group were predominantly working class and male with a power base centred on the diaconate. On the other side were those whom I term innovationists, representing a predominantly younger age group. They were often incomers who had been members of Pentecostal congregations elsewhere but who had moved or returned to Pontnewydd largely for employment reasons. As such they were both a socially and geographically mobile group creating a distinct middle class enclave in what had traditionally been a working class chapel. This group established its point of reference upon the new minister and one of the senior elders, a local businessman, both people with middle class credentials. In these early days, despite an underlying potential for polarization along class and lifestyle lines, there remained a common unity of purpose in the work of evangelism.

Traditionally, recruitment strategies had revolved around the Sunday evening Gospel Service and sporadic forays into doorstep evangelism. Given that the former was mostly the converted preaching to the converted and the latter was reliant on 'cold calling', it is perhaps unsurprising that these strategies had not resulted in much discernible growth. The introduction of special 'revival' meetings and evangelistic film shows were no more successful in attracting new recruits. This fairly bleak picture changed, however, with the recruitment to Libanus of one individual, a young man heavily involved with the countercultural youth scene of the day. Within the context of Pontnewydd, this was a loose social network in the town incorporating those individuals engaged in surfing, recreational drug use and petty crime. Up until this point none of the Pontnewydd churches had made any significant contact with this group. This was now all to change with the possibility of access to this new social network of largely previously unchurched individuals, which was soon to prove a fertile recruiting group for Libanus. As more individuals were successfully recruited from this social network they in turn utilized their social ties to recruit kin and friends. At the high point of recruitment in the late 1970s serious consideration was being given to purchasing a redundant 1000-seater cinema building to house what was seen as a rapidly expanding congregation. Obviously there was something going on here in terms of recruitment strategies that represented a radical departure from previous experience, not least in the remarkable success rate being obtained. If nothing else, recruitment strategies had begun to resemble something far more typical of Charismatic congregations rather than traditional Pentecostal practice, in that the informal social links of individual adherents were exploited rather than relying on collective formal evangelistic initiatives to bring in converts. Nigel Scotland notes that 'Charismatics have gradually evolved their own pattern of church extension. It is clearly a network pattern. People are drawn into charismatic churches through the social networks in which they operate the other aspects of their daily lives' (Scotland, 1995, p.262).

Sociological research in this area has tended to employ concepts of ideology and deprivation to explain why people allow themselves to be recruited to religious groups. However, recent American research (Stark and Bainbridge, 1985) suggests that interpersonal bonds between members of religious groups and potential recruits are an essential element of recruitment. Stark and Bainbridge argue that interpersonal relationships are at the centre of the recruitment process and membership spreads through social networks. Faith itself constitutes conformity to the religious worldview of one's intimates and final conversion is acceptance of their worldview. Max Heirich's research into Catholic neo-Pentecostalism (1977) traces the origins of this movement to a specific geographical location and a distinct set of friends and acquaintances. He notes that direct social relations in the form of affective bonds were a crucial element in the spread of Catholic neo-Pentecostalism in the USA. Affective bonds work by making a different understanding of one's personal experience possible and by the legitimation of this new understanding through the ties of friendship. Another way of looking at this would be through the concept of identity. Recruiters in Pontnewydd were able to exploit their erstwhile identity as members of the counterculture while offering the possibility of a new source of identity, that of a Christian, to their friends. Friendships, or affective bonds, remained of the one constant in this process allowing for the smooth transition from one cultural identity to another. Social identity, whether as friend or kin remained unchanged thereby lessening the anomic impact of a change in cultural identity. This was in essence the secret of the new found success in recruitment in Pontnewydd.

However, the nature of the recruits being gained from this loose network began to be seen as increasingly problematic by the Libanus traditionalists. The newcomers had been drawn from a milieu immersed in the counter-culture of the time and recruited by their friends or kin. A key constant was the retention of those affective bonds that had facilitated their prior recruitment and this ensured that the new recruits would retain at least a partially separate social identity within the congregation. As the new recruits were drawn into the orbit of the church there was a radical reorientation of their worldview, typical of evangelical conversion, but not in line with the normative expectations of the traditionalists in the congregation.

The reoriented normative structure the new recruits initially identified with and increasingly adopted was not that of the traditional Pentecostalist, but something much nearer in philosophy and style to the counter-cultural milieu they had been recruited from, the American Jesus Movement.

The Jesus Movement, an evangelical grouping which had appeared in the USA in the late 1960s, retained the visual elements of counter-cultural style as well as an emphasis on communal living and alternative lifestyle. By 1972, Bromley in London had become the recognized centre for the dissemination of these new ideas in Britain and cultural elements from this movement had also been coopted by some of the new Charismatic congregations in England. However, opinions within Libanus about the acceptability of this orientation were divided. The minister and innovationists saw the adoption of a cultural identity based on the Jesus Movement as essentially a half-way house for their young converts before their eventual full incorporation into the normative structures of mainstream evangelicalism. This relaxed position on their behalf was probably quite astute. The American sociologist James Richardson argued that the Jesus Movement, unlike the 'real' counter-culture, was basically a conservative movement, frowning on drug use and extramarital activity and fundamentalist in its theological orientation. He argued that it was more likely than not that adherents would eventually make the transition, probably as they advanced to the next stage of the lifecycle, to full incorporation into conservative evangelicalism (Richardson, 1977). The traditionalists in Libanus did not see it this way. They saw only a failure on the part of new recruits to acceptably integrate into the traditionally defined norms of the Elim Pentecostal Church. This was unsettling for them, as past experience had led them to expect integration almost immediately after conversion, which in their eyes was the hallmark of a successful conversion.

Increasingly, minor issues such as 'acceptable' codes of dress in church services began to take on the characteristics of major fault lines within the congregation as individuals began to identify with one or

the other position. These fault lines indicated a measure of strain within
the congregation that pointed towards a potentially conflict producing
situation. In David Clark's Oakcroft study (1970–1) the existence of
strains within the congregations studied by him were also noted. Significantly, both in the Oakcroft study and in Pontnewydd, interpersonal
influences played a significant role in the internal politics of the congregation, reflecting positions in class, power and prestige hierarchies.
John Wilson, in his article 'The Sociology of Schism', notes that
'schism . . . requires a structure that is susceptible to easy fragmentation' (Wilson, 1971, p.10). It was precisely the existence of fault lines
that contributed to the fractures that took place in Libanus and beyond.

By 1978, three distinct categories of individuals or reference groups
were to be found within Libanus. These were, traditionalists, innovationists and what we might term the 'radicals'. This latter group
was based around the young converts and those children of existing
members who were attracted to the ethos of the Jesus Movement. Each
group carried its own set of distinct normative values within a more
comprehensive set of congregational values based on evangelical principles. Progressively, each began to see their own set of normative
values as best expressing the evangelical principles the whole congregation should subscribe to. Even as the congregation was being held
up locally as a model example of a church which could effectively
recruit and hold young people the reality was very different, in that
schismatic processes were already in motion. Polarization was now
increasingly situated on the one hand in the diaconate supported by
the traditionalists and on the other hand with the minister and elders
supported by the innovationists and the radicals.

The traditionalists now became increasingly vocal about what they
saw as the worldly lifestyles of the others and these criticisms began
to centre on the person of the minister. Complaints began to be directed by the diaconate to Elim headquarters in Cheltenham and the
minister was forced to defend his own position and the middle class
lifestyles of his supporters. A number of failures on the part of the
minister and elders to adhere to the procedural rules and regulations in
the denominational constitution were exploited by the diaconate and
concessions were made to the traditionalists, leaving others in an ex-
posed position within the congregation. The cleavage along social lines
was now complete and a power struggle, over the appointment of one
of the innovationists to the eldership, developed which resulted in formal schism. The denomination was not supportive towards the minister and he left taking most of the congregation with him. Now completely

dominated by traditionalists, the rump Libanus congregation went into a rapid decline from which they appear never to have recovered. Conversely, the new congregation centred around the former minister and operating as a house church in the Charismatic mode, had at its high point over 200 adherents.

This new fellowship, which I shall call 'Dunamis' was the first independent Charismatic congregation to operate in Pontnewydd, incorporating weekly housegroups, and meeting together for worship on Sundays in various public venues. The church was soon networking with other like-minded groups, and senior figures in the Charismatic movement such as Bob Mumford were among the visiting speakers. Dunamis had now to all intents and purposes made a decisive break with traditional Pentecostalism, and given that the traditionalists were now out of the picture, it could have been expected that any strains within the new group would have all but disappeared. This was not to be the case. Two distinct categorical groups still remained, the innovationists and the radicals, distinguished by different normative orientations and increasingly demarcated along age lines. Whereas these two groupings had previously been united by the opposition of the traditionalists in Libanus, in the absence of this binding force, it is unsurprising that strains developed. John Wilson, in his analysis of schismatic tendencies within the Brethren writes, ' . . . strain was implicit in the movement from the beginning and members probably entered the movement on different premises – that is, with different assumptions as to just which normative patterns were implied by the set of values on which they all agreed' (Wilson, 1971 p.7). Wilson notes 'two distinct attitudes' (ibid.) and, really, he could be describing exactly the situation present at the formation of Dunamis.

The radicals saw themselves as more committed in their attitudes towards Christianity than the innovationists, who they suspected of an over-attachment towards the middle class lifestyle. As far as they were concerned, it was ideological differences that distinguished them from the innovationists. Conversely, the innovationists saw the radicals as enthusiastic but theologically and socially immature converts. Any differences, as far as the innovationists were concerned, were expressed in terms of social identity rather than ideology. Indeed, one of the main points of mutual incomprehension between the two groups was the refusal of the innovationists, on the grounds of the immaturity of the radicals, to take seriously anything they thought or said. This situation was exacerbated by the emergence of informal leaders within the younger age cohort. These were two musician brothers and a surfer who had recently returned from theological college, all three aspiring to formal recognition of what they and others in their age cohort perceived as their leadership status among the young people and co-option into the formal leadership structure. Increasingly these three came to suffer from status frustration as their individual positions did not improve and this frustration appeared to be progressively reflected throughout their age cohort. On the one hand, this group saw themselves as the dynamic element in the congregation, ideologically radical and still responsible through their access to outside social networks for the bulk of recruitment into the church. On the other hand, they saw themselves as a devalued section of the new congregation, marginalized from any experience of real power by virtue of their perceived inexperience and immaturity.

Given the importance of status frustration as one of the factors which draws previously marginalized individuals towards religious groups (Lofland and Stark, 1965), it is unsurprising that the denial of these aspirations for improved status both at the individual and collective level should set in motion significant strains. There is little doubt that before conversion these individuals had been marginalized in the town by their counter-cultural identity, encompassing as it did the three demons of sex and drugs and rock and roll and accompanied by a perceived reluctance to engage in gainful employment. However, they continued to remain marginalized within their church careers, initially because of their failure to live up to the normative expectations of the Libanus traditionalists, and then in Dunamis by virtue of their age. It was inevitable that the failure of the church to accommodate their expectations for enhanced status would create problems. Eighteen months after the first schism, following a full-blown polarization along the lines of social relations and a series of clandestine meetings held by the radicals, a second schism took place with the younger age cohort leaving to form a separate congregation, which I shall call 'New Covenant'.

Led by the three erstwhile youth leaders, New Covenant was initially committed to reflecting the ideals of the Jesus Movement. Tentative experiments in communal living and a highly democratic church structure indicated that the congregation might be successful in realizing their aims of establishing a new type of church culture and one that was appealing to those unchurched individuals who were alienated from traditional church and chapel culture. Significantly, women were now afforded equality with men and were able to preach and teach freely. The congregation still retained links with the local counter-culture and were able to continue mining this network with some success. In their rejection of the 'straight' church, they presented a very low tension model to this social group. However, recruitment was increasingly from kin and near neighbours, reflecting the changing social status of most group members who were marrying, purchasing houses and starting families of their own. The principle of utilizing interpersonal bonds for the purposes of recruitment remained in place, even if alternative social networks were being mined.

By 1984 the need to look to alternative networks for purely demographic reasons was becoming obvious. The counter-cultural scene was not large and only a small number were susceptible to religious recruitment. Adopting a conversion process model based on that of Richardson and Stewart (1977) we might note two sets of conditions at work. These are *predisposing conditions*, including an openness to the religious message and various forms of status derived deprivation, and *situational contingencies*, the interpersonal networks that initiate and act as a channel for recruitment. Conventionally, sociologists have tended to emphasize tensions that *push* individuals towards conversion, while my emphasis has been on the interpersonal factors that *pull* potential recruits towards a religious group. Both factors are of crucial importance in conversion and the latter is ineffective if the former are not in place. Lofland and Stark (1965) note that tensions are a necessary but not sufficient condition of conversion. Tensions only indicate a predisposition to act and they may be resolved in non-religious ways. Affective bonds, however, constitute powerful social forces, and as Stark and Bainbridge (1985) maintain, the crucial step in joining a religious group is the prior existence of or subsequent development of strong social ties with members. Put more simply, there needed to be a strong measure of trust before individuals would commit themselves to the group. This trust was exemplified by the commitment of new recruits and existing members to the prevailing group ethos and initially there was no sign of a cleavage based on social relations. However, kin relations were becoming increasingly important, particularly as they related to the leadership structure. An inner core coalesced around two family groups and their long term friends and increasingly the church began to resemble a large extended family, similar to the religious group researched by Hardyk and Braden (1962). By 1984 there had begun a collective reorientation from a low tension to a high tension model of a religious group. An expanded leadership, incorporating the female partners of the male leaders, began to adopt a progressively authoritarian stance. Access to television and radio was restricted and eventually proscribed, there was renewed emphasis on communal living, members were discouraged from having any social life outside the group and the group became progressively isolated in their social relations.

Whereas formerly the group had been relatively loosely bounded, their collective lifestyle began to operate as an impermeable barrier to the maintenance of normal relations with what was increasingly perceived as the 'outside world'. In characterizing this change from a low tension to a high tension model (that is in high tension with the world outside the group), we might usefully employ Mary Douglas' grid/group theory (1970) the better to understand the reconstituted social structure of this group. There appears to have been a definite shift to a high grid/high group model, in that there was both strong pressure on individuals to conform to highly defined roles, corresponding to 'high grid', and an increasing subordination of individuals to the collectivity and the establishment of a rigid boundary separating insiders from outsiders, both corresponding to 'high group'. The shift took place at the expense of the previously egalitarian ethos of the group, associated with a 'low grid' model and heralded the end of any significant individual out-networking, associated with a 'low group' model.

The leadership increasingly demanded the highest levels of commitment, not least in the area of ideological conformity, and leadership pronouncements were now presented as the outworking of prophetic utterances and as such, constituted the direct will of God. New Covenant now began to perceive themselves as somehow more in tune with God's purposes than the other churches in the town. Conversely, local ministers began to be concerned about these developments and began to perceive New Covenant as a deviant group. At this time the name of the group was changed to reflect symbolically this radical ideological and behavioural reorientation. Despite individual disquiet about some of these developments among what we might term the outer core of followers there was no significant cleavage along social lines and consequently, no collective schism. On the collective level, control by the leadership was so tight that the formation of parties necessary for schism was impossible and on the individual level, group members effectively regulated themselves.

This self-regulatory process seems to be characteristic of successful Charismatic congregations where the 'gifts of the Spirit' are operating, particularly prophecy. Prophecies are accepted as God's direction of the congregation and they operate in a process whereby they cumulatively feed off and bolster each other. Important prophecies usually emanate from individuals in leadership positions or recognized prophets, that is recognized by *the leadership*, and may refer to either the group direction, or in the case of 'words of wisdom', to the individual condition. Bill Davies, Principal of Cliff College, notes that generally within Charismatic groupings, 'Prophecies, tongues, interpretations, words of knowledge mostly come from the leaders on the platform' (Davies, 1986, p.101). This opens up possibilities of control by the leadership, either explicitly or implicitly. Useful consideration might be made of the work of Peter Berger as it relates both to the social construction of knowledge, the collective creation of what he terms 'plausibility structures' (Berger, 1967, p.134), and the way in which this process assists boundary demarcation and maintenance, through the establishing of a distinctive religious identity and worldview. In terms of social control, given the general dynamic of revivalist and eschatological religion, what we might term its linearity, that feeling of moving towards a goal laid down by God, and the psychological factors associated with this, then it becomes very difficult for individuals to go against what they believe might be a genuine move of the Spirit.

Objectors will either be perceived by others as 'not in the Spirit' themselves (or more forcefully, as having Satan working within them), or much more commonly, individuals will perceive themselves as not in the Spirit. This self-regulation is most pronounced in a revival situation where God can be 'seen' to be working, usually through the steady recruitment of new members. In the situational context of a successful church, therefore, where individuals are out of step, they are in their own and others' perception primarily out of step with God and not the leadership or congregation. What might be proper disquiet about developments is transformed into a *sin*, with all the psychological baggage that this entails. Only where the movement of the Spirit is not so apparent (that is, where the process of recruitment begins to falter or threatens to falter due to internal developments), will lines of cleavage form. Tensions are often a result of frustration and if God is seen to be working then there will be low levels of group tension and it becomes increasingly difficult for individuals to express their disquiet or withdraw from the group. This was compounded in New Covenant by the refusal of the leadership to allow members to hold 'strong opinions' (that is, for individuals actually to express their thoughts) about any aspect of the corporate church life and the equating of any individual reservations about leadership policy with sin. On the question of dissent, Bill Davies observes that, 'House Church members are encouraged to be free in sharing any question, but to avoid being contentious at all costs! The important thing throughout is the submissive spirit.' (Davies, 1986, p.56). The situation was further complicated in New Covenant by the existence of extensive kinship networks tied to the leadership. As Hardyk and Braden (1962) argued in their analysis of a similarily constituted group, this makes the emotional costs of challenging or leaving such a group particularily high. Both in the 1962 study and in New Covenant, it was those members tied by family links who were among the last to express their dissent publicly and defect from the group. Nevertheless, as recruitment became harder (a byproduct of the increasing social isolation of the group) taking away an important legitimating prop for the leadership's authoritarianism, people associated with the outer core began to leave the group in a piecemeal manner, either voluntarily or because they were ejected from the group for dissent. As far as the leadership was concerned there was no room for compromise. In their own words, individuals were either 'on the bus or off the bus'. It is perhaps telling to contrast accounts of ex-members relating the increasing climate of fear and uncertainty underlying the public face of New Covenant, with Gilbert Kirby's uncritical (and fairly typical of Charismatic apologists) description of the ideal typical neo-Pentecostal congregation. 'Probably the most striking feature of all about a house church is its atmosphere of love and fellowship. Only Christian names are used, members greet one another with a loving embrace and the atmosphere is that of a closely-knit family.' (Higton and Kirby, 1988, p.8).

With a slimmed down membership largely comprising the inner core, the final phase of the group began. A small housing estate owned by the local police authority came onto the market and it was decided by the leadership to purchase it with a view to the whole church making it their place of residence. This was financed by the sale of remaining members' houses and the taking on of a collective mortgage to convert one pair of houses into a Christian school for their children. Some ex-members feel they were coerced into this move, others went willingly but were given no choice in which house they were allocated or even how they could decorate it. Again there were also some individual reservations about the school itself. A common purse was also set up, which was later to lead to severe financial hardship among some families. The location of the estate was geographically isolated and with the absence of unchurched neighbours the group was now almost totally isolated socially. Given the central importance of networking in the growth of the church, this had profound ramifications for recruitment leading to a crisis of expectations among the group. On the one hand the group saw itself as especially favoured by God and thus the appropriate vehicle for revival in Pontnewydd. On the other hand, however, the bald facts were that recruitment had dried up and the other church fellowships in Pontnewydd were distancing themselves from New Covenant and its activities.

The response from the leadership was threefold. Firstly, a call for an increasingly rigorous lifestyle from members and a 'purification from sin'. Secondly, the mass adoption of a group of Brazilian orphans, which can be seen essentially as a recruitment strategy. Thirdly, the launching of a high profile moral crusade directed at the inhabitants of Pontnewydd. The call for a rigorous lifestyle appeared superfluous given that only the most simple of lifestyles was open to many families living under the austerity of the common purse. The mass adoption now brought the group to the attention of both the local social services department and, subsequently, the media. The negative impression that this created locally was further compounded by the moral crusade. This alienated large sections of the local populace by its use of extreme shock tactics, which included the house to house distribution of a newsletter containing pictures of aborted foetuses and the erection of a large banner across the main shopping street that baldly stated 'God Has a Case Against This Town'. These combined activities, supplemented by high profile street preaching in which the townspeople were castigated for their sinful ways, excited much comment in the local press and eventually prompted Welsh television coverage. Needless to say, none of this furthered the conversion of Pontnewydd in any way, merely increasing local antipathy towards New Covenant.

Despite the fact that there was now a high level of internal tension, associated with the crisis of expectations and all the unfavourable publicity that accrued from their activities, the level of defections was minimal. Ex-members cite the high level of emotional (and financial) investment they had put into the church, fear of judgement if they were seen to be critical of leadership strategies, intellectual confusion, family ties and the pressures of living side by side in community with the other church members, as reasons why they were reluctant to break with New Covenant. However, any defection at this point would have had important financial implications. The costs of the many church activities always put a constant strain on the common purse and many members had been encouraged to take out second mortgages to finance the shortfall. Even one or two families withdrawing their financial support was potentially devastating to the common purse. The stock market crash of 1987 and the subsequent rise in interest rates had placed added financial strain on members (some of whom lost significant amounts in the crash) and on the church finances generally. This strain became increasingly apparent in both the secrecy that the leadership adopted over finances and increasing disputes over the common purse that were breaking out between individuals and the leadership.

Members now found a critical voice and a mini-coup followed in which the two highest profile leaders were ousted and the common purse abandoned. However, many members felt nothing fundamental had changed as an authoritarian structure remained in place even if its effects were now muted. The crisis of expectations over recruitment remained, a situation exacerbated by the pressing need for new recruits to restore the precarious financial position of the church. When the end came, it came quietly and without much fuss. There was no major split, no formal schism as before, merely a steady stream of defections through 1988 and 1989. The leadership was no longer able to keep up the mortgage payments on the school and the bank was now pressing the church trustees for a settlement of the outstanding debt. As far as most members were concerned, the credibility of the remaining leaders was in tatters and the group collapsed in a state of exhaustion. Some individuals left to join other congregations in the locality, some moved away or dropped out of religion altogether. A small rump centred around the remaining leaders remained (basically four families) and these individuals have attempted, with some difficulty, to restore their fortunes under a different name and in a different location. Effectively, New Covenant had ceased to exist.

It might appear that New Covenant was a 'house church from Hell' and as such untypical of the many neo-Pentecostal fellowships flourishing in Britain today. Certainly, New Covenant *is* an extreme example of what can go 'wrong' in a house church but it does not necessarily follow that it was untypical of the house church type. New Covenant's origins lay in a fairly ordinary Pentecostal church, progressing through an unremarkable transitional neo-Pentecostal fellowship, Dunamis, into the final grouping, New Covenant, which itself did not manifest signs of dysfunctionality for some time. Nevertheless, in outlining the processes whereby New Covenant came into being it is possible to discern the seeds of its later failure as a religious group. I would argue further that this failure also reflected a particular structure common to all house churches.

The schismatic processes that worked themselves out in Libanus are what we might term of a general type, that is they may be present in any religious grouping (or indeed in any social group) and as such are not restricted to neo-Pentecostal house churches. The paramount factor was the structural weakness of the church, with the existence of three distinct categories of members creating dangerous fault lines and leaving the church open to fragmentation. Wilson's (1971) source material for his theorizing of schism is largely drawn from the Brethren and it might be assumed from this that it is highly pertinent to the house church, as both are organized along sectarian lines. I would argue that it is not, in that Wilson examines the origins of the Brethren and the fragmentary consequences of differing attitudinal orientations brought into the movement at its inception. Wilson's theorizing is thus pertinent to the cases of Libanus and Dunamis but less so in the case of a typical house church where ideological conformity is often (through the medium of 'commitment' classes) a prerequisite for membership (Scotland, 1995; Davies, 1986). The type of processes that Wilson outlines are therefore more likely to affect those congregations operating in mainline denominations, where Charismatics are present but where not all in the congregation are Charismatics. In this type of case we would expect to see formal schism along group lines possibly leading to the formation of a new grouping. More typical of fully-fledged Charismatic fellowships, I would argue, is the piecemeal defection of individuals or families over time.

Frank Pagden's study of Liverpool Churches (1968) suggests that the size of a congregation can affect a church's effectiveness and that too large a congregation can prove dysfunctional. He places the maximum size of a congregation at about 240 persons (the approximate size of Libanus and Dunamis just prior to schism), before dysfunctionality sets in. Recent interview material gathered by me from a schismatic Charismatic fellowship based in a Welsh city, suggests that growth in the church directly triggered schism in that the structure of direct control broke down, allowing parties to form within the congregation. Large congregations can operate efficiently but I would argue that there is an implicit recognition of the inherent instability of large fellowships within the Charismatic community. Kensington Temple, with an average Sunday attendance of 3500, has been responsible for planting 75 satellite churches in the London area (Scotland, 1995). Many other Charismatic fellowships are also committed to church-planting. I would suggest that apart from the explicit intention of evangelization, church-planting also operates to take pressure off large congregations, pre-empting the possibility of splits along party lines.

Within the Pontnewydd experience, there were particular situational factors operating. Returning to the idea of conversion process models which incorporate concepts of prior religious disposition, tension (including status deprivation and prior marginalization) and interpersonal influence, we might utilize these to explain the split in Dunamis. What appeared to be a simple intergenerational dispute was, I would argue, a failure to resolve preconversion status deprivation through the continued marginalization of the younger element. After the schism with Libanus, status remained a contentious issue. Status issues had not been resolved on conversion, they were only resolved through schism. This second schism can only be understood in terms of a conversion process model. The schism was in effect a collective reconversion process, incorporating all three aspects: prior religious disposition, tension and interpersonal influence, functioning to resolve a relative deprivation situation.

Conversely, it is quite clear why there was no formal schism within New Covenant. Structural innovations had created a tightly bounded body that was not susceptible to fragmentation. The tight kin networks made the personal costs of defection very high for some members and individual identification with the group was given particular emphasis by the leadership. Everyone was either 'on the bus or off the bus' and those deemed off the bus were given a very hard time by the leadership. To be off the bus was considered a very dangerous place to be. Increasing social isolation eventually meant no more recruits but there seemed no reason why the group could not have maintained itself given its tight structure and the self-regulating processes associated with the deployment of prophecy, both typical of Charismatic congregations. Nevertheless, the tightest knit group can experience significant numbers of defections if there is a major crisis of expectations (Hardyk and Braden, 1962), and the lack of recruits and increased financial troubles indicated to the congregation the withdrawal of God's favour and thus the legitimation for an authoritarian structure and costly lifestyle. Without this legitimation there was little to hold individuals as they began to question the costs of remaining within the group.

In examining how sociological theory might illuminate events in Pontnewydd it should be recognized that in essence many of the theoretical elements deployed might apply to any religious group, neo-Pentecostal or not. The question remains as to whether it is possible to generate a distinctive and generalizable theory relating to neo-Pentecostal groupings. I believe we can and that through this, we may understand how what might appear as an extreme type, New Covenant, is nevertheless typical in structure of most independent neo-Pentecostal churches. The recruitment processes outlined elsewhere would be fairly typical of Charismatic churches, as are the levels of commitment required.

The Charismatic congregation represents more than Sunday church attendance and is a recognizable social grouping with a distinct identity. Moreover, this is a group identity predicated on a shared worldview and a distinctive perception of what the church should be. This knowledge is encrypted in the practice of the group: Biblical teaching, prophecy, words of wisdom, confession and personal witness. This collective identity is carried in and driven along by a distinctive linguistic code that is largely unintelligible to outsiders and is typical of a sectarian structure. As such it corresponds to Bernstein's (1965) concept of restricted codes, which he identifies with closed social systems. We might consider restricted codes as a sort of ideational shorthand that is a system of both communication and control – what Mary Douglas describes as 'a common backcloth of assumptions which never need to be made explicit . . . used economically to convey information and to sustain a particular social form' (Douglas, 1970, p.55).

Douglas identifies two independent variables effecting structural relations: grid and group. We have touched on this in relation to New Covenant and I would argue that all Charismatic groups are structured along high grid/high group lines. For Douglas, the relation of the self to the group varies according to the constraints imposed by grid and group. For example, in a low group/grid context, the idea of wrongdoing is largely internalized, a matter for individual conscience and therefore relativistic. Conversely, the stronger the group and grid, the stronger the idea of wrongdoing which is externalized as *sin*. Douglas characterizes sects as groups where roles are ambiguous, leadership is precarious, there is a tendency towards schism and the group boundary is the main definer of roles. In a priesthood of all believers where leaders 'emerge', I would argue that roles are particularly ambiguous. In Charismatic fellowships ministry is open to everyone in the group, through the gifts of the Spirit. We might contrast this with most mainline churches where there is an unambiguous division of labour between religious professionals with formal accreditation and a lay congregation. The typical mainline church will have unambiguous relations and a loose boundary. Conversely, Charismatic fellowships are characterized by ambiguity within the group linked with very tightly controlled boundaries. These boundaries operate to reinforce notions of goodness within the group while establishing the wrongness and even danger of the world outside. Douglas argues that, 'The cosmic implications of God and the devil; inside and outside; purity within, corruption without; here is the complex of ideas that is associated with small groups with clearly marked membership and confusion of internal roles' (Douglas, 1970, pp.118–19).

This can lead to an almost Durkheimian picture where the group itself appears as an aspect of the Deity. If this seems far-fetched, a quote from an interviewee might throw this statement into perspective: 'the thumbscrews were put on in terms of agreeing with their proposals or basically you were not a Christian.' In this case allegiance to God was firmly equated with allegiance to the group, a common characteristic of Charismatic experience. Even other Charismatic groups can become suspect. Another interviewee describes attitudes to other Charismatic fellowships: 'they would be careful of outright criticism of other churches but it was always felt that **** was the place to be and no alternative would come up to it.' In interviews with ex-members of a number of Charismatic fellowships, one common element emerges. This is the overwhelming feeling of loss, rejection and anger that people experience on leaving. This remains a constant even where abuses of power and control are not readily apparent and it would appear that alienation from the group itself is the primary factor.

This returns us to questions of identity, both individual and collective. I would argue that individual identity is subsumed within group identity. Who people are and what they do is predicated in terms of the group and it is this loss of self-identity that is so traumatic. Simply put, people are ousted from the purity and safety of the group into the danger and pollution of the world, constituting a second expulsion from Eden. The effects of this can often lead to a total collapse of Christian faith in the leaving individual, where the group itself has been deified. Douglas' typology of high grid/high group, I would argue, establishes a framework in which to place independent Charismatic churches, a framework that reflects the essentially sectarian nature of these types of fellowships. It also allows us to distinguish neo-Pentecostals who remain within the mainline denominations and whose religious practice cannot be described as sectarian. The grid/group model also enables comparative theorization along the lines of identity, ideology, structure and group dynamics that is readily generalizable. Therefore the social dynamics operating in Pontnewydd can be viewed both as a particular case study of a Charismatic fellowship and, through the deployment of sociological theory, as a generalizable example of the neo-Pentecostal house church in action.

BIBLIOGRAPHY

Berger, Peter, *The Sacred Canopy* (Garden City, NY: Doubleday, 1967).
Bernstein, Basil, 'A Socio-Linguistic Approach to Social Learning', in Gould, J. (ed.), *Penguin Survey of the Social Sciences* (London: Penguin, 1965).
Clark, David B., 'Local and Cosmopolitan Aspects of Religious Activity in a Northern Suburb', in Martin, D. and Hill, M. (eds), *A Sociological Yearbook of Religion in Britain*, vol.3 (London: SCM, 1970).
Clark, David B., 'Local and Cosmopolitan Aspects of Religious Activity in a Northern Suburb: Processes of Change' in Hill, M. (ed.) *A Sociological Yearbook of Religion in Britain*, vol.4 (London: SCM, 1971).
Davies, William, R., *Rocking The Boat: The Challenge of the House Church* (Basingstoke: Marshall Morgan and Scott, 1986).
Douglas, Mary, *Natural Symbols* (London: Barrie & Rockliff, 1970).
Hardyk, J. A. and Braden, M., 'Prophecy Fails Again: A Report of a Failure to Replicate', *The Journal of Abnormal and Social Psychology*, vol.65 (1962) pp.136–41.
Heirich, Max, 'Change of Heart: A Test of Some Widely Held Theories about Religious Conversion', *The American Journal of Sociology*, vol.83 (1977) pp.653–80.
Higton, T. and Kirby, G., *The Challenge of the Housechurches* (Oxford: Latimer House, 1988).
Lofland, J. and Stark, R., 'Becoming a Worldsaver: A Theory of Conversion to a Deviant Perspective' *The American Sociological Review*, vol.30 (1965) pp.862–75.
Merton, Robert, K., *Social Theory and Social Structure*, 2nd edn (Glencoe: Free Press, 1957).
Pagden, Frank, 'An Analysis of the Effectiveness of Methodist Churches of Varying Sizes and Types in the Liverpool District' in Martin, David (ed.) *A Sociological Yearbook of Religion in Britain*, vol.1 (London: SCM, 1968).
Richardson, J. T. and Stewart, M., 'Conversion Process Models and the Jesus Movement' *The American Behavioral Scientist*, vol.20 (1977) pp.819–38.
Scotland, Nigel, *Charismatics and the Next Millennium* (London: Hodder & Stoughton, 1995).
Stark, R. and Bainbridge, W. S., *The Future of Religion: Secularization, Revival and Cult Formation* (Berkeley: University of California Press, 1985).
Wilson, John, 'The Sociology of Schism', in Hill, M. (ed.), *A Sociological Yearbook of Religion*, vol.4 (London: SCM, 1971).

8 Charismatic Politics: The Social and Political Impact of Renewal

William Thompson

INTRODUCTION

During the last three decades British sociology and political science maintained a consensus concerning Christian political activity. Labelled the 'New Moral Right', the movement supposedly consists of Protestant fundamentalists drawn from the declining middle classes who, motivated by status discontent and appearing during a legitimation crisis, emulated the US Moral Majority by bandwaggoning the rise of the New Economic Right (Hall *et al.*, 1978; Tracey and Morrison, 1979; Weeks, 1985; David, 1986; Levitas, 1986; Kavanagh, 1987; Sked, 1987; Mort, 1987).

As I have demonstrated elsewhere, this neo-Marxist reading rests upon a simplistic acceptance of the secularization thesis and a paucity of knowledge about the individuals and organizations involved (Thompson, 1992). Similar criticism can be applied to accounts applying post-modern imperatives for mobilization, given the previous consensus that fundamentalism was a reaction to modernism (see Poloma, (1982) and Durham's (1991) observation that all accounts underestimated the independence of the activists).

This chapter offers an alternative account, concentrating upon the religious facets behind the resurgence of Biblical based and motivated political action in Britain during the last three decades. Given the lack of research this is not an easy task, as even the best US studies frequently fail to distinguish between Charismatic, evangelical, fundamentalist and Pentecostal initiatives. Consequently, we need to establish a framework within which that enquiry can take place.

THE FALL OF FUNDAMENTALISM

Presumptions regarding the Christian activists' 'sudden' appearance and their 'right-wing' orientation can be traced back to the fundamentalist–modernist split in the Protestant church earlier this century. Those subscribing to *The Fundamentals*, a series of booklets condemning the modernist tendency in Protestant denominations, seminaries, and colleges, resisted attempts to refine the faith by incorporating contemporary scientific beliefs, such as evolutionary theory. The fundamentalists insisted upon an inerrant interpretation of the Bible; and either joined churches declaring for *The Fundamentals* or founded their own. Fundamentalists, therefore, were – and still are – to be found in numerous churches rather than constituting an exclusive and distinct group. Also, contrary to popular belief, they did not automatically dismiss politics as 'unworldly' in favour of individual salvation; the situation is far more complicated.

Between 1800 and 1920 evangelizing Protestants, as well as seeking converts, adopted two political strategies to help prepare and convert the world. First, they influenced social agendas about the family, sexuality and the corrupting effects of popular culture through a series of moral crusades: against alcohol, ballet, brothels, the low age of consent, contraception, dancing, erotic literature, gambling, ice-rinks and prostitution; and in favour of chastity and temperance (see Bristow, 1977; Thompson, 1994). As a result, evangelicals on both sides of the Atlantic effectively ensured that the state imposed a religiously informed social morality upon society. This cultural or 'lifestyle' politics had as much effect upon citizens' consciousness and actions as any class motivated ideology during the same period, as did the second strategy: 'humanitarian' social reforms such as the abolition of slavery, the introduction of mass education and the remodelled penal system (Lipset, 1964). While the first strategy has been simplistically associated with fundamentalist pleasure-negating 'puritanism', and the latter with the 'progressive' modernists, the two camps were not that clearly divided, as Wilberforce's dual interests in slavery and obscene literature suggest. Neither do contemporary evangelicals make the distinction (Stott, 1984). Consequently, though their post-1920 political agendas became another means of differentiating fundamentalists from the modernists, the former had a political tradition and were not inactive following the split either. What really needs to be determined is why the Pentecostals who appeared after 1905 did not take up the mantle of the nineteenth century conservative evangelicals.

One reason was the US experience, where the 1925 'monkey trial' destroyed the credibility of fundamentalism, and the repeal of prohibition inhibited lifestyle politics. The subsequent demands of the Second World War and the social effects of the expanding capitalist market and urbanization made fundamentalism appear anachronistic on both sides of the Atlantic (Simpson, 1983). Yet, if Biblical based political crusaders before the advent of the 1970s US Moral Majority were 'like prohibition . . . a vestige of the past [rather] than a vital dimension of the present' (Liebman and Wuthnow, 1983, p.1), the criteria being used to judge them were often suspect.

Another possibility, that conservative evangelicals, fundamentalists and Pentecostals ignored wordly politics in favour of personal salvation (see Stark *et al.*, 1971), has some validity, but it ignores the fact that most churches have been divided over political activism at one time or another, and that individual Christians' convictions are subject to change during a lifetime (see Brown, 1995; Randall, 1995). Even though contemporary evangelicals also speak of a 'great reversal' from social action, and point to disillusionment after the First World War and the rise of pre-millenialism, along with the other-worldly preoccupations of the religious middle classes (Stott, 1984; Bebbington, 1995), we have all been blinded by the corollary of the personal salvation thesis which argued that fundamentalism, like millenarian movements, being based amongst economic and socially dispossessed groups, would always be politically marginal. This theory is belied by the promotion of 37 anti-evolution bills in 20 state legislatures by fundamentalists between 1921 and 1929, and frequent Christian involvement before 1970 in various right-wing compaigns which provided political expression to commonly held Pentecostal eschatological scenarios (see Wood and Hughes, 1984). We also know that before 1976 fundamentalist orientated clergy were more likely to preach sermons on social and political issues than their, apparently, more politically aware liberal counterparts (Wuthnow, 1983). Clearly, much depends upon one's definition of what constitutes a political act.

A third potential reason is that internal theological disputes concerning priorities within the evangelicals' shrinking constituency after 1900 coincided with reduced extra-parliamentary effectiveness due to the rise of the British party political system (Brown, 1995). While this would mitigate against repeating the previous century's successes when 100 evangelical MPs sat in the House of Commons, fundamentalists and Pentecostals hardly needed to mount extra-parliamentary moral crusades when the conservative evangelical moral agenda laid down during the Victorian period was upheld by both the established church and the secular magistratory until the late 1950s (Thompson, 1987) – though they can be found fighting the odd 'threat' during the interwar period (Thompson, 1994).

THE RETURN OF FUNDAMENTALISM

In any event, given their origins, it is hardly surprisingly that fundamentalists and Pentecostals were preoccupied in the process of regrouping, proselytizing and creating culturally self-sufficient communities – stressing traditional family values, submission to authority, and clear moral guidelines concerning sexuality – based around a local church. While this could be seen as a defensive strategy expressing 'a sense of estrangement from the dominant values' (Gusfield, 1963, p.144), it should be recognized that this approach also proved to be a perfect preparation for entry into the lifestyle politics of the late twentieth century.

To apply a right-wing label to the re-emergence of those groups into what is defined as mainstream politics ignores the religious dimension involved. US commentators, like the British, favour anomic inspired mobilization, albeit more sophisticated versions point to the ability of Falwell and others to take advantage of the post-Watergate malaise (for example, Simpson, 1983). Yet, while such accounts can identify the moment, their rationales for mobilization are potentially misleading. What was new about the so-called 'New Fundamentalism' of the 1980s was its ability to transcend the continuing disputes regarding political activism in some churches (see Liebman and Wuthnow, 1983; Ammerman, 1987) convincing both Pentecostals and 'born-again' Charismatics to mobilize.

While the Moral Majority did work with the New Economic Right, even those sections seeking to mobilize Protestant Christians in defence of capitalism like Third Century Publications were morally motivated initiatives, as Bill Bright's Your Five Duties as a Christian Citizen – which encouraged entry into both party organizations in order to place moral issues on the political agenda – demonstrates (Liebman, 1983). Christian Voice, which enrolled 150,000 laypersons and 37,000 ministers from Pentecostal churches like the Assemblies of God and Charismatic groups, sought to unite existing single-issue moral crusades (for example, against the normalization of homosexuality and pornography) in order to make more effective their opposition to the immorality spread by the demonic forces of secular humanism

(Himmelstein, 1983; Liebman, 1983). Jerry Falwell's Moral Majority, which targeted the Baptist and independent evangelical constituency gaining four million members including 70,000 ministers (Leibman, 1983), aimed, as Falwell's book *Listen America* makes clear, to call America 'back to God, back to the Bible, back to morality' (quoted in Willoughby, 1981). And if Religious Roundtable brought Presbyterian, Methodist and Southern Baptist Ministers into contact with conservative Republicans like Jessie Helmes, it did so in an attempt to promote issues such as prayer in public schools (Guth, 1983).

Whatever political positions were adopted during the alliance with resurgent republicanism, which Jim Wallis and Sojourners demonstrate was not the only neo-Pentecostal option, no political mobilization could have occurred without the phenomenal rate of church growth amongst Pentecostal and neo-Pentecostal churches and the political groups' ability to convince the born-again to become politically active (Guth, 1983; Thompson, 1987). The British experience is no different.

From the mid-1960s and 1970s, the British constituency of conservative evangelicals, fundamentalists and Pentecostals not only grew, they were swelled by Charismatics in the old line denominations and the house church movement (see England, 1982; Walker, 1985). The importance of this Charismatic revival and input cannot be exaggerated for the emphasis upon the role of the Spirit and subsequent gifts enabled a common purpose across numerous church traditions. This was seen in the extensive platform-sharing during the yearly Christian festivals and the dramatic increase in both para-church organizations and neo-Pentecostal culture during the 1980s, which in turn was perceived by believers as confirmatory evidence that the Holy Spirit was at work (see Thompson, 1987).

Before 1971 overt Christian political activism, apart from anti-abortion groups such as the Society for the Protection of the Unborn Child, consisted primarily of The National Viewers and Listeners Associations (NVALA) which emerged from the 1964 Clean Up TV crusade. Growing to some 30,000 supporters by 1975, the NVALA lobbied parliament, initiated court action and collected nationwide petitions. Self-reference as 'National VALA' (pronounced Valour) reflected the organization's aim to defend 'traditional' cultural standards, based upon Judaeo-Christian values, which were under attack from 'permissive' legislation, the liberal Gospel, and secular humanism (see Caulfield, 1975; Whitehouse, 1977 and 1982; Thompson, 1987). Mrs Whitehouse's desire to see television 'encourage and sustain faith in God and bring Him back to the hearts of our family and national life' (Clean Up TV

Manifesto, reprinted in Whitehouse, 1982, pp.14–15) harked back to the days when the Director of the BBC, Lord Reith, used the Corporation to promote Christian values. VALA reflected its founders' coldwar generation political outlook, which appealed to fundamentalist orientated former policemen, returning colonials, aging pastors and churchmen, and earnest young youth and community workers who saw little difference between secularization and communism [see letters in *The Viewer and Listener*, Spring 1991].

However, with revival came change; and during the 1970s VALA's torch-bearing for the conservative evangelical tradition was transcended by the rise of the Community Standards Associations, reflecting increased political awareness amongst Pentecostals and Charismatics. Throughout the 1980s the CSA movement, initiated by VALA supporter Ms Whitaker, quickly expanded beyond her Cornish group as single issue campaigns in various towns and cities and became permanent organizations. Portsmouth's CSA, for example, emerged from an anti-sex shop campaign. The groups – whose membership ranged from a score or so dedicated members to hundreds, including whole church congregations – sought to change their local moral environments in two ways. First, they supplied platforms for national speakers such as Mrs Gillick, promoted Christian film shows such as Francis Shaeffer's *What Ever Happened To The Human Race* in evangelical and Pentecostal churches, collected signatures for national petitions such as the 1977 ABUSE campaign, and organized transport and publicity for national rallies. Second, they led vigorous local campaigns against abortion, electronic video game violence, teenage contraception provision, choice of English literature and religious instruction in local schools, pornography, prostitution, recreational drug use, and secular sex-education materials. While such issues could be seen as a continuation of conservative evangelical concerns, CSA opposition to popular Dungeons and Dragons games and pickets of occult stores reflected the Charismatic approach to spiritual warfare, and the 'modernist' tradition could be detected in Merseyside CSA's concerns for the care of the urban elderly, crime victims, offender policies, domestic violence, cruelty to animals and environmental ethics. A major political reconvergence reflecting active Pentecostal and the new Charismatic converts was apparent (Thompson, 1987 and 1992).

To secure their aims, CSAs not only addressed Christian and secular organizations such as PTAs, published newsletters, wrote protest letters to newspapers, and lobbied councillors and MPs; they also enthusiastically embraced radio phone-ins and TV studio debates and were not averse to directly intervening in local council politics. In Harrow, for example, one member stood as a local councillor on a moral standards platform, and supporters distributed 20,000 leaflets, forcing the other candidates to comment upon the issues raised. Worthing CSA also circulated some 47,000 homes during a 1980 local election (see Thompson, 1987).

These activities helped spread the word and began to affect their communities. Local councils refused certificates to films such as *Caligula* and *The Life of Brian*. Schools and colleges closed down 'evil' clubs and societies, and opened their doors to initiatives such as Portsmouth CSA's own audio-cassette presentation on *Sex and Personal Relationships*. Companies agreed to withdraw advertising from soft core pornographic publications. And CSA monitoring of businesses and organizations breaking the law, led to more than one police raid, culminating in the most dramatic episode in CSA history: the late Charles Oxley's infiltration of the Paedophile Information Exchange and provision of damning evidence at its trial (Thompson, 1987, 1994).

Yet, if the CSAs saw Charismatics and neo-Pentecostals joining conservative Evangelicals, it was the Nationwide Festival of Light's metamorphosis into CARE (Christian Action Research and Education) which demonstrated the extent and nature of Charismatic impact upon British politics, aided by the largest group of house churches, Harvestime, adopting a post-millennial position (Bebbington, 1995). CARE's origins can be traced to the 1971 Trafalgar Square 'Rally Against Permissiveness' and the subsequent founding of the National Festival of Light, which was seen by house church participants as evidence that God was working within the revivalist church groups (Walker, 1985). The NFOL enjoyed steady growth under Raymond Johnston, an Anglican evangelical; but became transformed under Lyndon Bowring, a regular Restoration Festival speaker and Elim church elder. Developing a comprehensive outlook and an American organizational approach, CARE went on the offensive providing extensive educational material, advice on political activism, and guiding political interventions by organizations of fundamentalists, Pentecostals and Charismatics employed in the medical, teaching and social welfare professions. Utilizing a 'mailshot' system for their magazines, prayer guides, resource packs, books, campaign posters, leaflets, conference notices, political briefings, and 'updates' on previous initiatives, CARE professionalized contemporary moral crusading. Their sophisticated handbook and briefing papers surpass anything ever produced by a political party or trade union, including as they do: theological justifications for campaigns, legislation briefings, relevant statistics, practical action checklists, as well as everything you would need to know about planning meetings, gaining media contacts, organizing press releases, and the best method to lobby government representatives. In the modernist tradition, CARE also practised what it preached: coordinating a nationwide network of Christian welfare programmes for the casualties of the permissive society (Thompson, 1987).

Collectively these three groups – VALA, CSAs and CARE – can take much of the credit for the Child Protection Act 1978, which outlawed 'child pornography'; the Indecent Displays (Control) Act 1981, which curtailed public advertisements for sexually orientated material; Clause 3 of the Local Government (Miscellaneous Provisions) Act 1982, which precipitated the closure of some 500 sex shops; the Cinematographic Acts 1982 and 1985, which eliminated the growing sex cinema industry; the Video Recordings Act 1984, which reintroduced pre-censorship; the new criminal offence of possessing child pornography in the 1988 Criminal Justice Act; and the 1990 Broadcasting Act's provision for a statutory Broadcasting Standards Council to act as an independent complaints procedure. The creation of the Broadcasting Standards Council to oversee the content of television programmes also fulfilled a long standing VALA demand.

In legislative terms this makes the British groups far more successful than the US Moral Majority, and this reflects the spiritual common cause held by Christians in the House of Lords, the House of Commons, and the hundreds of local activists from Charismatic, evangelical Anglican and Pentecostal churches involved in local CSAs and CARE groups (see Thompson, 1987).

MOTIVATION

When Christian activism is not dismissed as the ideological exploitation of moral panics initiated by others (Hall *et al.*, 1978; Barker, 1984; Ben-Yehuda and Goode, 1994), it is invariably regarded as an indignant symbolic political gesture motivated by secular concerns such as economic dissonance (see Zurcher and Kirkpatric, 1976; Tracey and Morrison, 1979; NDC, 1980; Sked, 1987). Such explanations rest upon Gusfield's (1963) suggestion that US temperance advocates were suffering a loss of social group status which they regained through a symbolic crusade seeking public affirmation of their group's values over those of their opponents. The link between status loss and religious mobilization is, however, undermined by the young, affluent, middle class origin of today's activists, not to mention their success. Likewise, their existing church affiliations would provide the personal affirmation of belief missing from the social isolates who do engage in symbolic political gestures (Wallis and Bland, 1978; Liebman, 1983; Toch, 1965; Poloma, 1982; Thompson, 1992).

Clearly, new explanations for mobilization are required and they can, ironically, be found in Gusfield's original theory. For, despite his insights regarding the role of 'status' considerations behind social movement mobilization, Gusfield was adamantly opposed to relegating 'moral' motives when they existed, and emphasized that prohibition's symbolic nature followed ineffective enforcement, not the crusaders' attempt to gain public affirmation of their values: activists did not use temperance as an agency for other motives (Gusfield, 1963, pp.32, 57, 121–2). For Gusfield, morals and status motivations were not a question of 'either or' differences, but part of the generalizing method of sociology:

> When we maintain that drinking has become a status symbol, we do not imply that religious movements were merely cloaks for status interest . . . A function of Temperance activities was to enhance the symbolic properties of liquor and abstinence as marks of status. This is not an assertion that this was the *only* function nor is it an assertion about motives. It is merely pointing out that as a consequence of such activities, abstinence became symbolic of a status level. (my emphasis; Gusfield, 1963, p.59)

In other words, religious beliefs can run parallel to secular motives and symbolic use of targets, and they can provide motivations outside and beyond economic and status factors. Consequently, those who ignore moral codes as value and norm defining belief systems and an impetus to motivation in their own right, and disregard faith in favour of alleged secular motives, are reducing moral positions to less than a justification, to the level of mere rhetoric masking the 'real' sociological factors. That amounts to promoting a latent function to a motivational force, and is an ideological position rather than a sociological observation.

While social–economic circumstances may produce a susceptibility towards taking social action, an individual's motives invariably come from within that person's own belief system (Toch, 1965); and for the religious, the values inculcated during their socialization and maintained by church culture (Thompson, 1987; Wood and Hughes, 1984).

The nearest sociology has come to differentiating between the two was the late Roy Wallis' attempt to understand how cultural and religious fundamentalism could merge to motivate a group like VALA (Wallis and Bland, 1978). His conclusion that VALA amounted to a movement of cultural defence was repeated in Bruce's (1988) study of the Moral Majority. However, Wallis' account still undervalued VALA's religious framework within which its members interpreted adverse secular trends, enabling Wallis to support a structural reading. Moreover, as we have seen, VALA represented a particular phase in Christian activism rather than the norm (Thompson, 1992).

EZEKIEL AND STEWARDSHIP

Whatever side of the Atlantic one starts, or whatever period one chooses, a set of common themes can be detected in the evangelical and neo-Pentecostal imperatives to mobilize irrespective of any social status considerations. Again and again, we see complaints concerning a lack of gospel preaching, the subsequent moral decline of a society, and the possibility of God's displeasure. These common laments, which undermine accounts prioritizing specific secular motives for mobilization, can be called the Ezekiel factor.

For some Christian activists sin is not merely an individual act, it is also a 'sign' of God's displeasure. The 'permissive era' in Britain, for example, is seen as a warning from God that we were turning from His grace; and it is believed that a failure to repent will ensure that Britain will go the way of the Roman Empire, because if one form of judgement fails to bring a people to repentance, other more severe judgements will follow (see Hill, 1984; Gardner, 1983). Such reasoning explains why crusaders like Mrs Whitehouse prioritize moral issues over the economic or social to the extent of even claiming that nude pin-ups are a greater evil than world famine (see *Daily Express*, 8 July 1986). In Charismatic eschatology, Britain's economic crisis followed the collapse in personal morality during the 1960s (Johnston, 1976) and improvements in public morality must precede successful public policies (Johnston, 1990).

The most important facet of collective judgement, however, is that Charismatics believe that Ezekiel warns that, no matter how devout they are, God's people cannot stand aside seeking personal salvation while God's judgement falls upon others. Unless they 'blow the trumpet', the blood of the fallen will be upon the believer's head (Ezek.

33:1–6; Johnston, 1990). Samuel's message for Eli is also used to justify the view that 'if the Christian knows of an evil and has the power
to restrain it, then he must do so' (Johnston, 1990, p.34).

Such beliefs and subsequent motivations to act cannot be explained
by imposing a socio-economic rationale upon believers, no matter how
relevant they may be, not least because the desire to avoid further
judgement by blowing the trumpet ever louder on moral 'signs' has
motivated Christians for over 300 years irrespective of class or economic circumstance. The fear expressed by modern crusaders is the
same as that expressed in the 1698 Royal Proclamation for Preventing
and Punishing Immorality and Profaneness:

> the open and avowed Practise of Vice might provoke God to with-
> draw His Mercy and Blessings from Us, and instead thereof to in-
> flict heavy and severe judgements . . .
>
> (cited in Bristow, 1977; p.18)

This Ezekiel factor, by linking private morality to collective public
good, has always meant that salvation cannot be a private concern; it
has to be public, collective, and national (Hill, 1982). As more
Charismatics become involved in contemporary crusading, another transcendent rationale – that of stewardship – is steadily replacing the
Ezekiel factor as a rationale for mobilization. For example, the Evangelical Alliance's recent contribution to political analysis, *Britain on
the Brink*, begins with the reminder that:

> Christians who deny social responsibilities and leave them to others
> are implying that they are unwilling to serve in the world as God's
> stewards.
>
> (Eden, 1993)

The concept of stewardship emanates from a Christian's obligations
of neighbour-love and the dominion mandate of Genesis 1:26 and 28
(Miller, 1992). It consists of serving others through utilizing one's
prophetic gifts, as Paul did in Acts 27. In general, this involves challenging the limitations of libertarian thought and the chaos caused by
pluralism in values (Miller, 1992). Politically, it consists of defining
and challenging the adverse social–economic effects of the 'cultural'
contradiction in capitalism between economic forces and social–cultural necessities such as the family. The most sophisticated, and influential attempt to apply this concept to date is Stott's *Issues Facing
Christians Today* which, including as it does nuclear, environmental,
north–south, human rights, and racial issues, widens moralizing way

beyond the 'New Moral Right' consensus (Stott, 1984). This ability to reunite fundamentalist and modernist traditions of social action clearly differentiates the British crusaders from the US Moral Majority, and has led to the possibility of a separate Christian political party.

FAMILY DEFENCE

The Christians' major public rationale for mobilization is 'family defence', exemplified by CARE's creation *Care For The Family* in 1988. Based upon the American group *Focus On The Family*, it holds countrywide seminars and distributes resource materials on issues such as parenting and teenage sexuality. Apart from reflecting the needs of the young Charismatic family, this rationale helps slot Christian concerns into existing political and 'rights' discourses, and it has ensured that the family is at the centre of political debate (see *CARE Magazine*, no. 2, Winter 90/91).

The British variant, devised by Raymond Johnston (1979) argued that families were not only the basic social and economic unit of society but provided the vital normative framework for monogamous sexual relationships which history demonstrated was vital for a civilized society's continued existence (Johnston, 1979). According to Johnston the family is under threat from the cults of individualism and feminism which had undermined the proper sexual division of labour consisting of the male's instrumental and women's expressive functions. The cognitive dissonance created by the subsequent social pluralism in values, ideals, roles and expectations could only be arrested by promoting laws which would: restore the concept of parental sacrifice; ensure that motherhood became 'the norm, the duty and the path of obedience as well as fulfilment for married women'; and enable fathers to reoccupy their divinely ordained patriarchal tasks (Johnston, 1979, pp.58, 60, 85, 87, 106). These laws – eliminating abortion, wife battery, child neglect and abuse, divorce, desertion, euthanasia, the 'glorification' of one-parent families, promiscuous sex and related diseases, pornography, and welfarism – were needed to ensure the non-religious complied with God's design. This 'declaratory or standard setting function of the law', however, could merely buy time as ultimate success would only be guaranteed by 'a renewed grip on scripture at every level of our churches', alerting Christians to their task of enlightening society, living the 'pattern of God' themselves, bearing witness, and adopting a 'renewed vision of the spiritual battle, one appropriate for our time', which included recognizing 'the demonic control of the unconverted' (Johnston, 1979 pp.115, 125–35, 144).

Convinced that Christian input over the centuries into society's laws and values had clearly profited the non-religious, Johnston and others hoped to revive the concept of the active Christian citizen engaging in active democracy and debate, promoting 'goodness and purity and justice' recreating the Christian social consensus which had been eroded by humanism and the crisis in values; for only Christians had the moral vision enabling 'coherence and identity and purpose' for the rest of society (Johnston, 1976; Schaeffer and Koop, 1982; Holloway, 1987; Johnston, 1990).

RIGHT-WING?

Placed within the context of Ezekiel, stewardship, and family defence, crusades targeting the 'public network of deviancy' that had arisen since the 1950s (Johnston, 1990) do not amount to a right-wing agenda. Trying to make them so, by pointing to the Moral Majority's association with the New Right and assuming British Christians vote Conservative, is difficult to substantiate (see Thompson, 1992). While Mrs Whitehouse has always backed the Conservatives, and Miss Whitaker has been linked with the Freedom Association (Durham, 1991, p.147), this reflects their generation's experience of 'permissive' Labour governments and left-wing pressure groups promoting permissive reforms.

The younger generation sometimes draw a direct link between their Charismatic experiences and support for the Conservative Party. For instance, Graham Webster-Gardiner believed he discerned God's will that he should stand as a Conservative when hearing an elder's prophecy at a healing service, and that the Lord led his friends – Dr Adrian Rodgers, Robert Whelan and Antonia Hopkins – to create the Conservative Family Campaign. However, this does not necessarily reflect the wider Charismatic experience.

In reality, the Conservative Party has constantly exploited the Christian crusaders. Throughout the 1970s, Ian Lloyd and the Conservative Lawyers Group failed to convince the Party that there were votes in moral issues. Mrs Thatcher only adopted her appeal to 'Victorian Standards' following the success of VALA's 1977 ABUSE campaign (McCarthy and Moodie, 1981). Once in power, however, the Conservatives merely offered the crusaders a legislative concession in time for each election in order to avoid the blatant contradictions between the Party's and the neo-Pentecostals' wider philosophies.

Unlike their US cousins, the British Charismatics do not believe that a free market automatically promotes moral responsibility. On the contrary, despite continuing debate (Chaplin, 1992), the Jubilee Centre (best known for its Keep Sunday Special campaign which brought Charismatics into an alliance with trade unions and the Cooperative movement), promoted an anti-Thatcher Biblically based economic programme called the Family Charter as early as 1987. Backed by 80 politicians across all parties this pro-family economic programme consisted of: credit controls; regional policies for lending, investment, and govenment contracts; family orientated personnel policies in firms with the government setting an example; more tax relief and allowances for family carers; tougher controls on takeovers and mergers to protect family businesses; and minimum Sunday trading (FamilyBase, 1987).

Once it became clear that the Conservatives, in blocking controls upon abortion and embryo research while extending licensing hours and Sunday trading, were unwilling to support the Christians' wider moral agenda, a search for alternatives reflecting the younger Charismatics' divisions on party allegiance began.

TOWARDS A CHRISTIAN PARTY

In February 1987, CARE issued a new briefing paper, *Becoming a Local Councillor* and extolled members to join a party, stand on their own account, or quiz prospective candidates on the 'vital moral issues': abortion law, obscene publications reform, moral education in schools, Sunday trading, financial support for marriage and the family, and an end to embryo experimentation and surrogacy. CARE groups were then established in constituencies to spread 'God's Agenda', with CARE arguing that party loyalties should be rejected in favour of any candidate who would support it. CARE's aim was to undermine the 'moral cul de sac of party politics', ending the period of isolation and mobilize an 'army of Christians' to go back into 'every area of society' (see *CARE News* Nos.17 and 18, 1987; Nos.19 and 20, 1988). This initiative, and the aim to increase the power of individual Members of Parliament *vis-à-vis* their parties (*CARE Campaigns*, Spring 1986), failed as CARE became involved in a dispute with VALA. Mrs Whitehouse and some CSA leaders were uneasy about CARE's willingness to work with Claire Short MP and radical lesbians. The move towards a specific

Christian Party, however, has since been taken up by the Movement for Christian Democracy (MCD).

Led by David Alton MP, this 'prophetic' interdenominational movement is endorsed by leading Charismatics like Gerald Coates. Patrick Dixon, the politically effective MD who influenced AIDS funding in Britain, believes that the Toronto Blessing is an indication that God is preparing the world for a revival that will 'perhaps . . . eclipse all others' (*Christian Democrat*, February/March 1995, p.16). Having secured public attention with their 1994 Video Violence campaign, the MCD's sixth Epiphany Conference at Stoneyhurst College in January 1995 considered founding a Christian Democratic Party after the next general election. Alton had had a 'prophetic insight' which perceived the possibility of a Conservative schism over European issues leading to a minority Labour government forced to grant proportional representation in return for Liberal Democrat support. This would then lead to numerous Conservative defections to the new party whose potential for success was apparently indicated by the failure of the Back to Basics campaign and Tony Blair's rise to leadership of the Labour Party.

Whether or not Alton's vision comes true, the MCD is heavily influenced by the Jubilee Centre's Michael Schluter who has extended the Family Charter and the concept of stewardship into a Charter of Human Responsibility. This promotes a 'free and just society' that is not in conflict with God and his creation. It does this by replacing the false idols of economic and material indicators as a yardstick for society's success with: a sense of responsibility to families and neighbours; an extensively resourced public education system; decentralizing ownership of large scale corporations; and focusing public policy around its effect upon improving the quality of human relationships (Westminster Declaration, reprinted in *Christian Democrat*, March 1991; *Christian Democrat*, February/March 1995). The model for this is the Relationship Foundation and the Mission in Hounslow Trust (*Christian Democrat*, February/March 1995); and the programme advanced is the closest one can get to the modernists' economic and social control populism of the early twentieth century. The MCD, however, admits that such a party would also involve creating a 'well-ordered' society (*Christian Democrat*, February/March 1995) and to understand what that might mean we have to turn to eschatology and Johnston's belief that the unconverted are demonized.

LIFESTYLE AND ESCHATOLOGICAL POLITICS

Far from subscribing to a simplistic conspiracy theory approach to politics (Durham, 1991, ch.9), contemporary neo-Pentecostals are entwined in a complex matrix of eschatological political analysis. Whereas Christian involvement in traditional political activity requires the prophetic gifts of the Spirit and intercessory prayer, eschatological politics stresses the discernment of spirits and inner-healing in an attempt to convince the world that miracles demonstrate the existence of God and the need to pay Him homage.

For many contemporary activitists the Bible not only provides an account of the past and the future in the Book of Revelation, it is also the means by which one discerns God's will about the present. The belief that the world and everything that happens in it is part of a spiritual war between the forces of Satan and the Christian community provides a dualistic bridge between the older Pentecostals and modern Charismatics, even if the former were apt to keep their demons to themselves (Walker, 1985). As believers defined this 'spiritual warfare' ever more expansively, political implications emerged from the Charismatics' attempts at interpreting Revelation passages and 'end-time' sign watching – the habit of recording and utilizing phenomena indicating the imminent return of Christ.

End-time sign watching has gone through distinct phases in recent history. During the 1950s, evangelicals and Pentecostals subscribed to the anti-communist or red scare, and subsequently opposed the United Nations and the World Health Organization because they amounted to the Anti-Christ's One World Government (Wood and Hughes, 1984). During the next three decades Charismatics contributed with an anti-cult crusade and rigorously opposed the alleged Hindu inspired New Age movement (see Watson, 1989; Miller, 1992). In the late 1980s, this worldview led neo-Pentecostals to campaign against manifestations of the occult, and ultimately led to the searching out of satanic ritual child sexual abuse (Pulling, 1989; Harper, 1990). Along the way, numerous social movements or trends which could be, and frequently have been, denounced as ungodly in their own right have, to a lesser or greater extent, been ascribed bit-parts in this 'sign-watching'. Opposition to rock and roll music, for example, has appeared in every phase since its initial denunciations in the 1950s as 'red' imported 'jungle' music to the contemporary assertions concerning back-masked satanic messages in heavy metal rock music (Pulling, 1989).

The benefit of using these multifarious 'signs' for believers is threefold. They avoid the more obvious problems which would occur 'when prophecy fails'; they enable subscribers to sustain unexpected defeats, as the final victory is assured; and they conveniently avoid doubts surrounding the perennial appearance of some of the more traditional 'signs' such as plagues and floods. It would be incorrect, therefore, to over-emphasize the anti-communist phase; although that does help explain, as Durham (1991, pp.168–73) realized, why some 'moral campaigners' leaned towards a right-wing perspective during the initial revival.

This previously unrecognized ability to link so many disparate trends into a systematic, worldwide conspiracy against 'traditional', 'family', or Christian values points to the fact that any and every target is conceived as part of Satan's opposition to, and his latest ruse to turn people from, God. In their own turn each target can be read as yet another 'sign' and manifestation that Satan's forces are mobilizing for the end-time. CARE, for example, see themselves opposing:

> the strong, invisible hold which Satan has in the lives of many, in many of our nation's institutions, and in those clear cut situations where God's influence and law is directly or subtly challenged
>
> (*CARE News*, No.15)

They are adamant that:

> Those who fail to take this spiritual dimension seriously, are those who give anaemic and ineffectual answers as Christians.
>
> (*CARE News*, No.15)

The social ramifications and political effects of such beliefs can be dramatic. Those involving satanic abuse allegations clearly reveal how Charismatic eschatological practice transcends the traditional terrain of political analysis, but can affect policy and resource issues.

During the 1980s, Charismatic anti-cult horror stories, deliverance practices (a form of lesser exorcism), the search for confirmatory end-time 'signs', and their ever expanding spiritual warfare hit-list was injected into the secular fear of child abuse to create a widespread fear of satanic sacrifice of children (see Jenkins, 1992; Victor, 1993). Thousands of families were adversely affected, social work agencies spent public resources that could have been used to help children truly in need, the courts and criminal justice system were overburdened while law breaking escalated, child abuse by staff in social service homes went undetected for years, and some of the falsely accused died (see Thompson, 1991; Nathan and Snedeker, 1995).

The core satanic scenario borrowed heavily from many previous conspiracies, asserting that there was a secret worldwide satanic cult kidnapping and sacrificing children while taking over governments, funded by drug running and child pornography. This evil conspiracy was being hidden from the public by Satan's legions including Masonic policemen who exploited the cynical secular public's refusal to believe 'adult survivors' and children saved from the Satanists by heroic social workers. Cases in the US centred upon allegations that in daycare nursery groups children were injected with drugs and were taken to other locations to be used as child pornography models and otherwise sexually abused by hooded figures, then made to eat the flesh or to drink the blood of other victims. British children were supposed to be endangered by their own families who in turn were controlled by top people in the local community.

Promoted by Charismatics associated with deliverance ministries, these satanic abuse allegations were fully endorsed by the Evangelical Alliance. With this support, proselytizers such as the Revd Kevin Logan, author of *Satanism and the Occult*, even gained parliamentary interest in his crusade against the 'Occult Explosion' (Logan, 1994).

US Charismatics sought to discredit the New Age movement through the satanic label to remove the First Amendment protection of satanic churches and outlaw the growing acceptance of Hell Week as an American festival. Having failed to outlaw 'occult' stores during a 1981 local government bill, British groups attempted to mobilize the forces of the state directly and indirectly in the service of spiritual warfare – directly, by convincing social service and police agency personnel of the validity of satanic abuse, indirectly by extending the influence of Charismatics in the medical and social welfare professions. As Dianne Core explained (1988):

> We're in the middle of the most massive spiritual warfare. The whole Satanic movement has decided to initiate as many young people as it can. We are at war. At this moment, in this country, Satan is winning, He's in the lead.
>
> Awareness must be raised. We're doing everything we can, causing reactions, receiving information, letters. If we can present a united front, and if the police support us more, I think we'd win. But often, the police deny it is really going on.
>
> The economic crisis creates fertile ground for recruiting kids to cults based upon despair and hedonism.

Satanism really gets hold where there is poverty and social deprivation. This is where the biggest harvest is.
I want Satan out and finished, He's causing dreadful suffering.

Core, whose Childwatch ministry was endorsed by CARE (*CARE News*, No.20, 1988), was promoting a self-fulfilling prophecy. Between 1988 and 1994 social workers invaded the lives of working class families living in housing projects, justifying their actions on the grounds that the children exhibited one or more 'signs' from satanic abuse indicator checklists supplied to them by Christian mental health professionals. Convinced that they had uncovered the proof that satanic victimization was a reality, social workers then subjected the children concerned to 'disclosure therapy' until they furnished the interviewers with what they already believed to be true.

Although this strategy began to fall apart in Rochdale after a concerted spoiling campaign conducted by half a dozen journalists, academics and child-care campaigner Judy Parry, British Charismatics still hoped that public fears could be mobilized against secular trends that were serving Satan's designs. The Evangelical Alliance's targets ranged from Halloween 'trick or treat' games to popular movies like *Ghost Busters*. VALA tried to exploit the satanic panic and similar allegations about 'snuff-movies' to justify criminalizing pin-up magazines (*The Viewer and Listener*, Autumn 1990). A video *Doorways to Danger* attacking 'the supernatural' was produced by Sunrise Video, and like the Revd Logan it asserted that there was a link between the New Age Movement, satanic crimes, and covens made up of 'high ranking civil servants, top industrialists and prominent city figures' who owed their wealth and power to demonology (see Logan, 1988, p.59).

In reality, far from emerging from the free and unexpected accounts of children or adult survivors, no allegation ever appeared before the intervention of secular therapists convinced that the allegations were true, or a deliverance ministry, as the Ayrshire case reveals. A later inquiry revealed that several Scottish Charismatic social workers, teachers, medics, and lawyers forming Ayrshire Lifeline, being convinced that God had called them to seek out a 50-strong satanic abuse gang across Scotland, turned a small family misunderstanding into a satanic abuse ring. Even the 'independent' educational psychologist who provided reports on the children was linked to Lifeline. By the time the inquiry criticized the children's interviewer's methods, this employee of the The Royal Scottish Society for the Protection of Children had exported the 'allegations' across Scotland. The dawn raids on four families on the Orkney Islands, following her discernment of satanic influence in another family, made international headlines, and led to public ridicule when it turned out that the satanic paraphernalia she had uncovered amounted to the results of a Sunday School exercise taken from an official Church of Scotland workbook!

While it has yet to produce the damage that satanic abuse allegations did, the Charismatics' belief in spiritual warfare also stands behind most moral crusades against popular films, TV shows, and fantasy games in Britain (Porter, 1986). As activists are intent upon seeking out the demonic channels by which satanic influence spreads (Johnston, 1976), similar campaigns can be expected in the future, and will demonstrate the continuing influence of religious beliefs upon the Charismatics' political targets (for examples see Thompson, 1992 and 1994).

THE FUTURE

Ironically, the recent emphasis upon 'healing' and the rise of the 'Third Wave' may encourage Charismatics to concentrate upon individual experiences, if not salvation, at the very time the possibility of a distinctive Christian party built upon neo-Pentecostalism has emerged. While Clive Calver, Secretary of the Evangelical Alliance, hopes that the new internal transformation symbolized by the Toronto Blessing could be accompanied by a new commitment to social action (Roberts, 1995), there is no proof that this is happening. On the contrary, the number of Christians who mobilize for political crusades has waned recently. As part of the initial launch, VALA gained half a million signatures for its Clean Up TV petition. This petition base rose to one and a half million for the 1972 Petition For Public Decency and the 1977 ABUSE Campaign, but has since declined to half a million for the 1982 STOPORN NOW and less than 400,000 for the 1992 Campaign to Outlaw Pornography (*The Viewer and Listener*, Spring 1992; Membership leaflet c.1984). Third Wave prophets also strenuously avoid discussion of worldly politics and re-emphasize the means towards personal salvation (see Wimber, 1985; Prince, 1994).

On the other hand their followers have been involved in the satanic panic which reflects the Third Wave's attempt to replace secular psychotherapy; and if concerns about excesses (for example, Jensen and Payne, 1990; MacArthur, 1992) go unheeded, such actions could have a dramatic effect upon future political activity. For example, British Charismatics have flirted with reconstructionism, a Calvinist trend which seeks to build a society upon God's law, chiefly by literally applying to today Old Testament civil legislation and Judaic law. (Enthusiasm for 'dominion theology' which has some similarities with reconstructionism is discussed by Paul Freston in Chapter 9.) In 1987, when Charismatic leaders met to hear a reconstructionist speaker, his reminder that this would include the death penalty for homosexuals was, according to Miller (1992), met with thunderous applause. CARE, amongst others, have dismissed this approach, pointing to the radical difference between Mosaic Law and the second covenant, but they do hold to the retributive role of punishment (see, for example, Johnston, 1990).

Consequently, when considering the future of neo-Pentecostal politics, much could depend upon the direction of the churches such as the Ichthus Fellowship whose 1988 March For Jesus led to the controversial denunciation of the demonic possession of the City by the Jesus Army (*Independent Magazine*, 8 April 1989), and the direction adopted by the Evangelical Alliance. The Alliance, which has brought the fundamentalist and modernist traditions together, has prioritized the traditional political path. In 1984. it funded the Leadership '84 Conference which brought together evangelical, Pentecostal and Charismatic leaders to consider political and eschatological political action for the next decade; to some extent emulating Religious Roundtable's Dallas Convention. Two years later, the Alliance distributed *How Much Longer Must The Silent Majority Remain Silent?* which included an overt call for Alliance members to take decision making away from 'politicians, doubters and secularists'. Economically, it backs the Jubilee Policy Analysis Group and hopes that the Movement for Christian Democracy will continue to link Christians across the political parties (Eden, 1993). Having the ear of over one million people, from the affiliated churches and institutions to its own groups such as the Evangelical Coalition on Sexuality, it is in a strong position to shape the future of Charismatic politics.

BIBLIOGRAPHY

M. Ammerman, *Bible Believers* (London: Rutgers University Press, 1987).
M. Barker, *Haunt of Fears: The Strange History of the British Horror Comics Campaign* (London: Pluto, 1984).
D. Bebbington, 'The Decline and Resurgence of Evangelical Social Concern

1918–1980', in J. Wolffe (ed.), *Evangelical Faith and Public Zeal* (London: SPCK, 1995).

N. Ben-Yehuda and E. Goode, *Moral Panics: The Social Construction of Deviance* (Oxford: Blackwell, 1994).

E. J. Bristow, *Vice & Vigilance* (Dublin: Gill and MacMillan, 1977).

K. D. Brown, 'Nonconformist Evangelicals and National Politics in the Late Nineteenth Century', in J. Wolffe (ed.), *Evangelical Faith and Public Zeal* (London: SPCK, 1995).

S. Bruce, *The Rise & Fall of the New Christian Right* (Oxford: Clarendon Press, 1988).

M. Caulfield, *Mary Whitehouse* (London: Mowbray, 1975).

J. Chaplin, *Politics and Parties* (Leicester: IVP, 1992).

D. Core, *The New Federalist*, 15 November 1988, p.4.

M. David, 'Moral and Marital: The Family in the Right', in R. Levitas (ed.), *The Ideology of The New Right* (Cambridge: Polity Press, 1986).

M. Durham, *Sex and Politics: The Family and Morality in the Thatcher Years* (Basingstoke: Macmillan, 1991).

M. Eden, *Britain on the Brink* (Nottingham: Crossway Books, 1993).

E. England, *The Spirit of Renewal* (Eastbourne: Kingsway, 1982).

FamilyBase, *The Family Charter* (Cambridge: Jubilee Centre, 1987).

D. S. Gardner, *The Trumpet Sounds for Britain: Vols 1 & 2* (Altringham: Christian Foundation Publications, 1983).

J. R. Gusfield, *Symbolic Crusades: Status Politics and the American Temperance Movement* (Urbana, IL: University of Illinois Press, 1963).

J. L. Guth, 'The New Christian Right', in R. C. Liebman and R. Wuthnow (eds.), *The New Christian Right* (New York: Aldine, 1983).

S. Hall *et al.*, *Policing the Crisis* (Basingstoke: Macmillan, 1978).

A. Harper, *Dance with the Devil* (Eastbourne: Kingsway Publications, 1990).

C. Hill, *Towards the Dawn: What's Going to Happen to Britain?* (London: Fount, 1982).

C. Hill, 'Address to the Order of Christian Unity', reprinted in *New Humanism* (Autumn, 1984).

J. L. Himmelstein, 'The New Right', in R. C. Liebman and R. Wuthnow, *The New Christian Right* (New York: Aldine, 1983).

D. Holloway, *A Nation Under God: What Role Should The Church Play In Public Life?* (Eastbourne: Kingsway, 1987).

P. Jenkins, *Intimate Enemies: Moral Panics in Contemporary Britain* (New York: Aldine de Gruyter, 1992).

P. Jensen and T. Payne, *John Wimber: Friend or Foe?* (London: St. Martin's Press, 1990).

O. R. Johnston, *Christianity in a Collapsing Culture* (Exeter: Paternoster Press, 1976).

O. R. Johnston, *Who Needs the Family?* (London: Hodder and Stoughton, 1979).

O. R. Johnston, *Caring and Campaigning* (London: Marshall Pickering, 1990).

D. Kavanagh, *Thatcherism & British Politics* (Oxford: Clarendon Press, 1987).

R. Levitas, *The Ideology of The New Right* (Cambridge: Polity Press, 1986).

R. C. Liebman, 'Mobilising The Moral Majority', in R. C. Liebman and R. Wuthnow (eds.), *The New Christian Right* (New York: Aldine, 1983).

R. C. Liebman and R. Wuthnow, *The New Christian Right* (New York: Aldine, 1983).

S. M. Lipset, 'Religion and Politics in the American Past and Present', in R. Lee and M. Marty (eds.), *Religion & Social Conflict* (New York: Oxford University Press, 1964).

K. Logan, *Paganism and the Occult* (Eastbourne: Kingsway Publications, 1988).

K. Logan, *Satanism and the Occult: Today's Dark Revolution* (Eastbourne: Kingsway Publications, 1994).

J. F. MacArthur Jr., *Charismatic Chaos* (Grand Rapids, MI: Zondervan, 1992).

M. A. McCarthy and R. A. Moodie, 'Parliament and Pornography: The 1978 Child Protection Act', *Parliamentary Affairs*, Vol.XXXIV, 1 (1981).

P. Miller, *Into The Arena* (Eastbourne: Kingsway, 1992).

F. Mort, *Dangerous Sexualities* (London: Routledge and Kegan Paul, 1987).

D. Nathan and M. Snedeker, *Satan's Silence: Ritual Abuse and The Making of a Modern American Witch Hunt* (New York: Basic Books, 1995).

National Deviancy Conference, *Permissiveness and Control* (London: Macmillan, 1980).

M. Poloma, *The Charismatic Movement: Is There A New Pentecost?* (Boston: Twayne, 1982).

D. Porter, *Children at Risk: Who Will Protect Our Children in the Modern Age?* (Eastbourne: Kingsway, 1986).

D. Prince, *The Spirit Filled Believers Handbook: Foundations For Christian Living From the Bible* (Milton Keynes: Nelson Word Ltd, 1994).

P. Pulling, *The Devil's Web* (Lafayette: Huntingdon House, 1989).

I. M. Randall, 'The Social Gospel: A Case Study', in J. Wolffe (ed.) *Evangelical Faith and Public Zeal* (London: SPCK, 1995).

D. Roberts, *The Toronto Blessing* (Eastbourne: Kingsway, 1995).

F. A. Schaeffer and E. M. D. Koop, *Whatever Happened to the Human Race?* (London: Marshall, 1982).

J. H. Simpson, 'Moral Issues & Status Politics', in R. C. Liebman and R. Wuthnow (eds.), *The New Christian Right* (New York: Aldine, 1983).

A. Sked, *Britain's Decline* (Oxford: Basil Blackwell, 1987).

R. Stark *et al., Wayward Shepherds: Prejudice and the Protestant Clergy* (New York: Harper and Row, 1971).

J. Stott, *Issues Facing Christians Today* (Basingstoke: Marshalls, 1984).

W. Thompson, 'PornWars: Moral Crusades, Pornography, and Social Policy', (Unpub. PhD Thesis: Essex University, England, 1987).

W. Thompson, 'Moral Crusades and Media Censorship', *Franco-British Journal* No.9, Paris (1990).

W. Thompson, 'Snuff, Sex and Satan: The Social Construction of Satanic Ritual Sex Abuse', (Unpub. paper presented at BSA conference, Manchester, 1991).

W. Thompson, 'Britain's Moral Majority', in B. Wilson, *Religious Contemporary Issues: The All Souls Seminars in the Sociology of Religion* (London: Bellew Publishers, 1992).

W. Thompson, *Softcore* (London: Cassell, 1994).

H. Toch, *The Social Psychology of Social Movements* (London: OUP, 1965).

M. Tracey and D. Morrison, *Whitehouse* (London: Papermac, 1979).

J. Victor, *Satanic Panic: The Creation of a Contemporary Legend* (Chicago: Open Court, 1993).

A. Walker, *Restoring The Kingdom* (London: Hodder and Stoughton, 1985).

R. Wallis and R. Bland, 'Who Rallied to the Call?', *New Humanist* (Autumn, 1978).

D. Watson, *Hidden Warfare: Conquering in the Spiritual Conflict* (Eastbourne: Kingsway Publications, 1989).

J. Weeks, *Sexuality and its Discontents* (London: RKP, 1985).

M. Whitehouse, *Whatever Happened to Sex?* (Hove: Wayland, 1977).

M. Whitehouse, *A Most Dangerous Woman* (Tring: Lion, 1982).

M. Whitehouse, *Mightier than the Sword* (Eastbourne: Kingsway, 1985).

W. Willoughby, *Does America Need a Moral Majority?* (Plainfield: Haven Books, 1981).

J. Wimber, *Power Evangelism: Signs and Wonders Today* (London: Hodder and Stoughton, 1985).

M. Wood and M. Hughes, 'The Moral Basis of Moral Reform', *American Sociological Review*, vol.49, pp.86–99 (1984).

R. Wuthnow, 'The Political Rebirth of American Evangelicals', in R. C. Liebman and R. Wuthnow (eds.), *The New Christian Right* (New York: Aldine, 1983).

L. A. Zurcher and R. G. Kirkpatrick, *Citizens for Decency: Anti Pornography Crusades as Status Defence* (Austin: Texas University Press, 1976).

Magazines

Care Campaigns
CARE News
Christian Democrat
Prophecy Today
The Viewer and Listener

9 Charismatic Evangelicals in Latin America: Mission and Politics on the Frontiers of Protestant Growth

Paul Freston

'God is, therefore he thinks', proclaimed posters in Oxford. The New Life Christian Church, recently arrived in one of the ancient seats of learning, advertised the visit of an Argentine evangelist, stressing that 'we belong to a family of churches from the UK, France, Spain, Portugal, Italy and South America'. The South American connection was the important one. Under the name of Ríos de Vida, the church had begun in Argentina in 1967 with young people newly baptized in the Spirit. Now with 40 churches in its homeland, it has spread to Europe (15 churches). Its apostolic leadership, predominantly Argentine, is international in composition. Two-way international contacts abound in the church's history: American missionaries played a facilitating role early on, and British Restorationist Arthur Wallis later collaborated in campaigns; in Europe, the Argentine leaders have preached in many countries. Another characteristic has been social work amongst the disadvantaged. Now, under a lay English university-educated man and his Argentine wife, Ríos de Vida takes its first steps in Oxford's competitive religious marketplace.

CHARISMATIC EVANGELICALISM: A GLOBALIZED RELIGION

Ríos de Vida is one example of a growing phenomenon: the international reach of Latin American Charismatic churches. The complex global dimension of Charismatic Christianity is coming to be appreciated. For example, the traditional history of origins (the Renewal started in 1960 in California with Dennis Bennett) is unsatisfying to anyone familiar with similar phenomena in Brazil, where Baptist pastors were preaching Spirit-baptism by the late 1950s. Poewe makes a scathing attack on parochial interpretations, whether propagated by American supporters or non-American academic critics. '"The beginning" is an American media-event [since Bennett's story reached *Time*], and has nothing to do with the actual history of worldwide Charismatic Christianity' (Poewe, 1994a:4). One might rather refer to the Renewal among black Anglicans in South Africa in the 1940s, usually ignored because preserved in oral history and because 'Americans have the resources to publish developments in their country . . . before those of other countries' (Hexham and Poewe, 1994:62). We may add Hollenweger's observation about English being only a secondary language among the world's Pentecostals–Charismatics (1994:207). The point is that the origins of a phenomenon (which may be anywhere or nowhere) must be distinguished from the (usually American) power to 'globalize' knowledge of it.

Similarly, Charismaticism is often portrayed as spreading from the US; in some versions, as part of an agenda to make Third World people more subservient to American interests. But as Hexham and Poewe counter, 'a multisource diffusion of parallel developments encompasses Europe, Africa, America and Asia' (1994:61). New churches are local expressions of a global culture, characterized by parallel invention, complex diffusion and international networks with multilateral flows. This is what globalization theory, which talks of 'the complexity of global cultural flows', leads us to expect. 'There is little prospect of a unified global culture, rather there are global cultures in the plural' (Featherstone, 1990:10).

Seeing Charismaticism as one of these global cultures helps avoid parochial interpretations. Discussions about religion under globalization must take into account what has happened to Christianity in recent decades: recession in Europe and stagnation (masked by political and media activity) in the US have been countered by the expansion of evangelicalism (at the expense largely of nominal Catholicism) in Latin America and impressive growth of all forms of Christianity in Africa and the Far East. The constitution of a global Christianity, largely Pentecostal–Charismatic, is often ignored because it has occurred mostly independently of western initiatives. The Toronto Blessing is interpreted in other chapters of this book as a craze (Walker) or a desperate search for the end-time revival posited by Restorationism (Richter), but similar fads in Brazil (such as the gold teeth fillings in believers' mouths from 1992 to 1994, interpreted as divine blessing) occur in the context of rapid growth and are explained more by the lack of an existential project for the individual believer.

Walker asks whether Charismaticism has become decadent, and whether Toronto has been not a new beginning but a last gasp. 'Pentecostalism rushed into [existence] like a hurricane at Azusa Street . . . Perhaps it has finally blown itself out at Toronto . . . We must ask whether Charismatic Christianity is well-equipped to survive in [post-modernity]. Of course, Pentecostalism will continue to be thoroughly modern in the Third World for some time to come . . .'. In reply, we must stress that no analysis of the global future can treat the Third World (two-thirds of the world's population and a majority of its Christians) as a passing appendix rather than a sign of the times. It is parochial to imagine that what happens in Anglo-Saxon evangelicalism is still determinant globally. Huge swathes of Charismaticism are hardly touched by Toronto. In Brazil (the largest evangelical community in the world after the US), it is better known through a hostile television documentary than through its impact in the churches. Argentina, on the other hand, had it before Toronto (I heard about it in Buenos Aires in 1993) – an example of how the North American church's resources enable it to 'expropriate' phenomena from elsewhere and ensure their globalization, or else to globalize their own parallel inventions.

Why is Charismatic evangelicalism successful as a global culture? Its evangelical nature may be part of the answer. The future of religion lies not only in association with localist opposition to globalizing trends, but also as personal choice within the thrust of globalization itself. Martin (1995) sees the salvageable essence of secularization theory as the process of social differentiation which breaks up monopolies, leading to a pluralism which vitalizes the religious field by competition. In this context, which characterizes ever larger parts of the globe, of individualism centred on expression of the self and putting together of fragments of traditions, evangelicalism seems better equipped to flourish, since it takes elements of expressive individualism but controls them with moral obligation and community loyalty.

Another factor is the 'translatability' (Sanneh) of Charismatic Christianity. It is not the abstract and elitist 'cosmic Christ' but the Jesus of the gospels and the Charismatic outpourings of the Acts of the Apostles which despite (or because of) their cultural rootedness seem able to found a global theology. In alliance with ecstatic worship which draws on primal religiosity, this theology has the same capacity as jazz to be truly universal and to sound indigenous wherever it is found (Cox, 1996:146).

Christianity has always had a global project, and its Pentecostal–Charismatic version was the most likely to spread once the Third World had indigenized the faith. If post-modernity is essentially 'incredulity towards metanarratives' (Lyotard), then the globalization of Charismaticism, perhaps the fastest growing metanarrative in the world, questions all Eurocentric interpretations of our future.

THE IMPORTANCE OF CHARISMATIC EVANGELICALISM IN LATIN AMERICA

Pentecostal–Charismatic Christianity is still marginal to church life in the developed west, but in Latin America it is central. Studies of Protestantism there distinguish Pentecostals–Charismatics and historicals (non-Pentecostals in churches of immigrant or missionary origin). Pentecostals have been present since 1909. Rapid growth in Chile and Brazil dates from the 1950s; by the 1980s it was continent-wide.

Protestants now constitute 10 per cent of Latin Americans. Brazil, 15 per cent Protestant, leads in absolute numbers (25 million). Guatemala, El Salvador and Chile are higher in percentage terms. Pentecostals–Charismatics are two-thirds of all Latin American Protestants.

In Rio de Janeiro (Fernandes, 1992) one new evangelical church (nearly all Protestants are evangelicals in Latin America) is registered per day. Evangelical churches outnumber Catholic ones; in the poorest districts, the ratio is 7:1. Of new churches registered in 1990 to 1992, 91 per cent are Pentecostal–Charismatic. Of the 52 largest denominations, 37 are of Brazilian origin, virtually all Pentecostal–Charismatic. Evangelicalism is national, popular and rapidly expanding.

I have elsewhere treated predominantly lower class Pentecostalism. Here, I shall talk of predominantly middle class Charismatic evangelicalism,[1] in its various forms: within the historical churches, in independent 'communities' and in transdenominational ministries.

As elsewhere, the distinction between Pentecostals and Charismatics, while not always clear-cut, is useful in Latin America. To the differences stressed by the *Dictionary of Pentecostal and Charismatic Movements* (Charismatics put less stress on glossolalia as a sign of Spirit-baptism, do not join classical Pentecostal denominations and do not share Pentecostalism's world-denying holiness roots), I would add two others. Charismaticism marked the arrival of Pentecostal phenomena in ample sectors of the middle class. As the secretary of the Latin American Evangelical Confederation proudly says: 'today the gospel reaches all social strata: the rulers, the legislators, the Armed Forces . . .' (*Boletín del Instituto Rutherford* May 1994:4). Related to this are cultural affinities, accentuated in Latin America by extreme social inequality, often creating a yawning cultural gap between Pentecostals and Charismatics. As elsewhere, there is a link with greater expressiveness, especially with the expressive professions. Awareness of international dimensions makes interpretations related to Brazilian politics (a mystical flight to compensate for political alienation imposed by conservative denominational hierarchies after the 1964 military coup) less plausible.

The Latin American middle class is becoming pluralist, and Charismatic evangelicalism must fit in between Catholic Charismatics, other Catholic movements, historical Protestants and esoterical tendencies. Brazil, with its solid historical churches and openness to foreign influence, led the way. Protestant Renewal preceded the parallel (also successful) Catholic phenomenon; being initially repulsed, there were schisms in all historical denominations by 1975.

However, these Charismatic offshoots have been less successful than expected. The flow from the parent denominations dried up, as the latter accommodated their Charismatics in an effort to overcome stagnation. This stagnation has to do with Catholic changes since Vatican II, allowing greater internal pluralism and discouraging conversion to Protestantism. Another factor is urbanization, making the middle classes more secularized or more attracted to privatized religion without dogmas or communitarian demands. Where historical churches do grow, it is often due to their Charismatics. Recent Protestant expansion in the middle class, however, has been mainly due to Charismatic 'communities', part of an international trend in which traditional denominations become less important in the religious field.

In most other countries of the region, historical Protestantism was too weak to produce a significant Renewal (whether inside the churches or in schismatic denominations maintaining the structure of the parent body), but Brazil mirrors the typologies of Charismaticism in the English-speaking world. The major difference is that the historical denominations were at first totally unable to accommodate the Renewal. Besides the theological rigidity of derivative churches, the search for respectability would not be served by appearing too Pentecostal. Nevertheless, the basic pattern of Renewal in historical churches in the 1960s and early 1970s followed by the rise of independent assemblies thereafter can be observed in Brazil, as can the division of the latter into those grouped into networks and those totally unlinked.

Charismatic evangelicalism has been little researched in Latin America. Only in the 1990s have studies appeared on Brazil (Mariano, 1995;

Freston, 1997), Argentina (Frigerio and Semán, forthcoming; Wynarczyk, 1993), Peru (Amat y León, 1996) and Guatemala (Stoll, 1990; Rose and Schultze, 1993). I shall use material from Brazil, Peru and Guatemala to discuss themes such as the youth culture, the media, gender, prosperity theology, spiritual warfare, influence on the Protestant field and political role.

CHARISMATICS IN BRAZIL: THE CONQUEST OF SOCIETY

Brazil's huge Protestant community (with a large internal market and considerable autonomy, and aided by the openness of Brazilian culture, media and politics) has begun to penetrate social spaces from which evangelicals were traditionally absent. Politics and the media are high visibility cases. Another is sport – Atletas de Cristo has 2000 members. Seven of the 22 footballers in the squad which won the 1994 World Cup were evangelicals who held high profile meetings throughout the tournament and were responsible for the scene after the final, in which the whole team huddled together on the pitch and prayed. Other examples include businessmen and executives, the military and police, gypsies (half of the Romanies in the city where the author lives are Pentecostals) and prisoners (in the most notorious prison in São Paulo there is a wing inhabited solely by converts). Famous people from various walks of life proclaim themselves evangelicals, often through contact with Charismatic churches: actors and singers; the best-known television newsreader; prominent politicians. Lifestyles previously frowned on by evangelicals are brought within the pale by high profile converts who retain their basic identities, as with the 'socialite for Christ', daughter of a famous playboy, who has a social column in an evangelical magazine. Charismatics pioneer the huge market for evangelical products (clothes and objects with religious phrases, and so on), evangelical productions (overflowing stadiums for music presentations, in styles including rock, funk and rap, as well as Brazilian idioms such as samba, pagode and baião) and even evangelical shopping malls.

Perhaps the greatest symbol of this process is the assault on the Rio carnival – not to abolish but to transform it. While some leading carnival figures convert to Pentecostal churches and abandon the festival, Charismatics put out their own carnival 'blocks' whose participants avoid excessive sensuality in (un)dress as they samba along the boulevards. Their lyrics talk of religious themes in contemporary language and onlookers are evangelized or exorcized as opportunity allows. 'God told us we should confront the powers', says a pastor from the Comunidade Evangélica of the wealthy South Zone of Rio (Mariano, 1995).

The Comunidades Evangélicas and Spiritual Warfare

The last phrase has overtones of spiritual warfare, a key concept of the churches usually known as the Comunidades Evangélicas. The network divided in the early 1990s due to disagreements between the main apostles, leaving one group centred on Goiânia and another on Brasília.

The initial nucleus (1973) of the Comunidades[2] in Goiânia consisted of middle class Brazilians in the American para-church organization, Youth for Christ. The main founder, Robson Rodovalho, has a degree in physics but is self-taught in theology. From a spiritist family, he was converted as a teenager after accidentally killing a man with a shotgun. Discovering Spirit-baptism, he left the Presbyterian Church and Youth for Christ. He now owns a publishing house, makes radio and television programmes (Brazil comes second only to the US in production of evangelical television programmes) and has written many books, mainly on spiritual warfare. His wife is also a pastor; in fact, half of the pastors in Rodovalho's network are women, since couples are ordained jointly. Considerable female leadership is characteristic of Brazil's charismatic evangelicalism,[3] as is the integration of pastoral and entrepreneurial activities and the transference of skills between them. Rodovalho's wife holds a cosmetics franchise, and the world-affirming faith this symbolizes is another trait of Charismaticism globally.

Many of the 100-plus congregations were founded by students and professionals who had moved. More recently, planned expansion has prevailed, together with the takeover of independent churches attracted by the Comunidade's media visibility and practical advantages. Although it has a Bible institute, pastors need not have theological training. Social projects and a school are run by a foundation connected to the church. Several footballers attend the church, and pastors were asked to give spiritual advice to both teams in the 1994 São Paulo state championship final, taking over a role traditionally filled by *pais-de-santo* of Afro-Brazilian religions.

Until 1992, congregations were only 'spiritually linked'. Today, they constitute a highly centralized denomination. The objectives are to avoid more schisms such as that between Brasília and Goiânia, and make expensive media projects viable.

The emotional and firmly directed services are oriented towards spiritual warfare. However, at the level of combat against individual demonic oppression, the Comunidades consciously differ from lower class churches such as the Universal Church of the Kingdom of God: they do not put possessed people through embarrassing situations (for middle class sensibilities) such as physical manhandling or interviewing the demons.

However, spiritual warfare, for churches of a higher social level, does not mean only dealing with people possessed by spirits, often identified with Afro-Brazilian religious entities. It includes macro-level ideas of spiritual warfare developed in the US in the 1980s. This is both a theory of evangelism, by which the 'strongholds of Satan' must be defeated before proselytism can succeed, and a theory of society and of evangelicals' role in it. Reflecting the re-enchantment of the world in post-modernity, it involves a 'sociologically well-informed but one-sided and ethnocentric focus' (Wynarczyk, 1995:117). The historical and cultural study needed to discern 'territorial spirits' is usually beyond the popular Pentecostal churches, the leadership in this realm falling to middle class Charismatics.

Latin American Pentecostals and Charismatics, despite living in religious contexts with elaborate celestial pantheons (peopled by Catholic saints or indigenous and Afro-Brazilian spiritual entities), cannot 'innovate much in the celestial sphere, under pain of expulsion from the evangelical field, [and therefore] innovate in the demonic sphere' (Brandão, 1986:215). With Charismatics, it is the middle class that innovates, the idea of a 'demon of corruption' hovering over Brasília expressing greater concern with press denunciations of political practices.

For Rodovalho, spiritual warfare has to do with the major problems of Latin America.

> Latin America has borne the weight of foreign debt for decades . . . due to the sins of negro slavery, exploitation of Indians and pacts with demons brought by Afro-Catholic syncretism . . . Of course, we are not such simpletons we don't see the action of First World imperialism against us . . . But they took the gold and wealth of Brazil to European banks and if we pray and break this spiritual curse . . . all this wealth will return.
>
> (Rodovalho, n/d:47, 6, 8ff)

Spiritual warfare is key for Charismatics and, increasingly, for other Brazilian evangelicals. The International Spiritual Warfare Network, founded by 'church growth' expert Peter Wagner in 1990, is headed in

Brazil by his former doctoral student Neuza Itioka. Its third national congress had 1600 attenders from 214 denominations. In the 1990s, 'Marches For Jesus' and like manifestations (morphologically similar to Catholic processions) have proliferated. They aim to 'break the curses over the city', 'declare the spiritual independence of Brazil', proclaim that 'blessed is the nation whose God is the Lord, and not a Lady' (a reference to Our Lady of Aparecida, patron saint of the country).

The last phrase highlights religious competition in Latin American concepts of spiritual warfare. For Itioka, the curse is linked to 'idolatry [Catholicism], spiritism [including Afro-Brazilian cults] and the occult [New Age doctrines]'. For Peruvian Humberto Lay, 'the idolatry in the past cultures of our country opened the doors to demonic powers . . . Their dominion is perpetuated by pilgrimages to sanctuaries [popular Catholicism] and the pagan rites of the Inca and pre-Inca past' (Amat y León, 1995:164).

In Peru, says Amat y León, 'we have never heard [Charismatics] reprehend the power of "savage capitalism" or the "demon of authoritarianism", still less the family curse of covetousness' (1996:141). In Brazil, many Charismatics have a political vision based on ritualism (exorcizing 'the demon of corruption' and national curses caused by social sins like slavery or spiritist religions) and the placing of Christians in power. The multiplication of demons can be a metaphor for ideological battles. As one Charismatic, the son of a politician, told me, 'people from the Workers' Party always look oppressed'; the oppression being demonic and not social.

It is also a way of empowering evangelicals. One candidate for congress asserted that 'a servant of the Lord, once elected, can establish an office employing only spiritual warriors, with daily intercession' to evangelize politicians. Evangelicals are handling their share of public money to other religions. 'Where in the Bible is it written that the Lord's servants should finance the expansion of the kingdom of darkness? Should it not rather be the opposite?' Social solutions will only come 'when we are politically dependent on the Lord', which in spiritual warfare concepts means dependent on evangelical politicians.

The language of spiritual warfare thus becomes a weapon for ambitious evangelical leaders. 'The purpose of God is that we should bind the powers . . . taking over government', writes a leader of the Comunidades (Augusto, 1984:38). Evangelical politicians so far (largely Pentecostals) have suffered from 'apocalyptic fatalism', thinking the world is getting inevitably worse. They do not realize the church has to take power before Christ returns (Rodovalho, n/d:56, 19).

The influence of spiritual warfare language is so great it has started to be invoked even by Brazil's evangelical left. In 1994, an evangelical committee supporting the left-wing candidate for president used the language of exorcism. 'The demons must be expelled from social life in the name of the vote, justice, organization and democracy . . . We desire a Brazil free from spiritual oppressions such as hunger, unemployment, inflation, corruption, organized crime . . .'.

What is the potential of Charismatics' abandonment of pietistic individualism in favour of ritualistic solidarity? As Stoll says of Guatemala, elite Charismatics seek ways of translating personal reform into public reform. Social exorcism could be the language of top-down reform, or else just a rationalization for not treating structural problems while giving elite believers an ideology of empowerment (Stoll, 1994:188). The latter seems more likely. Spiritual warfare symbolism often reflects desire for a place in civil religion. Besides, exorcizing individuals (of the 'spirit of laziness') can produce results, but exorcizing collectivities (of the 'spirit of corruption') would require a social environment similar to the aboriginal 'effervescent assembly' identified by Durkheim.

Beyer emphasizes that religious leaders, if they want public influence today, must control a service that not only supports adherents' faith but is seen as indispensable for 'profane' spheres. While globalization has made it more difficult to personify evil, the reappearance in some religious currents of the devil as that which defines the transcendent, signals a return to a traditional way of making religion communicate publicly essential information (Beyer, 1994:71–91). Spiritual warfare fits this definition precisely.

Renascer em Cristo and the Youth Scene

One of the best known churches today in Brazil is Renascer em Cristo (Reborn in Christ). It exemplifies, even exaggerates, many aspects of Charismaticism in Latin America.

The founder, Estevam Hernandes, son of a Spanish immigrant of modest origin, was converted as a teenager and attended several churches before starting Renascer in 1986 with a group of executives and professionals. They began in a pizza parlour in São Paulo, but in 1989 acquired a cinema. In 1991 they rented a radio station and then started a television programme. The media presence and the organization of mega-events gave Renascer visibility. By 1995, it had 46 churches, including five in Spain, one in France and one in Italy. Some are in poor suburbs; some are acquired by franchising. But the mother-church in São Paulo sets the tone, with its emphasis on middle class youth and professionals. A Prophets' School trains pastors (including some women). A foundation administers the denomination, centralizing resources and overseeing a network of social projects. A production company makes material for their four television programmes.

Hernandes has no theological studies. He did business administration and was marketing manager of Xerox before founding a consultancy in information technology. Still a partner, he now dedicates himself to the church. Hernandes illustrates a trend: not only do religious leaders absorb business practices and even branch into other fields, but now entrepreneurs from modern sectors transform themselves into religious leaders.

In 1994, Hernandes did an apostleship course in Los Angeles. He now calls himself apostle and his wife Sônia is bishop. Sônia used to own a boutique and is now Renascer's main television presenter. She has achieved fame in the secular media. Her references to God as 'a cuddly, fluffy warm thing, a Super-Mouse', and the fact she won a BMW in a church raffle ('do you think our preaching doesn't work for us as well?'), have provoked mixed reactions inside and outside the evangelical world. For some time, Renascer benefited from the sympathy (and one visit) of world-champion racing driver Ayrton Senna. Senna's sister was a member, but broke with Renascer just before Senna's death, a sequence of events which (allied to the exclusion of the Renascer leadership from the funeral service) is said to have been given a sinister interpretation.

In the late 1980s, Renascer spearheaded evangelical expansion into the youth culture. Rock musicians were converted and transformed into evangelical rock musicians. Hernandes became effectively the impresario of a career shift based on personal transformation. The converted musicians maintain their external appearance, but with a changed lifestyle in relation to drugs, sex and time-discipline. Methods of resocialization included community life, physical work, the spiritual disciplines of Charismatic Christianity (baptism in the Spirit, prayer, fasting, spiritual warfare) and participation in musical evangelism. On Monday nights, the main church reverberates to evangelistic rock concerts.

Renascer has had a demonstration effect on other churches. But while the style can be imitated, there is a limit to the model. Renascer, as the pioneer, could take advantage of the fact that, for a certain number of musicians, the evangelical market offered considerable opportunities. There was no penetration of the secular artistic milieu, since none of the converts continued in it. They were not well established in their careers at conversion, due to drug dependency and unstructured lifestyle, or to lack of contacts with recording companies. The investment Renascer made in their personal transformation and integration into its web of economic activities meant the chance to reorient their careers towards a market largely capable of supporting them. But it could not absorb too many converts of this sort.

Renascer was the driving force behind the take-off of what is known in Brazil as the 'gospel' movement. 'Gospel' (in English) is the fashionable term for anything associated with evangelical penetration of the youth culture: 'gospel' music, 'gospel' clothes companies, 'gospel' newspapers . . . In music, 'gospel' is any song which talks of God, in any contemporary musical idiom (Brazilian or foreign). Renascer's radio station, almost exclusively musical, has one of the highest audiences in São Paulo. 'Gospel' shows in stadiums raise food donations for anti-hunger campaigns. Renascer has also been responsible for the Brazilian 'March for Jesus', the largest in the world.

Adhonep and the New Evangelical Elite

Adhonep (Associação de Homens de Negócios do Evangelho Pleno) is the Brazilian version of the Full Gospel Businessmen's Fellowship International. Like the American founder, Demos Shakarian, the founder in Brazil, Custódio Rangel Pires, was an Assemblies of God businessman who chafed under lifestyle taboos and clerical tendencies. Having met Shakarian in an aeroplane, Pires founded Adhonep in 1975. It has outgrown its AG origins, and nowadays its converts end up in Charismatic churches.

The expensive locales of its events incarnate Adhonep's prosperity theology. Testimonies are supernaturalistic, but the business culture appears in the streamlined presentation. Members are taught to give a testimony in three minutes. If this packaging is parallel to market tendencies which allow wide distribution while maintaining quality control, there is also an inverse movement by which training in personal presentation and technical rationality received in Adhonep can be fed back into business.

Along with Renascer and the Comunidades, Adhonep is a popularizer of prosperity theology. One entrepreneur testified: 'when I joined Adhonep I prayed: "Lord, I need to get out of this recession fast, and thus point other businessmen towards you". I raised my tithe to 30 per

cent'. Large tithes are part of a package of new attitudes which re-
structure the convert's life. It is difficult to select 'rationally' from the
package, as this would expose the economic motivations which generally come enveloped in a set of complex personal motivations.

Adhonep does not preach an ascetic 'Protestant ethic' because Brazilian reality is different. Professional ethics, or theological reflection
on the economic system, are scarcely mentioned. It is the religion of
the merchant (Weber), emphasizing elective affinities with material
interests. Like ancient deities of prosperity, Adhonep offers an adequate
representation of their needs and hopes.

Although sometimes considered evidence of Americanization of Third
World religion, the spread of prosperity doctrine, with its concept of
faith as a force and giving as investment, is due rather to its resonance
with much primal religiosity. However, it would seem to find a sounder
cultural base in Africa (from traditional religion and current political
culture) than in Latin America where, besides ideological criticism from
intellectual sectors, it faces opposition from the 'populist' Pentecostal
tradition which values the poor as more open to the gospel. This theological idealization of the poor lives in tension with new desires for
social respectability in denominations such as the Assemblies of God.
For Charismatics, prosperity doctrine legitimates conspicuous consumption: one Charismatic congress taught 'how to take possession of unbelievers' wealth'. It is also functional for expensive media ministries
and for pastors' personal aspirations, since the latter's own wealth pro-
claims the efficacy of their preaching. This has contributed to the recent deterioration in the public image of evangelical pastors in Brazil.

Adhonep is officially apolitical but in 1989 and 1994 the leadership,
alleging divine revelation, was heavily involved in the presidential
campaigns of Iris Rezende, the most prominent evangelical politician.

The ideological implications of prosperity doctrine remain, in my
opinion, enigmatic. The Brazilian left's proposals for strengthening the
domestic market and small-scale enterprise could be as pleasing as
neo-liberalism to Charismatic groups which, besides giving to the church,
encourage members to strike out on their own economically.

**Caio Fábio and the Charismatic Style in the Wider Protestant
World**

In Latin America, historical evangelicals and Pentecostals–Charismatics
are all known as *evangélicos*. Recent studies of Argentina's Protestant
field stress its Pentecostalization (diffusion in historical circles of Pen-

tecostal worship and theological themes (Wynarczyk *et al.*, 1995)), and development of a pan-evangelical allegiance, with shared identity, common goals and unifying public figures (Marostica, 1994).

In Brazil, the multiplication of pan-Protestant representative entities has increased transit between historical and Pentecostal–Charismatic tendencies. Tele-evangelism has popularized models of preaching and worship beyond denominational boundaries. Ambition for power leads to alliances which overlook denominational polemics.

A key actor in this is Caio Fábio, president of the Brazilian Evangelical Association, one of two entities which claim to represent all Protestants. Caio is paradigmatic of the new Protestant moment: a charismatic leader (sociological sense) of elitist origin, but self-taught after a lost youth; a Presbyterian pastor with Charismatic tendencies (theological sense) and acceptance among historicals and Pentecostals; head of his own para-church organization and presenter of television programmes.

Long-known among evangelicals, Caio has recently gained famous converts (gang-leader, state governor) and started a huge social project. He criticizes Bishop Macedo of the Universal Church of the Kingdom of God (owner of a television network) for the 'terrible visibility he has given all *evangélicos*'. Unlike Macedo, who called left-winger Lula 'the devil's candidate' for president, Caio voted for Lula because 'I thought not of myself but of the millions of destitute people'.

In 1994, the secular media projected Caio as an 'anti-Bishop Macedo'. The main TV network introduced an 'ethical pastor' into a popular soap-opera. The growth of *evangélicos*, making them an important market and electorate, and the perception that generalizations in reporting did not isolate Macedo from the Protestant community, were behind the search for an 'anti-Macedo'.

Caio's para-church organization is supported mainly by Brazilian businessmen and has links with American evangelists Leighton Ford and Pat Robertson. For this he is distrusted by the evangelical left, but still cultivates friendships with leading left-wing politicians.

In 1995, Caio launched what he calls the first 'gospel' magazine in Brazil, printed by a leading secular publisher. It represents the mainline face of the Charismatic transformation of evangelicalism and penetration of society. Its social column talks of socially prominent evangelicals. Caio himself takes 'neopilgrims' to Israel for tours which include baptism in the River Jordan.

CHARISMATICS IN PERU: THE CONQUEST OF THE EVANGELICAL WORLD

If Brazil's Charismatics influence the Protestant world, in Peru they have near hegemony. Amat y León (1996) talks of three phases. The first, from the late 1960s, was Renewal in the historical churches, which remained limited because the strong holiness tradition in Peruvian Protestantism (emphasizing personal holiness, community life and evangelism) undercut its novelty.

In the second phase (1980s), Charismaticism was established through three routes: influence in historical and Pentecostal denominations; independent churches; and Charismatic para-church groups. An example of the first route is the transformation of the Assemblies of God, whose aspiration to reach the middle class was frustrated until joined in 1987 by a Charismatic breakaway (led by the pastor) from the main church of the largest holiness denomination, the Alianza Cristiana y Misionera.

In the third phase (early 1990s) Charismaticism became hegemonic in Peruvian evangelicalism. Its worldview and language were popularized and its concept of mission widely accepted. Spiritual warfare 'decongested the discussion about evangelism and social action – neither one nor the other, but a return to the sacred . . . The essence of this re-enchanted world is interconnection between things the modern world had treated as separate' (Ibid:205f). FIPAC (International Fraternity of Christian Pastors), a charismatic connection for groups outside the National Evangelical Council, grew due to the aura of ministerial success its affiliates exuded and the financial facilities it offered. There is nothing comparable in Brazil where Protestantism, more successful, does not offer Charismatics such relative power. In Peru, however, Charismatics are now 'the main ideological force in Protestantism, with power to define relations with government and attitudes towards society' (Ibid:211).

CHARISMATICS IN GUATEMALA: THE CONQUEST OF THE STATE

Guatemala is the supreme example of Charismatic penetration of politics. In Peru, Charismatics have taken little political action. But in Brazil, although the key players in evangelical politics are Pentecostals, there have been notable interventions by Charismatics. Two examples from 1994 will suffice.

Francisco Rossi, an experienced politician, reached the run-off election for governor of São Paulo, making intensive use of his new identity as member of a Charismatic church (whose pastor is vice-president of the largest private Brazilian bank, with which Rossi has political connections). His campaign song was an evangelical hymn. (Two years later, campaigning for mayor of São Paulo, Rossi, having been baptized in the Spirit in the interim, was to speak in tongues in a campaign meeting.) He was supported by Renascer and tele-evangelist Valnice Milhomens ('let us struggle in spiritual warfare so this servant of God becomes governor').

Rossi represents a phenomenon with which Guatemala is familiar: a career politician who converts and continues in evangelical style. The case appealed to Protestant triumphalism, the idea of a divine right to govern Brazil. The president of the rival entity to the Evangelical Association campaigned for Rossi. 'As spiritual beings, born again, we are the "cream of society". The church is on a higher level to normal people . . . because the church has the answers politicians are looking for.'

In congressional elections, this triumphalism was expressed by Lamartine Posella. A prosperous tele-evangelist, he had the support of prophecies from Valnice and Hernandes. As Lamartine said: 'if we evangelicals are one day literally going to dominate on earth, why can't we start taking power now, as a foretaste? . . . The social chaos is due to spiritual curses on our country [idolatry, spiritism] . . . God is raising up men full of the Spirit to take over the positions of power.'

If Charismatics in Brazil are flexing their political muscles, in Guatemala they have produced presidents. Throughout Latin America, Charismatics have a greater propensity than other evangelicals to adopt an American political theology called reconstructionism. This replaces pre-millennial pessimism about the world with optimistic post-millenialism. It is the destiny of Christians to govern by a mixture of extreme neo-liberalism and Old Testament laws. Few politicians adopt the whole package, but use it selectively to meet their programmatic deficiencies. The optimism and emphasis on analysis are culturally more attractive to middle class Charismatics than to lower class Pentecostals.

Guatemalan Charismaticism took off in the 1970s. After Vatican II Catholic reforms, 'socially prominent Catholic professionals . . . had begun to explore other religious options' (Smith, 1991:134). In addition, the 1976 earthquake stimulated the arrival of Charismatic groups from the US, including the Church of the Word (Verbo) which soon recruited future president Ríos Montt. The model was copied by members

of the Guatemalan elite, such as the founder of El Shaddai from which
sprang another future president, Jorge Serrano.

General Ríos Montt had been presidential candidate in 1974. In 1978,
after failing to regain nomination, he joined Verbo. In 1982, after a
military coup in which he denied involvement, he was invited to take
power. He governed for a year, being deposed by another coup. He
had few Protestant ministers, except for some Verbo advisors, but gave
weekly televised sermons exhorting civil servants to honesty. He invited an American reconstructionist to make recommendations for economic policy. Tele-evangelists Falwell and Robertson launched an aid
programme. Only about $200,000 were donated, and impact was mini-
mal. At the same time, human rights abuses continued apace in the
countryside, as part of the anti-guerrilla campaign. But Ríos still enjoys popularity as an upright military man, having been favourite for
two presidential campaigns (1990 and 1995) in which he was impeded
from running (as a former coup participant). He did manage to become president of Congress.

The trajectory of Jorge Serrano was different. A businessman, he
joined the Elim Church in 1977, but a family tie with a Verbo elder
earned him appointment as head of the Council of State under Ríos
Montt. With redemocratization, he stood for president in 1985. Not
finding favour for his ambitions at Elim, he joined El Shaddai. At the
time of his successful presidential campaign in 1990, the church was
engaged in a spiritual warfare project promoted by Serrano to free the
country from an ancient curse related to pre-Christian religion. In 1993,
facing opposition in Congress to his economic stabilization plans, and
scarred by revelations about his private life and probity, Serrano sus-
pended the constitution. He was overthrown within a week.

Both Ríos Montt and Serrano were politicians before converting.
Born-again religion has reached social strata habitually engaged in politics
(Stoll, 1994:107). Serrano's election was not due to the Protestant vote;
it reflects Protestant penetration of the elite and the social respectability acquired.

Guatemala is a pioneer example of what can happen when Protestantism begins to be practised by a significant minority of the elite.
The combination of elite presence, popular base and a weak State is
transforming Protestantism into a new source of political and cultural
hegemony. The State's weakness has led it to take up with Protestants
in educational and social programmes (Rose and Schultze, 1993). But
the question Stoll asks in the early 1990s (can Charismatic-led top-
down reform change political and economic reality?) seems to get a

negative answer in a later work: the social capital generated is wasted in costly experimentation at taking power rather than altering the basic landscape of politics by encouraging the spread of trust (Levine and Stoll, 1995).

Perhaps in Brazil, with its larger internal market, stronger democratic life and vibrant social movements, plus a more varied evangelical world in which Charismatics are less dominant and more subject to critique, results will be different. Certainly it is rash to evaluate Charismatic politics in isolation from variable contextual factors. Hexham and Poewe's (1994) critique of the exaggerated criticism of Charismatics in South Africa is valid. They are rarely under foreign control and certainly not uniformly reactionary. But Hollenweger's (1994) concern about the insulation of elite Charismatics from dialogue with poor Pentecostals is justified. The post-millennial dreams of church growth and accession to power of Charismatic elites are scant comfort to the disadvantaged of Latin America, an increasing proportion of whom are evangelicals. The political implications of prosperity theology, spiritual warfare and the triumphalist doctrine of a divine right of evangelicals to rule, could be very different from those of classical Protestant ethics and political doctrine in Europe and North America. In addition, in a Latin America still marked by the old monolithic relations between religion and society, the supposed 'logic' of voluntarist religion (Martin, 1978) may be modified. In short, while recognizing that the future is open, both the regional context and the type of evangelicalism growing in Latin America raise concerns as to the long-term political effects of Charismatic religion there.

CONCLUSION: LOCAL REFRACTIONS OF A GLOBAL
CULTURE

The general picture of Charismatic evangelicals in Latin America is of initially limited space in historical denominations, due to the latter's intransigence or numerical weakness, followed by the growth of independent churches which later influence the wider Protestant field. The space for Charismaticism, however, varies widely from country to country, depending on the strength of historical Protestantism and Catholic Renewal, as well as social factors favouring the growth of Protestantism generally. Its social visibility is affected by the space available in the media and politics. In no developed English-speaking country have Charismatics become as dominant in the Protestant field, much less as important in politics, as in Guatemala. Nor do they operate within an expanding and triumphalist evangelical community, as in Brazil.

Amat y León stresses the fit between Charismaticism and post-modernism. But it is 'not a simple imitation of a post-modern religious structure, but a creative adaptation with clear elements of a Christian worldview' (1996: 76). He also asserts that it 'distances itself from the need for scriptural support' and 'de-emphasizes the social dimension of the gospel'. This is contradicted in Brazil by heavy investment in social projects, and by the fact that prosperity, spiritual warfare and political manifest destiny are all given exhaustive Biblical justification.

Whatever the ethical ambiguity, Charismaticism represents a new stage in the inculturation of Protestantism in Latin America. The penetration of the youth culture, the assimilation of musical rhythms, the adoption of secular communication styles, the reinterpretation of spiritual warfare in terms of local religious rivalries, the acceptance of social categories and symbols of prestige once placed under taboo, the renewal of religious language, the belief in the destiny of their countries under evangelical leadership – all point to an unprecedented 'naturalization' of Protestantism in this previously most Catholic of continents.

Latin American Charismaticism is thus at the same time a global culture, with multiple foreign influences and multiple foreign extensions, and a creative local adaptation. As Smith (1990: 178f) says, new traditions must hew close to vernacular motifs. 'It is one thing . . . to package imagery and diffuse it . . . It is quite another to ensure the power to move and inspire . . . Meanings of even the most universal of imagery for a particular population derive as much from the historical experiences and social status of that group as from the intentions of purveyors'. A global culture, says Smith, is memoryless and therefore impossible – unless, we might add, it is based on an 'adoptive memory', the Christian adoption of the Biblical past. It is as a universality which embraces particularity that Charismatics' 'first-century Christian schema' (Poewe) finds its power to create a global culture.

One can therefore see Charismaticism in Latin America not so much (as Wright does in this volume) as a 'sign against the excessive institutionalization of the churches', but, in a context of generalized evangelical growth, as a reaction to cultural changes which render the middle class more open to conversion and enthusiastic religion but which the historical churches are incapable of taking advantage of. In addition, one can surmise that Latin American Charismaticism may be capable of a unique role in any future re-evangelization of Europe, since unlike its African counterpart, it combines a Western cultural heritage with an unashamed embracing of primal religiosity.

NOTES

1. Or 'neo-Pentecostalism', as it is known in some literature on Spanish-speaking countries. I have avoided the term because it is used in Brazil for the newer mass Pentecostal churches, sociologically very different.
2. The section on the Comunidades is based on my own research and on Mariano (1995), as is my later section on Renascer.
3. The most watched tele-evangelist in Brazil is Valnice Milhomens, who has founded her own denomination (with 50 per cent women pastors) and criticized other churches for reproducing the machismo of Brazilian society.

BIBLIOGRAPHY

Amat y León, Oscar, 1996. 'La Propuesta Misionera y el Desarrollo del Movimiento Carismático Evangélico en el Perú', Masters thesis, CEMAA, Lima.
Augusto, César, 1984. *Guerra Espiritual* Goiânia: Koinonia Comunidade.
Beyer, Peter, 1994. *Religion and Globalization*, London: Sage.
Brandão, Carlos Rodrigues, 1986. *Os Deuses do Povo*, 2nd edn. São Paulo: Brasiliense.
Cox, Harvey, 1996. *Fire From Heaven: The Rise of Pentecostal Spirituality and the Reshaping of Religion in the Twenty-First Century*. London: Cassell.
Dictionary of Pentecostal and Charismatic Movements, 1988. Burgess, Stanley and McGee, Gary (eds.), Grand Rapids, MI: Zondervan.
Featherstone, Mike, 1990. 'Global Culture: An Introduction' in Featherstone, Mike (ed.) *Global Culture: Nationalism, Globalization and Modernity*, London: Sage, 1990, pp.1–14.
Fernandes, Rubem César, 1992. *Censo Institucional Evangélico CIN 1992: Primeiros Comentários*. Rio de Janeiro: ISER.
Freston, Paul, 1993. 'Protestantes e Política no Brasil: da Constituinte ao Impeachment', PhD Thesis, University of Campinas, Brazil.
Freston, Paul, 1994. 'Popular Protestants in Brazilian Politics: A Novel Turn in Sect-State Relations', *Social Compass*, 41(4), pp.537–70.
Freston, Paul, 1995. 'Pentecostalism in Brazil: A Brief History', *Religion*, 25, pp.119–33.
Freston, Paul, 1996. 'The Protestant Eruption into Modern Brazilian Politics', *Journal of Contemporary Religion*, 11, 2, pp.147–68.
Freston, Paul, 1997. *Evangélicos no Brasil: Suas Igrejas e Sua Política*. São Paulo: Ática.

Frigerio, Alejandro and Semán, Pablo, Forthcoming. *Giménez, El Pastor: El Fenómeno Religioso de la Década.*

Hexham, Irving and Poewe, Karla, 1994. 'Charismatic Churches in South Africa: A Critique of Criticisms and Problems of Bias' in Poewe, Karla (ed.), *Charismatic Christianity as a Global Culture.* Columbia: University of South Carolina Press, pp.50–69.

Hollenweger, Walter, 1994. 'The Pentecostal Elites and the Pentecostal Poor: A Missed Dialogue?' in Poewe, Karla (ed.), *Charismatic Christianity as a Global Culture.* Columbia: University of South Carolina Press, pp.200–14.

Levine, Daniel and Stoll, David, 1995. 'Bridging the Gap Between Empowerment and Power in Latin America', mimeo.

Mariano, Ricardo, 1995. 'Neopentecostalismo: os pentecostais estão mudando'. M.A. Thesis, University of São Paulo.

Marostica, Matt, 1994. 'La Iglesia Evangélica en la Argentina como Nuevo Movimiento Social', *Sociedad y Religión*, 12, June, pp.3–16.

Martin, David, 1978. *A General Theory of Secularization*, Oxford: Blackwell.

Martin, David, 1995. 'Sociology, Religion and Secularization: an Orientation', *Religion*, 25, pp.295–303.

Poewe, Karla, 1989. 'On the Metonymic Structure of Religious Experiences: the Example of Charismatic Christianity', *Cultural Dynamics*, II, 4, pp.361–80.

Poewe, Karla, 1994a. 'Introduction: The Nature, Globality, and History of Charismatic Christianity' in Poewe, Karla (ed.), *Charismatic Christianity as a Global Culture.* Columbia: University of South Carolina Press, pp.1–29.

Poewe, Karla, 1994b. 'Rethinking the Relationship of Anthropology to Science and Religion' in Poewe, Karla (ed.), *Charismatic Christianity as a Global Culture.* Columbia: University of South Carolina Press, pp.234–58.

Rodovalho, Robson, n/d. *Regendo a História da Nossa Geração.* Goiânia: Koinonia.

Rose, Susan and Schultze, Quentin, 1993. 'The Evangelical Awakening in Guatemala: Fundamentalist Impact on Education and Media', in Marty M. and Appleby, S. (eds.), *Fundamentalisms and Society*, University of Chicago Press, pp.415–51.

Smith, Anthony D., 1990. 'Towards a Global Culture?' in Featherstone, Mike (ed.) *Global Culture: Nationalism, Globalization and Modernity.* London: Sage, 1990, pp.171–91.

Smith, Dennis, 1991. 'Coming of Age: A Reflection on Pentecostals, Politics and Popular Religion in Guatemala', *Pneuma*, 13, 2, Fall, pp.131–9.

Stoll, David, 1990. *Is Latin America Turning Protestant?* Berkeley: University of California Press.

Stoll, David, 1994. '"Jesus is Lord of Guatemala". Evangelical Reform in a Death-Squad State', in Marty, M. and Appleby S. (eds.), *Accounting for Fundamentalisms*, University of Chicago Press, pp.99–123.

Wynarczyk, Hilario, 1993. 'Las aproximaciones a la sociología del campo evangélico en la Argentina', in Frigerio A. (ed.), *Ciencias Sociales y Religión en el Cono Sur*, Buenos Aires: Centro Editor de América Latina, pp.61–71.

Wynarczyk, Hilario, 1995. 'La Guerra Espiritual en el Campo Evangélico', *Sociedad y Religión*, 13, pp.111–26.

Wynarczyk, Hilario, Semán, Pablo and De Majo, Mercedes, 1995. *Panorama Actual del Campo Evangélico en Argentina*, Buenos Aires: FIET.

10 The City on a Beach: Future Prospects for Charismatic Movements at the End of the Twentieth Century

Martyn Percy

INTRODUCTION

Joseph Bell is often remembered for being the doctor and surgeon who inspired Arthur Conan Doyle, the creator of Sherlock Holmes. Doyle was a student of Bell's at the Edinburgh Medical School in the mid-nineteenth century, at a time when the city's medicine led the world. What especially impressed Doyle about Bell was his eye for detail. His reputation as a medical 'sleuth' was legendary. By looking at a man's walk, he could reputedly say which regiment he had served in. When examining a woman, he could often say where she lived and worked, her accent and the 'factory smells' on her clothes being the principal indicators. His powers of deduction, all based on acute sensory perception, were put to work in an age that knew nothing of DNA testing, X-rays or tissue analysis. Of course, Bell's deductions worked because the populace of Edinburgh was essentially settled: districts were specialized and identifiable units of socio-economic development. The way someone walked or talked was quite likely to tell you something about the person's class, origin, employment – and maybe their health too. Bell's deductive powers rested on taking many things for granted, making premises, and assuming a priori knowledge.

No doctor could get away with this today. Neither for that matter could a sociologist, especially one engaged in the analysis of contemporary religion. In the nineteenth century, the way an Anglican clergyman dressed would often indicate his churchmanship. Styles of worship clearly delineated between 'high' and 'low', between Established and Free, between Catholic and Protestant. Even in the early twentieth century, boundaries between denominations such as the Assemblies of God and Oneness Pentecostals were firmly fixed. However, at the end of this century the religious world is an altogether more mixed economy. The divisions tend to be less about denominational identity, and more about 'conservative' and 'liberal' dispositions. Added to this, the 'outbreak' of Pentecostalism at the turn of this century has introduced progressive and radical change into nearly all existing Christian denominations, besides spawning its own groupings. In the nineteenth century, careful observation and questioning of an individual could have revealed much in a short space of time about his or her religious allegiance. Not so today: Charismatics may be Anglican, Catholic, Methodist or any other denomination. Pentecostals and neo-Pentecostals can be any colour or class. Historically, there had been a chasm between black Pentecostals, who had once focused mostly on glossolalia and the healing and prophecies of their middle class white Assemblies of God counterparts for whom they had little time. Yet the present situation is much more conflated. The varieties and vagaries of contemporary religious expression are seemingly endless. Today, Charismatics, Pentecostals and neo-Pentecostals significantly influence each other and the rest of the world's Christian population, as well as secular social, political and moral arenas. From 20,000 in South America in 1920, their projected numbers are 20,000,000 by the year 2000. Globally, Charismatics, Pentecostals and neo-Pentecostals may number as many as 400,000,000, which is one third of the world's Christian population. No part of the world is untouched by Pentecostalism and Charismatic Renewal.

In the Gospel according to Matthew, Jesus tells two parables about size and structure that are relevant to our discussion. In the first pericope in Matthew 5:14, Jesus likens the Christian community to 'a city on a hill that cannot be hid': the suggestion is that in its growth, Christianity should be both progressive and visible. In a second parable (7:24–27), which has a 'Sunday School' familiarity about it, Jesus suggests that the foundations for a stable religious life need to be built on rock, and not on sand. Building on rock is thorough but slow, although it ultimately outweighs the short-term attractions of building on sand. When the rains and floods come, the house on the sand is washed away. The suggestion is that rapid expansion may not be the desideratum of Christianity: extensive growth should not be overvalued at the expense of intensive development.[1] I want to suggest, at least for the moment, that we should think about neo-Pentecostalism at the end of the twentieth century as being like 'a city on a beach'. I have deliberately conflated the metaphors Jesus uses to get to the heart of the present and (potential) future state of Charismatic Renewal, which is what we shall be discussing here. Another advantage of the metaphor is that it resonates with images that have already been deployed in describing the state of contemporary religion. One thinks immediately of Matthew Arnold's poem 'Dover Beach' (1867) which questioned where faith would go once it had left the stable rocks and shores of modernity. Building on this image, Anthony Thiselton sees the present (post-modern) religious situation as one in which 'everything is shifting, as every stable meaning is deferred and erased in an ever-moving, never-ending flux'. The image of Pentecostalism as a city sited on these foundations has been suggested by commentators such as Harvey Cox in his works *The Secular City* (1965), and later again in *Religion in the Secular City* (1984).[2]

Let me say more. There is no question that neo-Pentecostalism is a major shareholder in the totality of Christian expression. But like a city, that expression is not monobehavioural: it is multifaceted, diverse and expansive, capable even of being at odds with itself. It has its own distinctive districts of belief and behaviour (for example, those who are 'pro-Toronto Blessing', those who are anti, those who speak in tongues, those who don't, and so on, and also like a city, it increasingly sprawls and expands. Indeed, following Melton, we can say that although it is a loosely clustered group, the movement still belongs together.[3] Yet the location of this expanding city is far from secure. Ironically, Charismatics frequently talk of being hit by 'waves' (of the Holy Spirit), of revival falling like rain, and of being drenched, soaked, washed and refreshed by the Spirit. These metaphors cover a multitude of occurrences, but it is safe to say that in each instance, whilst bringing energy and revival to some, they bring schism, erosion and disaster to others. Waves of the Spirit tend to fragment the neo-Pentecostal community, washing some away, whilst bringing others in. Part of the reason that Charismatic Renewal is so prey to the tides of revival lies in its foundations; namely, identity being heavily reliant on religious experience as the ground of actuality, even though there may be (often latent) fundamentalist or evangelical foundations. More will be said about this later, but for the moment, it is enough to reflect on and note how various 'waves' – or fashions – in revival have expanded Pentecostalism yet also destabilized it: health and wealth movements, the Toronto Blessing, house churches, 'shepherding' movements, dancing in the Spirit, healing ministries and flamboyant Charismatic leaders have all played their part. The city on the beach, in spite of its size, has major structural problems that make its long-term future far from secure. As many sociologists have noted, charisma fades over time, enthusiasm wanes, institutionalization sets in, and the individual communities that housed motifs of adventure and excitement tend to fall flat.[4]

I am more than conscious that this is a controversial and potentially offensive 'lens' through which to view neo-Pentecostalism at the end of the twentieth century, but the subjects of the preceding chapters bear out my thesis, at least in part. Yet in order to suggest some future possibilities for Charismatic Renewal, it will be necessary to offer a portrait of the present, which will give birth to the future. That portrait will inevitably be 'sketchy', but I propose to illustrate the basic characteristics of Charismatic Renewal as it occurs globally. This will be followed by a discussion of the sociological and theological issues that concern neo-Pentecostal groups. Some of the main ones are linked to identity. For example, can sectarianism and syncretism be avoided when religious experience is the essential ground of being? A further section will examine the likely shape of neo-Pentecostal identities in the future, and suggest potential fissures and federations. The concluding remarks will be addressed to how a sociological method can be used to 'map' the 'shifting sands of Charismatic Renewal' in its restless struggle for security in the post-modern world. But let us begin with the present.

NEO-PENTECOSTALISM: A GLOBAL PICTURE

David Martin's *Tongues of Fire* (1990) assesses the explosive growth of Protestantism in Latin America in recent times. It is a predictably excellent survey, and it is his treatment of Pentecostalism that we are primarily concerned with here. Noting that Pentecostal churches are experiencing numerical growth at a time when 'liberal' or traditional denominations are declining, Martin presses the question as to how this shift has come about. Clearly, part of the answer lies in the successful enculturation of Pentecostalism into contemporary society, which itself is moving towards fragmentation, new autonomies and a willingness to create and participate in a 'free spiritual market'.[5] Whilst it is true that there are only a handful of mainline neo-Pentecostal denominations in South America, which accounts for most followers, there are nonetheless hundreds of offshoots and alternatives. Martin also notes that their expansion is linked to their acceptance by a wide range of social classes. For the poor, Pentecostalism can represent a popularized, accessible version of Protestantism. Yet the movement also appeals to the middle classes, because of its focus on conservative values mixed with adventurous and novel religious motifs. Testimony to the success of Pentecostalism in the middle classes of South America is chiefly visible in the types of buildings now emerging, but also in energetic evangelistic campaigns and forays into the media.[6]

The strength of Martin's work is his appreciation of how Pentecostalism both creates and is created by society, is a reaction against it yet adaptive of its trends. For example, he is mildly critical of accounts of Pentecostalism that indulge in what he would probably call 'crude parallelism'. That is to say, simply linking the growth of Pentecostalism to changes in social and economic situations, thereby implying that Pentecostalism is somehow 'a religion of the gaps'.[7] But Martin does not retreat into naive positivism in response to this: he is more subtle. He recognizes that Pentecostalism does offer a 'sacred canopy' under which individuals and groups can shelter, and then make decisions about their response to modernity, secularization and the incessant ravages of pluralism. Thus, he notes that Pentecostalism 'offers participation, mutual support, emotional release, a sense of identity and dignity . . . [it] provides a substitute society.'[8] Clearly, this functions in different ways for different social classes. For the middle classes, this form of religion can be escapist, offering mythical legitimization for their affairs, without really pressing social questions. Yet for the poor, it can be essential: a means of social and psychological survival, with religious hope issuing a form of security and the promise of liberation. So, it seems in South America at least, that Pentecostalism has become a peculiarly adaptable expression of Christianity that benefits from the breaking up of old religious monopolies, which in turn mirrors a more general fragmentation in society. Traditional Protestants and Roman Catholics alike are losing their grip on the souls of the people, as the search for authentic, transformative and convincing religious experience gathers pace. In South America, this process is accelerating with some rapidity, so it is safe to suggest that the forms of neo-Pentecostalism that will emerge in the near future will most likely be more novel and particular than before. Fissure will increase, and enculturation and conflation of beliefs in relation to society and culture will require continual redrawing of the Pentecostal map.

In North America, the picture is no less diverse. Catholic neo-Pentecostalism has been explored in some depth in important works by Meredith McGuire and Mary Jo Neitz.[9] Their contributions to the study of contemporary Charismatic Renewal are vital because they

shrewdly identify the 'suburbanization' of neo-Pentecostalism in North
America. Quite simply, the religion of perennial revival is at home
there. The focus of McGuire's work is on healing, a subject that persistently absorbs the American mind. In her view, there is no question
that part of the reason for the appeal of neo-Pentecostalism in the USA
lies in the notions of power that underpin healing ministries: groups
and individuals who practise these therapies operate as brokers of power,
enabling a sense of healing energy to flow into people. Participants
are caught up in a dynamic matrix in which agents of power give rise
to experiences that help individuals feel closer to one another and closer
to God.[10] This occurrence forms the church: it is a framework in which
one can simply be.[11] Neitz's work, although more general, is valuable
for its portrayal of the diversity of Catholic Charismatic Renewal. We
shall explore this in more detail later, but for the moment it is worth
noting that neo-Pentecostal groups have formed themselves into a significant subculture within American Roman Catholicism through informal 'home groups' and cells. At the same time, high profile individuals
and influential publications have placed Charismatic Renewal firmly
on the church's agenda.[12]

   The mapping of contemporary Protestant Pentecostalism in North
America could begin almost anywhere and end just about everywhere.
From tele-evangelists such as Swaggart and Bakker, to Pat Robertson's
or Oral Roberts' universities, then to churches the size of small towns,
right down to snake-handlers in the rural mid-west.[13] Phenomenologically, Protestant Charismatic Renewal is both behaviourally and doctrinally diverse, and is also dispersed through all denominations besides
having many of its own. Are there any generic characteristics that bind
the movement together? Harvey Cox suggests that neo-Pentecostalism
has fallen prey to new theologies that are enhancing the numerical
growth of the movement, but at the same time, betraying its original
fundaments. Working with a fairly positivist notion of the origins of
Pentecostalism, Cox notes its present preoccupation with 'dominion
theology', excessive demonology, health and wealth movements and
'spiritual' phenomena more usually associated with the New Age.[14]
The first of these, dominion theology, particularly concerns Cox as he
sees it as a way of inculcating politically conservative values and fundamentalist social attitudes into Pentecostalism. The preoccupation with
establishing God's reign on earth now – righteously dominating individuals and institutions in the name of God – has led to the dissolving
of distinctions between pre- and post-millennialists. Dominion theology syncretizes these positions, and invites neo-Pentecostalism to move

forward to make a brave new world, in preparation for the return of Christ. Yet in spite of this new social dimension to neo-Pentecostalism, it would be a mistake to assume that concrete galvanization and authentic socio-political integration is taking place. In North America, it is still true that neo-Pentecostalism continues to incline towards being 'divisive, anti-intellectual, self-righteous and reluctant to assume responsibility for social and institutional reform'.[15]

In Britain and Europe, the picture is slightly different. House churches have led the way in Charismatic Renewal for many years. Andrew Walker's seminal *Restoring the Kingdom* (1985) charts the rise of restorationism, the principle vehicle for neo-Pentecostalism in the last quarter of the century. Walker describes the house church phenomenon in sociological terms that categorize churches according to whether they are 'R1' or 'R2'. The taxonomy employed allows for differentiation over styles of leadership, attitudes to authority, women, dialogue with other groups, ecumenism and orders. Sociologically speaking, R1 churches are tightly controlled, with an aggressive sectarian mentality. R2 churches on the other hand, are more relaxed, though both types may well share similar fundamentals and core beliefs. However, since the 1980s, there is plenty of evidence to suggest that some house church movements, at least in terms of their sociological identity, move between the R1 and R2 categories. This is no doubt caused by such variables as the particular Charismatic leader or situation, what issues the church might be addressing, and how it continues to consolidate and expand in the plural and post-modern world.[16] Interestingly, Roman Catholics have a similar structural variant on the house churches as an agent of renewal, in the form of the neo-catechumenate movement and communities such as the Mother of God, founded in Gaithersburg, Maryland, in 1966. Whilst those involved in these movements would argue that they have not left the Church, and are therefore communitarian, not sectarian, there is mounting evidence to suggest otherwise.[17]

Of course, neo-Pentecostalism has reached well beyond the house church movement. Charismatic Renewal is one of the most potent forces of change and development in existing denominations. Revivalists and healers such as John Wimber, Benny Hinn, Morris Cerullo, Bill Subritzky and Reinhard Bonnke have reintroduced the principles of revival in recent times with some force. In Britain, Europe and the Commonwealth, they attract considerable audiences for their conferences, yet do not necessarily press for a change in denominational affiliation. Cynics would say that this ensures that their 'market' is consequently much

larger than those who remain with the house church movement, such
as Terry Virgo and Bryn Jones. In my view, there is no question that
Wimber and others are sensitive to being overidentified with their own
denominational expansion, lest they lose widespread ecumenical support in the process. But it would be unfair to suggest that Charismatic
Renewal has only been stimulated in traditional denominations by forces
external to them. True, many agencies in the 1960s such as the Full
Gospel Businessmen's Fellowship International (FGBMFI) did engender a form of dispersed ecumenical revivalism, that tended to be rather
personal. Yet there were more corporate examples of renewal emerging in the 1970s and 1980s. For example, the Church of England has
seen bodies such as Anglicans for Renewal Ministries (ARM), Sharing
of Ministries Abroad (SOMA), the Fountain Trust and assorted healing ministries become an established part of the established church.[18]
Added to this, major Anglican centres for revivalism – Holy Trinity,
Brompton, St Andrew's, Chorleywood and St Thomas Crooke's, Sheffield
– attract people in their hundreds if not thousands, to experience the
very latest and freshest experiences of renewal, usually winged in on a
jet and a prayer from North America.

The last area of neo-Pentecostal expansion that needs mentioning is
not so easily confined geographically. I am referring to the 'syncretic'
revivalist churches that have mushroomed in recent years. Sociologists
are in general agreement that the principal locations for study in this
field are Africa and the Pacific-Asian Rim, which includes countries
like South Korea. Indeed, David Martin uses both Korea and South
Africa as 'instructive parallels' in his discussion of neo-Pentecostalism
in *Tongues of Fire* (1990). Martin notes, as others have, that the relationship between revivalist religion in these places and the existing
structure of primal religion goes far beyond what many western Christians would find acceptable.[19] For example, it is no accident that churches
that strongly emphasize demonology flourish in mainly animistic areas
of Korea, whilst those that press the Protestant work ethic in conjunction with healing ministries do extremely well in the new urban areas
and overcrowded inner cities of Africa and Asia. Harvey Cox goes so
far as to describe the situation as one in which shamanism has met
entrepreneurialism, and been largely adopted by neo-Pentecostalism.
Looking at the work of pastors such as Paul Yonggi Cho, with his
church membership numbered in hundreds of thousands, this is a difficult thesis to defeat.[20] Similarly, Africa, through primal religions that
emphasize healing, God as deus ex machina, and with the world of
spirits and demons, is also prey to novel and heady concoctions of

revivalism and local religious belief. However, it is important not to patronize Africa and Asia for their alleged syncretism; the idea that the First World somehow has a 'pure' version of the Gospel which is being corrupted and diluted is deeply offensive. Are healing ministries, health and wealth movements, dominion theology and the Toronto Blessing not also examples of (post-modern, middle class) syncretism? Nonetheless, it is estimated that 'indigenous African churches', many of which are strongly influenced by Pentecostalism, already number 100 million Christians, and are the biggest growth area in revivalism today.[21]

KEY SOCIOLOGICAL AND THEOLOGICAL ISSUES FOR THE FUTURE

The previous section with its global sketch of neo-Pentecostalism has been necessarily brief, but already some of the key issues for the future are beginning to emerge. For example, if communitarian groups like house churches or the Roman Catholic Mother of God communities are to succeed, how will they avoid becoming increasingly sectarian? In Africa and Asia, how far can syncretism go before fundamental beliefs are changed, and core Pentecostal values lost? How will all these movements avoid routinization, as Weber would call it, and what are the implications of that for new denominations and movements? And are times of spiritual revival, renewal or refreshing really capable of being the ground of being for religious identity? Placing so much stress on religious experience is perennially problematic: how can anyone be sure that the ultimate sources of revival rest not in God, but in the restless human psyche, searching for certainty at the end of a millennium? Equally, how do Charismatics cope with the tension between word and Spirit when strange phenomena like the Toronto Blessing hit town? As before, the brevity of this discussion necessitates a somewhat sweeping portrayal, but it is important if we are to arrive at sensible suggestions and options for Charismatic Renewal in the next century.

Nigel Scotland, in his sympathetic portrayal of Charismatic Renewal provisionally highlights some areas of concern that he hopes those within Renewal movements will address. The most obvious concern, echoing Weber, is the 'routinization of charisma' over a period of time. Although Charismatic Renewal has had a substantial effect on traditional denominations, it has largely failed to transform the structures in which it finds itself operating.[22] Thus, instead of displacing the liberal hierarchy, it finds itself placed within it – just another 'also ran'. So, radical agendas for growth are often ignored, sometimes justifiably due to their theological and sociological paucity.[23] By the time the movement has come of age and is ready to dialogue, it has lost its cutting edge. Allied to charisma being routinized and controlled, is the difficulty of Charismatic divisiveness, which can occur over a range of issues. Nigel Scotland sees a number of problems arising already: disagreement over interpreting religious experience in relation to the authority of scripture, worship that 'focuses on the self', and (generally) poor theological methodology (although he is optimistic about this point).[24] Harvey Cox sees Charismatic Renewal becoming a 'battlefield', a kind of phenomenological war that is waged between fundamentalists and experientialists, and then again between separatists and ecumenists.[25] Jean Jacques Suurmond's treatment of Charismatic Renewal opens up yet more possibilities, arguing that the movement could become theologically and morally liberal, as a direct result of its playful engagement with post-modernism.[26] The future, it seems, is still an open one for neo-Pentecostalism, although I am not inclined to be as positive as scholars such as Nigel Scotland are, for the following reasons.

First, there is no escaping the sociological dimensions that accompany Charismatic Renewal, 'Latter-Rain' and neo-Pentecostal movements. No matter what theological story is being articulated in these groups, there is a sociological script to follow as well. Following scholars of charisma such as Sohm and Weber, Thomas O'Dea has indentified 'five dilemmas of institutionalization' that affect Charismatic movements.[27] Each dilemma reflects a fundamental antinomy between charisma and the pressure to routinize it for the sake of the institution, so that religious experience is rendered continuously available for the masses to provide stability. The first dilemma concerns the status of the original message, and the maintenance of its prescient power. Clearly, this places great emphasis on the original messenger, although post-modern revivalism apparently seems to be quite 'decentred' in this way. The second dilemma is over how the 'sacred' or the experience of the numinous is to be objectified and reified. Typically, this is done in the context of worship, ritual 'clinics' or in preaching. But in spite of the organization, perceptions remain highly subjective. A third dilemma arises directly out of this, namely assessment of the appropriate structures for inculcating Charismatic experience: there will always be disagreements over how it is routinized, and the consequent hegemonic ecclesiology. This leads to a fourth dilemma: delimitation. Definitions of Charismatic phenomena tend to 'kill the spirit', but some limits have to be placed on acceptable phenomena, or the movement risks gross subjectivity and eventual relativity. Fifth, the exercise of power also poses a dilemma. 'Power language' is common to theology and sociology, and there is a great temptation in Charismatic groups to conflate sacred and profane notions of power in order to protect 'the religion' itself.

O'Dea's observations begin to bear out the initial thesis of this concluding chapter. Namely, that religious experience is insufficient in terms of the provision of a foundation for neo-Pentecostalism. The very basis of the movement is riddled with basic antinomies, that ensure fracture, fissure and instability. My second point therefore, is that 'the routinization of charisma' always occurs in relation to contemporary social norms. At the end of this millennium, Charismatic Renewal finds itself reacting to an increasingly post-modern society. Naturally, following Niebuhr, its self-perception is that it leads the way in asserting 'Christ above culture', but the movement would be more adequately expressed as representing the 'Christ of culture'.[28] The movement taps into the contemporary preoccupations with empowerment, fulfilment, healing and meeting individual needs. It treads lightly on complex social issues. It is playfully ambiguous in its treatment of absolute values, tending towards pneumatological situationalism in moral and theological questions. It is becoming a radically 'decontextualized' movement, that has more time for the symbolic and less for texts, yet is profoundly 'dislocated', capable of instantly operating at any time, in any place, and anywhere.[29] Ironically, this may be a subconscious missiological response to the cultural challenge of the new millennium; the provision of an adaptive, experiential religion that is accommodating of the new, emerging world, neither rejecting it too strongly nor affirming it too easily.[30]

Third, and linked to the above point, a theological observation that has sociological consequences needs to be made. If the foundations of the neo-Pentecostal city are weak (built on sand: cf. endnote no.2), what about the structures themselves: how do they cope with the 'rain' or dramatic religious experience? It is ironic that the theologian who first posited experience as being important for the Christian community should unintentionally offer a critique at this point. Friedrich Schleiermacher suggested that religion could be located in feeling and intuition, not just in dogma, and that the doctrine of the Trinity could therefore be seen as a 'coping stone' that sits atop the Christian faith. It provides no support for the walls, but its function is rather to prevent corrosive external elements from entering the walls and building and corrupting it from within. There is a sense then, in which a 'coping stone' is an essential burden to any building: it is supported by the walls, but without the stone, the walls are very vulnerable.[31] Clearly, Schleiermacher saw the doctrine of the Trinity as a way of keeping out heresy and thus uniting the body of Christ. The question is, how does neo-Pentecostalism achieve the same ends? In spite of Nigel Scotland's assertion that contemporary revivalism has 'renewed its interest' in this doctrine, it is fairly apparent that it may be too little too late. True enough, neo-Pentecostalism does know the persons of the Trinity individually, but that is not the same as knowing a doctrine of the Trinity that might serve as a 'coping stone'. So, sociologically speaking, there is a theological account for the fracture and fissure so endemic to contemporary revivalism, namely the absence of a doctrine that promotes openness, mutuality, unity, coherence, and is also anti-hegemonic.[32] In short, an economic doctrine of the Trinity. This means that neo-Pentecostalism is constantly open to the vagaries of 'Charismatic weather': every time there is a 'latter rain' (for example, the Toronto Blessing), the body divides against itself on grounds of authority, the interpretation of experience, or other factors. Renewal over erosion, sometimes severe, is a constant factor in neo-Pentecostalism.

It is perhaps worth commenting at this point that the house in Jesus' parable that is built on sand and falls flat does so for two reasons. First, it is built on sand; second, it rains. This suggests that the socio-theological observation concerning the absence of a dogmatic 'coping stone' will have important implications for the future. Clearly, the fragmentation that is common to post-modernity will be in some way copied in neo-Pentecostalism. In turn, this will result in some abandoning an experiential-based religion and opting (again?) for the more 'solid' fundaments of conservative evangelicalism or fundamentalism. Either way, the future does not look likely to develop into one of consolidation and unity, in spite of the inevitable routinization of charisma.

A fourth point that needs making in this section concerns the value of religious experience itself in relation to theology and sociology. Following Barth and Rahner, I am rather inclined to distinguish between religion and revelation, and therefore see much of the (alleged) 'fresh' rain or phenomena in contemporary revivalism as a matter of 'religious questing'.[33] There is a sense of contemporary shamanism in much of neo-Pentecostalism, that suggests that the phenomena have more to do with expressing religious aspiration and maintaining group boundaries (cf. Durkheim) than anything else. In a sense, a phenomenon like the Toronto Blessing shows this most starkly. Theologically speaking, it is dubious (and offensive?) to believe in a God that would indulge a small, Caucasian-based, international and mainly middle-class group with great blessings, whilst leaving the lot of the poor largely untouched. Any argument about the particularity of God over the universality would still have to address why this group is 'blessed', and not others. It is preferable therefore, to see the Toronto Blessing as representing a search for God, rather than a revelation from God. At the same time, we should indicate that the reasons for this search are sociologically accountable. The alienation of the middle classes, their gradual loss of identity, status and deprofessionalization has led to a profound crisis.[34] Religiously speaking, their angst and neurosis get dealt with in revivalism by neo-Pentecostalism acting as a transformer, reifying neurosis into mania, and issuing new identity to the believer based on notions of empowerment and fulfilment.[35] This is partly why contemporary revivalism is so sociologically and theologically appealing for the middle classes in the west, and the emerging middle classes in the burgeoning economies of South America, Africa and the Pacific-Asian Rim.

THE FUTURE OF CHARISMATIC RENEWAL: SOME PREDICTIONS

Given the remarks made above in this chapter, we are now in a position to speculate about the next millennium. I have already suggested that neo-Pentecostalism is increasingly mirroring post-modernist trends, so it seems appropriate to define more precisely what is meant by that. Modernism could be characterized as a movement that searched for inner truths behind surface appearances: the origins of sociology, phenomenology and psychology are birthed in this vision. Modernism was also expressed in cultural and aesthetic ways: it was or is progressive, secularized and consciously opposed to classicism. Fundamentalism and classic Pentecostalism represent the cognitive and intuitive reactions to modernity. In contrast, post-modernism, supposedly, represents the recovery of the romantic outlook. Yet it is not a reversion to tradition, because post-modernity sees the search for truth as a mirage; thus, it is decentred, with 'a profusion of style and orientation . . . any attempt to penetrate to a deeper reality is abandoned and mimesis loses all meaning'.[36] There is a sense in which neo-Pentecostalism reacts against this vision of truth, culture and life. Yet to be a reaction against it, it has to be a reaction to it, and the inculcation of post-modernist values

is thus unavoidable, unless a strict communitarian line is imposed.
Generally, it is not, and neo-Pentecostalism therefore finds itself accommodating the new world, and in some ways, affirming it, Thus,
many in Charismatic churches have quite unconsciously abandoned their
modernist foundations of evangelicalism or fundamentalism, and traded
them in for the experiential forms of personal certainty so beloved of
post-modernity. Therefore, they now share in Lyotard's description of
post-modernism (including its sacred forms) as 'incredulity towards
metanarratives'.[37]

Systematizing the future of religion is something few academics would
attempt, especially given the potentially turbulent and truculent nature
of post-modernity, coupled with a new millennium. However, two worthy
of note are Haddon Willmer and Robert Wuthnow.[38] Willmer offers a
positive prescription for Christianity on how it can meet the challenges
of pluralism in the future. Ironically, it is a pluralist response that is
advocated: Willmer suggests not one future for Christianity, but several.
In general, he is affirmative of becoming 'missionaries to our own
culture', recognizing that the post-modern situation has eroded the benign
acceptance of Christianity in Britain. In other words, the way to engage with pluralism in the post-modern situation is to be sharper and
more particular about your religious beliefs, since it is a competitive
'spiritual and quasi-spiritual market place'.[39] Wuthnow's, whilst not
disagreeing with Willmer's book, is a more systematic work that outlines the major areas for engagement on a more global scale. These
include the relationship between Christianity and culture, the future of
fundamentalism and the quest for identity amongst the middle classes:
all areas we have already touched on. Ultimately, Wuthnow calls for a
resacralization of the critical moral and political questions post-modernity
poses. Yet this is to take a subtle form, with Christianity making sure
that 'life is breathed' into these issues, rather than simply privatizing
them or resorting to assaulting society in a 'crusading' fashion.[40]

Clearly, neo-Pentecostalism is capable of carrying forward this agenda:
Cox, Suurmond, Hocken and others all see considerable potential for
engagement and growth at this point. However, the strength of the
pluralism in relation to post-modernity should not be underestimated,
particularly in its capacity to turn revivalism into a form of cultural
expression.[41] I have already suggested that the Toronto Blessing should
probably be read like that, as should healing movements and methods
of empowerment and fulfilment. So how might the future shape up for
neo-Pentecostalism if it fails to engage with post-modern pluralism in
a way that is discerning and distinctive? I see six possibilities, fitting

under one 'sacred canopy'. The canopy is this: fissure and specializa- tion in post-modernity are inevitable. The sacredness comes from the religious legitimization that is given to the opportunities that pluralism brings, and most especially the sacralization of particularity. The city is already too big, too insecure and too fragmented to be governed by central fundaments or core experiences. Thus, it will consciously or subconsciously assume a decentred nature, in order to attain a form of local and provisional certainty and faith expression.[42] In effect, the probability is that the movement will gradually fall apart. The possible futures then become:

(1) *Apocalyptic*: Some revivalist groups will focus their millennial beliefs (pre-, post-, and so on) on the year 2000, and look for portents, visions and signs of the end. Some groups on the Charismatic peri- phery, such as the Branch Davidians (Waco), seem to suggest that some communities may even attempt to 'hasten the end' them- selves, possibly through violence or retribution.

(2) *Novel*: Movements such as the Toronto Blessing, with its specious particularity of experience, point to an increased interest in exotic encounters with the numinous. Indeed, fiction may start to guide truth: the supernatural thrillers of authors such as Frank Perretti seem to serve as a template for some Christians, guiding them in their demonology, prayer and exorcism.[43]

(3) *Communitarian*: Groups such as the Mother of God Community and the Jesus Army suggest that a withdrawal from society will be advocated by some. Following Wallis (1984), these groups are set to become 'world-rejecting'.

(4) *Sectarian*: The absence of a doctrinal 'coping stone' for neo- Pentecostalism ensures that some Christian Charismatic groups will evolve into sects. This has already occurred with the Californian Children of God ('The Family'), which was originally Charismatic. [Indeed, at the time of writing, the Toronto Airport Vineyard had just been 'excommunicated' by the International Vineyard Minis- tries, allegedly for 'cult-like and manipulative practices'. However, it is more likely that the secession is to do with the perennial clash between prophetic and apostolic ministries that bedevils most Charismatic churches, and Wimber's desire to delimit his 'circuit' of churches and their reticulate power structure. With the accom- panying dynamics of charisma, this always leads to schism, and often to outright sectarianism.

(5) *Political*: Some within neo-Pentecostalism will turn to more moral or politicized agendas that reflect right-wing or left-wing tendencies. Some will simply be seeking social justice in this turn, whilst others might look more towards the creation of a theocracy.

(6) *Fundamentalist*: Effectively a return to dogmatic, cognitive security, moving away from the 'shifting sands' of experiential-based religion. For many, this will be manifest in a rediscovery of conservative evangelicalism.

These possibilities are not exhaustive, though they are in my view the leading contenders. Naturally, one cannot lightly dismiss the status quo continuing well into the next century, but the fracture and fissure I have outlined suggests otherwise. Other possibilities do exist, however. Suurmond's thesis that neo-Pentecostalism could turn liberal is ideologically enticing, but unlikely. The only real evidence that would support this thesis (so far) is the experimental/alternative worship that has been popularized through the 'Nine O'Clock Service' in Sheffield, that has embraced aspects of post-modern ideology (sexuality, ecology, non-textual/visual worship, and so on). Equally, the stress on experience could ultimately be routinized in a form of sacramentalism for some, taking the form of a renewed interest in the formal-symbolic, grounded in Trinitarian belief.[44] But again, I do not think this a serious option for most within neo-Pentecostalism. Neither should one underestimate the effect Roman Catholicism will have on neo-Pentecostalism, and vice versa. Although Gordon Urquhart's thesis is rather alarmist in respect of the Neo-catechumenate, if the Magisterium of the Church becomes much weaker, it may be hard for the Roman Catholic Church to depend on the benign sacramental routinization of charisma that has kept neo-Pentecostal ideology in check thus far. Clearly, some of the options outlined above can be combined with others or adapted: that would be appropriate in a post-modern context. Thus, the most likely scenario is that the 'sacred canopy' that I intimated earlier will dominate the pattern for the future. So, in these concluding sections, we must now assess how sociology can keep track of and make sense of the fissure that is to come. In short, can a sociological method cope?

SUMMARY: SOCIOLOGY AND THE SHIFTING SANDS OF NEO-PENTECOSTALISM

Let me say first of all that I think that a sociology of religion that 'reads' neo-Pentecostalism in the future will need to be radically open to working with other disciplines. Critiques of sociology have been present since the 1950s, challenging the basis of rational accounts of the sublime. The work of Peter Winch is most prescient in this respect, questioning the explanation of and interpretation of human affairs in relation to social science. Winch has argued that disciplines such as sociology fail adequately to comprehend the nature of intention and therefore the actual constitution of acts. This leads to a kind of false relativism, which might suit certain types of 'liberal' thinking, but in fact, does not assist us much in the task of finding the underlying truth or meaning of a belief system.[45] More recently, John Milbank has critiqued the notion that there can be a 'social' vantage point from which to survey religion. He suggests that religion can always invert the relationship and deconstruct sociology, making it a faith; but Milbank only does this to attack the idea of a sociological 'metacritique', which he considers bogus, or at least something that should be significantly scaled down.[46]

Following Milbank, I think that part of the problem is the assumed nature of relations in sociology: bipolar, dialectical and essentially humanist. However, we should at least acknowledge the possibility of a ternary relationship, consisting objectively of the individual, society and God. This is why, when those within contemporary revivalism read the sociology of their religion, they often fail to recognize themselves, because 'God' has been ignored. or reduced to a notion of projection or social legitimization. The theory does not correspond to their inner experience, and only (just) to their ecclesial polity. This really won't do when it comes to interpreting the complex and rich nature of neo-Pentecostalism. What is required is a multidisciplinary approach to a multifarious phenomenon. Insights from phenomenology can be useful here, since at least it attempts to eschew rationalist or idealist accounts of religion, and to initially 'see things as they are'. Careful anthropological study often confounds sweeping grand narratives from sociology. The psychology of religion can open up debates on the delicate area of intention. Lastly, theology itself also has something to offer in articulating the strengths and weaknesses of belief systems, and their ultimate coherence in relation to 'orthodox' or 'mainstream' religion, which is partly what I have attempted here.

That said, I believe that the sociology of religion still has a part to play in interpreting neo-Pentecostalism. Metacritiques have their uses; they are rather more like maps than close-up studies, a kind of ideological cartography, useful for charting complex data, but from a distance. Also, since ecclesial polity does reflect faith, it seems that sociology will always be in business when it comes to analysing belief systems. Notions of power, charisma, order can never be entirely monopolized by one discipline: their dynamics and language are always shared by theology, sociology and psychology, and more besides. So, it seems appropriate to say a little more about the structure of the city on the beach to conclude.

First, the general direction of neo-Pentecostalism does seem to lie in a more 'playful' engagement with truth. This is partly because it is tending to abandon textually-centred religion in favour of the visual, symbolic and intuitive.[47] One of the implied ideas in describing neo-Pentecostalism at the turn of this century as a city on a beach is that it connotes the notion of pleasure, leisure and play. But we are entitled to ask at this point, has the 'pleasure principle' in phenomena such as the Toronto Blessing become divorced from reality? It would certainly seem so: such phenomena seem escapist and self-indulgent to those outside the city, yet to those within, it is the very presence of God, in playful activity with his children. The playfulness with truth – guaranteed by the experiential nature of late neo-Pentecostalism – leads to a number of problems for the movement and its onlookers. Conservative evangelicals find it hard to accept phenomena that are not explicitly reflected in the canon of scripture. Neo-Pentecostals partly respond to this by searching for texts that connect with their experience, but the connections are usually very thin, if appropriate at all. In turn, the failure to locate 'Biblical proof' or scriptural legitimization for neo-Pentecostal practice leads them to the very heart of the post-modern abyss. Namely, contenting itself with a movement from the pre-critical phase to a post-critical phase, without ever passing through a critical stage; in other words, abandoning the search for any ultimate truth, and engaging in methodological pragmatism and playful experientialism.[48] The real problem with this position is that it reflects post-modern culture only too well. If it does transpire that post-modernity will permit liberalism or totalitarianism, but without an 'agreed ethical heart', neo-Pentecostalism might end up by offering a religion that has no real head for discernment.

Second, there is a finite limit to the number of times one can say, 'behold, I am doing a new thing'. Such proclamations are essential to the Charismatic situation, and especially for the leadership. But there is a boredom threshold that has to be negotiated by the neo-Pentecostal movement at the turn of the century. What happens when prophecy fails? How can the community of romantic and adventurous ideology be maintained? Will followers not become weary of quasi-immanence? There is already some evidence to suggest that neo-Pentecostalism is losing the present generation of 'twenty-somethings', who are turning their backs on a form of religious expression that is too narrow and particular, in favour of 'alternative' modes that are sacramental, ecological and more avowedly post-modern. Where this will leave neo-Pentecostalism remains to be seen, but Bryan Wilson notes that Charismatic communities always ultimately disappoint: 'the specific prophecies . . . fail, the essential miracles are heard about rather than seen . . .'.[49] Because charisma and charismatic phenomena are such a shaky commodity, it does seem justifiable to speak of neo-Pentecostalism as founded on the shifting sands of religious experience and charisma. As such, the ground of being is subject to all the elements, including the wind: and who knows where it will blow in the future? And as for 'rain', is not the safety of that metaphor in conveying revelation and renewal doubtful? The source of rain appears from heaven; but its source is the earth, created by hot air and complex climatic conditions.

Third, the core or centre of neo-Pentecostalism, if it exists at all, seems to be an interest in power. The exercise of power, both human and divine, characterizes the movement at the end of the millennium. The power of God is deemed to be a counter-power against the world, yet working within it. The task of the renewed ecclesial community is seen as identifying that power (especially new and novel sources, such as the Toronto Blessing), reifying and controlling it, and finally expanding its influence. What is confusing in the analysis of neo-Pentecostalism is that many studies focus on the agency of renewal (a guru, text, phenomena, and so on), without seeing that the interest in the agency ultimately rests in its capacity to deliver power. Ironically, although neo-Pentecostalism can be said to be 'power-centred', this does not invalidate my earlier point, that the movement is becoming decentred, because it remains power-related. The subtlety of argument lies in the alliance between power and its agents.[50] At the end of the century, the reticulate nature of neo-Pentecostalism is expansive, with new agents for empowerment constantly being added: yesterday the Kansas City Prophets, today Toronto, and tomorrow . . .? These agents are increasingly distanced from each other, assuming their own particularity, making the boundaries and communicative links in the city difficult to track. Yet 'power-centredness' still exists notionally as the desideratum of core experiences. The problem for neo-Pentecostalism is that the ways of accessing that power have now become so myriad, the movement as a whole is losing its corporate identity and is beginning to break up.[51] The poet W. B. Yeats expresses the situation like this:

Things fall apart;
the centre cannot hold . . .
The ceremony of innocence is drowned.
The best lack all conviction,
the worst are full of passionate intensity.[52]

A CODA ON THE BEACH

We are standing on the threshold of a new millennium and are now returning to our original image: the rain, the tides, the wind, and the city on the beach, founded on the shifting, playful sands of charisma, showy religious experience and the culture of post-modernity. If this is an appropriate way of seeing neo-Pentecostalism at the turn of the century, can there be a vision for a secure future? Clearly, one possibility is a realignment with fundamentalists or conservative evangelicals, which will act as a corrective to unrestrained experientialism. Another possibility is accepting the impact of post-modern culture on the belief system, and letting nature take its course. This will guarantee a kind of pragmatic relevance, but it will be a religion that is prone to becoming a victim of fashion. A third possibility lies in a deeper engagement with theology and the social sciences. If neo-Pentecostalism became more politically, socially and psychologically self-aware, theologically critical of its self, and open to new horizons in its own hermeneutics, it is just possible that we are actually looking at a religion for the third millennium. Anyone for post-Pentecostalism?

NOTES

1. See K. Barth, *Church Dogmatics* (Edinburgh: T & T Clark, 1958), Bk IV, ii, Chap. xv, p.648: 'we cannot strive for greater vertical renewal merely to produce greater horizontal extension and a wider audience.'

2. See A. Thiselton, *Interpreting God and the Postmodern Self: On Meaning, Manipulation and Promise* (Edinburgh: T & T Clark, 1995), pp.81–5. Harvey Cox, *The Secular City: Urbanization and Secularization in Theological Perpective* (New York: Macmillan, 1965); *Religion in the Secular City* (New York: Simon & Schuster, 1984).

3. J. G. Melton, *Encyclopedia of American Religion* (North Carolina: McGrath, 1978). Melton uses the notion of 'family' to describe the federation of charismatic movements, but the notion of city or polis is just as appropriate.

4. For a discussion of charisma in relation to institutions, see M. Weber, *Charisma and Institution Building* (Chicago: Chicago University Press, 1968). For a discussion of adventure as a prominent theme in contemporary revivalism, see James Hopewell, *Congregation: Stories and Structures* (London: SCM, 1987).

5. D. Martin, *Tongues of Fire: The Explosion of Protestantism in Latin America* (Oxford: Blackwell, 1990), p.52.

6. Martin cites the Jotabeche Cathedral in Santiago, which holds 18,000 people, as an example. Much of the work in radio and television is still in debt to North American efforts.

7. Martin, 1990, p.82. Martin especially has in mind Cornelia Butler Flora's *Pentecostalism in Colombia: Baptism by Fire and Spirit* (Cranbury, NJ: Fairleigh Dickinson University Press, 1976). The basic thesis is to treat Pentecostalism as the religious aspect of economic dependency.

8. Martin, 1990, p.258.

9. Meredith McGuire, *Pentecostal Catholics: Power, Charisma and Order in a Religious Movement* (Philadelphia: Temple University, 1982) and *Ritual Healing in Suburban America* (New Brunswick: Rutgers University Press, 1988); Mary Jo Neitz, *Charisma and Community: A Study of Commitment within Charismatic Renewal* (Oxford: Transaction Books, 1987).

10. MacGuire, 1988, pp.38–78.

11. A likeable account of this phenomenon can be found in Harvey Cox's *Fire From Heaven: Pentecostalism, Spirituality, and the Shaping of Religion in the Twentieth Century* (Reading, MA: Addison-Wesley, 1994) pp.263ff.

12. Individuals who are prominent include the Dominican Francis Macnutt, a popular healer and author, and Peter Hocken of the Mother of God Community, Gaithersburg, USA, publishers of *The Word Among Us*.

13. See entries in S. M. Burgess, G. B. McGee and P. H. Alexander, *A Dictionary of Pentecostal and Charismatic Movements* (Grand Rapids, MI: Zondervan, 1988).

14. Cox, 1994, pp.281ff.

15. J. Thomas Nichol, 'The Charismatic Movement', in *Christianity in America*, eds M. Noll, N. Hatch, G. Marsden, D. Wells and J. Woodbridge (Grand Rapids, MI: Eerdmanns, 1983) p.484.

16. A. Walker, *Restoring the Kingdom*, 2nd edn (London: Hodder & Stoughton, 1988).

17. See 'Charismatic Communities' in *A Dictionary of Pentecostal and Charismatic Movements* (Grand Rapids, MI: Zondervan, 1988) pp.127ff, and Gordon Urquhart, *The Pope's Armada* (London: Bantam, 1995).

18. See M. Harper, 'Renewal in the Holy Spirit', in *Christianity: A World*

Faith, ed. R. Keeley (Tring: Lion Publishing, 1985) p.103. A full, if over-positive, account of Charismatic renewal in Britain can be found in Peter Hocken's *Streams of Renewal* (Exeter: Paternoster Press, 1986).

19. Martin, 1990, pp.1135ff.
20. Cox, 1994, pp.213ff. See also Ro Bong-Rin and Marlin Nelson (eds), *Korean Church Growth Explosion* (Taichung, Taiwan: Asia Theological Assoc. & Word of Life Press, 1983). There is a short article in this volume by Paul Cho, but his 'prosperity Gospel' teaching is more clearly articulated in his *Salvation, Health and Prosperity* (Altamonte Springs, FL: Creation House, 1987).
21. cf. D. Barrett, *Dictionary of Christianity* (Oxford: OUP, 1982).
22. Nigel Scotland, *Charismatics and the Next Millennium* (London: Hodder & Stoughton, 1995) p.251.
23. See for example B. Skinner and D. Pytches, *New Wineskins* (Guildford: Eagle Press, 1991), in which the authors effectively argue for the privatization of the Church of England, so that parishes can compete for success.
24. N. Scotland, 1995, pp.249ff.
25. Cox, 1994, pp.310ff.
26. Jean Jacques Suurmond, *Word and Spirit at Play* (London: SCM, 1994) pp.74ff.
27. T. O'Dea, 'Sociological Dilemmas: Five Paradoxes of Institutionalisation' in *Sociological Theory, Values and Sociocultural Change* (New York: Free Press of Glencoe, 1963) pp.71–89, and *The Sociology of Religion* (Englewood Cliffs, NJ: Prentice Hall, 1983).
28. H. R. Niebuhr, *Christ and Culture* (New York: Harper & Row, 1951). cf. Frank Brown, 'Christian Theology's Dialogue with Culture' in the *Companion Encyclopaedia of Theology* (London: Routledge, 1995) pp.314ff.
29. Some of these insights are derived from David Lyon, *Postmodernity* (Buckingham: Open University Press, 1994), and Richard Roberts, 'Power and Empowerment', in *Religion Today*, vol.9, no.3, 1994, pp.3–23.
30. See R. Wallis, *The Elementary Forms of the New Religious Life* (London: Routledge, 1984), for a discussion of accommodation, rejection and acceptance. For a discussion of Pentecostal mission in relation to the millennium, see David Bosch, *Transforming Mission: Paradigm Shifts in the Theology of Mission* (Maryknoll, New York: Orbis, 1994) pp.313–27.
31. F. Schleiermacher, *The Christian Faith* (Edinburgh: T & T Clark, 1928) pp.740ff.
32. My observation of Charismatic communities such as the Jesus Army is that their 'Trinity' is a theological hegemony that matches their ecclesial hegemony. A ruling Father, suffering Son and serving Spirit mirrors the structure ('Godly order') imposed on men, women and children. Michael Harper has expressed similar views in some of his more recent works.
33. Barth distinguishes between the two in many ways and in many places, but the most obvious exposition is found in the *Church Dogmatics* (ET: Edinburgh: T & T Clark, 1975) Bk 1.1, pp.295ff, and Bk 1.2, pp.280ff, where Barth clearly teaches that revelation abolishes religion. Karl Rahner takes a more subtle view in his *Foundations of Christian Faith* (London: DLT, 1978) pp.155ff, in which he argues for a more interdependent view between religion and revelation, eschewing Barth's dogmatic chasm. For

a sympathetic phenomenological approach, see R. Torrance, *The Spiritual Quest* (California: University Press, Calif., 1994).
34. 'Middle class' here is used rather loosely. I really mean the Marxist category of 'bourgeois', which might include the emerging managerial and commercial classes of recent times. Although they may be prosperous, they are nonetheless undergoing a profound process of alienation brought on by an excessive dependency on the free market, which identifies them as tradeable units of production, and then again the gradual loss of corporate notions of work, society and responsibility. See A. Giddens, *The Class Structure of Advanced Societies* (London: Hutchinson, 1980), p.106ff; N. Chomsky, *Keeping the Rabble in Line* (Academic Press: Edinburgh, 1994) pp.124ff, and my 'The Power Trip: Adventure Tours for Charismatic Christians', *Church of England Newspaper*, 23 Feb. 1996.
35. For a fuller discussion, see my *Words, Wonders and Power* (London: SPCK, 1996).
36. See A. Giddens, 'Uprooted Signposts at Century's End', *The Times Higher Educational Supplement*, 17 Jan. 1992, pp.21–2. See also Grace Davie, *Religion in Britain, 1945 to the Present* (Oxford: Blackwell, 1994) p.192, and D. Lyon, *Postmodernity* (Buckingham: Open University Press, 1994).
37. See Jean-Francois Lyotard, *The Postmodern Condition: A Report on Knowledge* (Manchester: Manchester University Press, 1984) p.xxiii.
38. I could also mention Wade Clark Roof, *Towards the Year 2000: Religion in the 90's* (London: Sage, 1993); cf., *Annals of American Academy of Political and Social Science*, vol.522, 1992, pp.157ff.
39. H. Willmer, *2020 Visions: The Futures of Christianity in Britain* (London: SPCK, 1992) pp.60ff.
40. Robert Wuthnow, *Christianity in the Twenty-First Century: Reflections on the Challenges Ahead* (Oxford: OUP, 1993) p.212.
41. cf. Melanie McGrath's excellent travelogue, *Motel Nirvana: Dreaming of the New Age in the American Desert* (London: HarperCollins, 1995).
42. So, this is related to Peter Berger's vision of religion needing to be 'marketed' and 'sold' to a public no longer constrained to 'buy'. The modernist response to pluralism is ecumenism – centralization of resources, not unlike economic cartelization. The post-modern response is to seize the opportunity the spiritual free market brings, and diversify and specialize. See P. Berger, 'A Market Model for the Analysis of Ecumenicity', *Social Research*, 1963, 30: pp.75–90, and *The Sacred Canopy* (Garden City: Doubleday), p.138.
43. See Frank Perretti, *This Present Darkness* (Eastbourne: Kingsway, 1990). Perretti's writings (demonology, horror and contemporary urban myths) have had a profound influence on constructing the reality of some revivalists.
44. cf. Heidi Baker, 'Glossolalia: Towards a Reconstructive Theology', unpublished Ph.D. thesis, King's College, London, 1996. Baker attempts to argue that glossolalia is consonant with Trinitarian and sacramental theology.
45. See P. Winch, *The Idea of a Social Science* (London: Routledge, 1958); 'Understanding a Primitive Society' in B. Wilson (ed.), *Rationality* (Oxford: Blackwell, 1970) pp.78–111. Other works that could be consulted include E. Gellner, *The Uniqueness of Truth* (Cambridge: CUP, 1992), G. Anscombe, *Intention* (Oxford: Blackwell, 1957), and D. Davidson,

'Actions, Reasons and Causes' in A. R. White (ed.), *The Philosophy of Action* (Oxford: OUP, 1968) pp.74–94.

46. J. Milbank, *Theology and Social Theory: Beyond Secular Reason* (Oxford: Blackwell, 1990) p.139.
47. cf. R. Porter and P. Richter, *The Toronto Blessing – Or is It?* (London: DLT, 1995).
48. cf. my review of Suurmond's *Word and Spirit at Play*, in *Anvil*, vol.12, no.3, 1995.
49. B. Wilson, *The Noble Savages: An Essay on Charisma* (Berkeley: California University Press, 1975), p.3. See also the work of James Hopewell on adventure and romantic notions in Charismatic communities. Readers interested in psychological studies of prophecy are referred to Leon Festinger's *When Prophecy Fails* (New York: Harper & Row, 1956), and *A Theory of Cognitive Dissonance* (Stanford: Stanford University Press, 1957).
50. cf. M. Foucault, 'Space, Knowledge and Power' in Paul Rabinow (ed.), *The Foucault Reader* (New York: Pantheon-Random, 1984) p.247: 'Nothing is fundamental . . . there are only reciprocal relations, and the perpetual gaps between intentions in relation to one another'. This quote is not intended to signify that I doubt such a thing as divine power.
51. For a fuller discussion, see my *Words, Wonders and Power* (London: SPCK, 1996).
52. W. B. Yeats, 'The Second Coming', in *The Collected Poems* (Basingstoke: Macmillan, 1921) p.110.

Index

Losing the Blanket

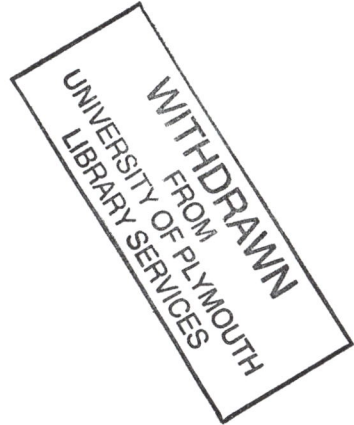